The Jews in Polish Culture

The Jews in Polish Culture

Aleksander Hertz

Translated by
Richard Lourie

With a Foreword by
Czesław Miłosz

Editor
Lucjan Dobroszycki

Northwestern University Press
Evanston, IL

Northwestern University Press
Evanston, IL 60201

ISDN0-8101-0758-9

Orginally published as *Żydzi w kulturze polskiej* by Instytut Literacki, Paris, 1961. The English edition of *The Jews in Polish Culture* has been prepared with the assistance and cooperation of the Aleksander Hertz Foundation.

Library of Congress Cataloging-in-Publication Data

Hertz, Aleksander.
The Jews in Polish culture.

Translation of: Żydzi w kulturze polskiej.
Includes index.
1. Jews—Poland—History. 2. Antisemitism—Poland—History. 3. Poland—Ethnic relations.
I. Title.
DS135.P6H413 1988 943.8'004924 88–12537

Contents

To My Wife

Foreword

by Czesław Miłosz

My friendship with Aleksander Hertz developed in the years 1937–1939 when we both were employed by the Polish Radio, a state institution, in Warsaw. That was an ominous period as the signs of the approaching war went together with the self-imposed blindness of many people. The political climate was ugly. Since the turn of the century, a division into two camps characterized the political life in Poland: liberals and socialists on one side and the nationalists on the other; but in the late thirties the second camp seemed to encounter no open resistance. Its chauvinism, its anti-Semitism, its fanning of hatred for other nationalities led to acts of violence, particularly at the universities, where gangs of students would attack their Jewish colleagues. The press was full of inflammatory articles directed against presumed conspiracies of Jews and Freemasons. For Aleksander Hertz to observe this gradual sinking into baseness and absurdity was an ordeal. He considered himself a Pole and placed himself in a certain Polish tradition going back to the Enlightenment and still alive among his friends, eminent Polish intellectuals—a tradition of humanism, tolerance, and equal rights for all men. Now it looked as if that frame of mind was proper only to an insignificant minority, unable to resist the pressures of the mobs. The paradox was that Poland was threatened by Nazi Germany and determined to defend itself, yet the majority of Poles seemed not to realize they were undermining in their own way the principles of democracy. Another paradox consisted in the relative strength of islands of resistance to the prevailing jingoistic mood of the country, and one such island was the Polish Radio. Hertz, in a book written at the end of his life, *Wyznania starego człowieka* (Confessions of an Old Man, 1979), writes: "I have to state clearly that in the Polish Radio I met many worthy, wise, and honest individuals. Most fondly I remember Halina Sosnowska, Vice-Director of Programs and my former university colleague. She was a person of great intelligence and exceptional civic courage, not afraid of experimentation, even risky experimentation. Unfortunately, her possibilities were limited by various considerations—political and not political. The first acquired more and more importance in the years directly preceding the war and disastrously influenced the work on programming; Halina was perfectly aware of this and tried valiantly to resist these various pressures."

Halina Sosnowska belonged to the generation of Poles for whom the independent Poland created in 1918 incarnated a possibility of justice, freedom, equality for all citizens, and social progress. I feel solidarity with Aleksander Hertz's praise of her, since I witnessed her desperate efforts to outplay her enemies, who used bigotry as their weapon. Aleksander Hertz, constantly full of new ideas about educational programs, could always count on her friendly attention if not always the implementation of his projects, for the obstacles were considerable. After 1939 Halina Sosnowska was to prove her indomitable spirit. Engaged in the Resistance against the Nazis, arrested after the war by the communist authorities, she received a life sentence because of her loyalty to the London government-in-exile. Released after twelve years, rehabilitated ("we are sorry, that was a mistake"), she died soon afterward.

I quote again from Hertz's above-mentioned book: "The Polish Radio obviously was a state organ. At the same time it had to be very sensitive to the moods of the public at large. It was forced to do things which for many people working in it were the source of pain and shame. In its programs the Polish Radio had to ignore the fact of the multinational composition of Poland. Only in local programs were some completely apolitical talks in the Ukrainian and Belorussian languages being broadcast. As far as I remember the subjects were mostly agricultural. In no way did those broadcasts satisfy the aspirations and needs of Ukrainian and Belorussian citizens of the Polish republic, several million strong. When, as a timid attempt, five-minute talks for Jews, *in Polish*, were introduced, once every two weeks, such a storm of protests followed that that miserable concession to over three million citizens of Poland was speedily withdrawn. The folly of chauvinistic nationalism, anti-Semitism—ills that like cancer were consuming Poland—showed their strength. That was the triumph of Roman Dmowski and his devotees; it was Poland's defeat."

Hertz belonged to those numerous Poles of Jewish descent whose love of Poland went unrequited. A teacher by vocation, he drew much pleasure from lecturing first at the Institute of East European Studies in Wilno, then at the State Institute of Theatrical Arts in Warsaw, but a gradual increase in discrimination after 1935 pushed him more and more toward reflection on his Jewishness and on the whole tangle of uneasy Polish-Jewish coexistence. Those last years before the war are at the origin of the present book, written in America, at the time when Jewish presence in Poland became only history.

He was a man free of bitterness, which simply did not go together with his open, generous, and enthusiastic nature. Till the end of his long life his mind burst with new plans and intellectual discoveries—and all of them had something to do with the rights of human beings to the respect and pursuit of happiness. The titles of the chapters in his *Confessions of an Old Man,* deliberately chosen by him to sound old-fashioned, Platonic, correctly convey his basic concerns: "In Search of Good," "In Search of Truth," "In Search of Beauty." Also, a title less easy to translate into English: "The Search of a Fatherland," of *Ojczyzna, Patria*. Poland was the country of his ancestors for many generations; his forebears participated in insurrections against Russia and paid for it with deportation to Siberia or exile. He was aware of the extreme oddity of Poland as a country. As he writes: "Every country is strange. But Poland belongs to those countries where strangeness is extreme. Contrasts are here striking, often astonishing." He acknowledges his indebtedness to a non-Jewish friend in acquiring his own self-awareness as a Jew: Stanisław Vincenz, a writer, called a "tsadek" or "rabbi," an admirer of Jewish culture, a man who for Hertz exemplified the old, multinational, and multidenominational Poland. Yet, calling himself a Pole and a Jew, Aleksander Hertz was fortunate enough to find a new attachment, this time to America. He learned to love America, to esteem its democracy and its openness to various cultures. He was happy in America, and the serenity that pervades his writings is due to his feeling of being settled at last.

Editor's Introduction

by Lucjan Dobroszycki

Aleksander Hertz's *Jews in Polish Culture*, which appeared in Polish more than twenty-five years ago in Paris, is unknown to the American reader, and the same may be said of its author. Hertz's writings are held in high regard in Poland, his native country. Before the war he was one of the most eminent social scientists in Poland, the author of important scholarly works, including a few books which to this day remain valuable contributions to knowledge. Students in the sociology departments of Polish universities must, however, exert some effort to track down the now rare *People and Ideas*, *Classics of Sociology*, or *Contemporary Sociology*, to name but three of Hertz's works, published in Warsaw in 1931, 1933, and 1938 respectively. After the war, the Polish reader knew Hertz as a frequent contributor to *Kultura*, the prestigious monthly published by Polish émigré intellectuals in Paris. The same Institut Littéraire which brings out *Kultura* was also the publisher of *Jews in Polish Culture*.

Hertz was, as it were, destined to write *Jews in Polish Culture*. He was not only a thoroughly trained sociologist who studied at universities in Vienna and Warsaw, but a profound thinker and keen observer as well. He seemed also to have been destined for the task, as a man immersed in those two cultures, Polish and Jewish. He came from a completely Polonized Jewish family which had traditionally been both actively involved in Polish culture and strongly loyal to Poland. His closest relatives included noted writers, scholars, and musicians as well as those who fought for Poland's independence. His father, Leon Hertz, took part in the insurrection against Russia in 1863, and, as late as the 1930s, was the acting treasurer of the association for veterans of that uprising which had captivated the whole nation. It was not, however, an easy thing to be a Jew in Poland, even if one were a Jew only by descent. And it is to that very problem that a considerable portion of *Jews in Polish Culture* is devoted. Hertz was to return to this question in his last book *Confessions of an Old Man* (published in London in 1979), although here his approach, as Hertz himself says, "had to be more intimate, more personal that anything I had thus far written."

Jews in Polish Culture was and in large measure remains an essentially pioneering work. Despite the passage of many years, the book's thrust has retained its initial, original freshness. This applies equally to its content and to its form. Hertz's subject is not easy. Its very framework imposes breadth, assuming an a priori need to conduct investigations of both a theoretical and empirical nature, and it also requires a mastery of nearly all the disciplines of the humanities—history, sociology, ethnography. Hertz did not have many precursors when he undertook this venture, though Jewish historiography in interbellum Poland could boast of more than a few fundamental works. Hertz was, however, justified in saying that those previous works had usually dealt with the life of the Jewish community in Poland or with some aspect of it "as a phenomenon in itself that, as a rule, eludes connection with Polish life as a whole." And it is precisely this which constitutes the principal subject of Hertz's reflections.

He was particularly interested in the mechanism of social intercourse on a variety of levels and by cultural interpenetration between Poles and Jews. He posed and attempted to answer such complex questions as: did interpenetration in fact take place, when and under what conditions did it occur, what forms and directions did it take, and, finally, what were its consequences. Working theoretically, yet basing himself on specifically Polish grounds, Hertz analyzes the place and role of the Jews in Polish society and that society in general. Here his inquiry focuses on the image of the Jews in the eyes of non-Jews: Did the Jews truly exist apart from the rest of the population of pre- and postpartition Poland? What was the basis of the belief that the Jews were alien? What determined their separateness and isolation? All of Hertz's thinking flows from his contention that the Jews in Poland were a caste and, in nearly every respect, displayed the principal traits characteristic of a caste group.

The question of whether or not the Jews in Poland did in fact constitute a caste may seem debatable to some. For Hertz, however, this was primarily a sociological concept, one that gave rise to his approach, categories, ideas, and even his style. The use of that sociological concept enabled the author to find a means both artistically vivid and historically accurate for presenting an image of the Jews as they had been seen in Poland for centuries and also as they had customarily seen themselves. In this context it might be worth recalling what Gunnar Myrdal wrote in his *The American Dilemma: The Negro Problem and Modern Democracy* (1944) concerning the term caste, which he applied widely in his investigation of American blacks: "The sole criterion in defining scientific terms is practicality. Concepts are our created instruments and have no other form of reality than in our usage. Their purpose is to help make our thinking clear and our observation accurate" (667–68).

Hertz's concept can in no way be separated from the fact that he wrote *Jews in Polish Culture* in the United States, where he had sought refuge during the war and where later he was to settle permanently. "This book is primarily the fruit of my American experience," wrote Hertz. And indeed he was able to observe in America processes that he would find quite compelling, given his range of interests. On the one hand, there was pluralism and the ongoing, intensive absorption of a great many heterogeneous ethnic groups (the so-called melting pot) and, on the other hand, there was the movement for genuine black emancipation, which accelerated during and after the war. To a considerable extent Hertz was inspired by the research conducted in America on all possible aspects of human relationships. He was particularly fascinated by the monumental projects launched by the Carnegie Corporation under Myrdal's direction, and their influence is detectable in Hertz's book. This chiefly applies to the frequent comparisons he makes between the situation of the Jews in Poland and the position of blacks in America. The passages which refer to the blacks' situation, especially in the southern states, are now anachronisms, though thirty years ago they reflected the reality.

Hertz's book still makes for inspiring reading, especially now when Polish-Jewish studies have undergone significant evolution. This has found expression not only in the proliferation of publications of every sort but in the founding of Polish-Jewish research centers in Israel, England, France, and the United States. Scarcely thirty years ago when Hertz commenced his work, however, the field was a complete blank and it was difficult to locate works written at that same time both within Poland and without. Hertz realized that what he had accomplished—and it was no small accomplishment—was only a beginning. As he wrote in the afterword to *Jews in Polish Culture:* "This book's task is to open the discussion, pose the problems, and discuss the methods that can be used in their solution. Further work should be taken up by others."

Finally, one last remark. *Jews In Polish Culture* was clearly intended for the Polish and Polish Jewish reader. This is evident not only in the language but in the form of the narrative, which assumes that the reader has a previous knowledge of the facts and historical figures mentioned in the text (hence the need to supply the present edition with brief but essential footnotes). Immediately upon its publication in Paris in 1961, this book was placed on the index in communist Poland because of its author, its publisher, and its subject. A certain number of copies did, however, make their way to Poland through various channels, mainly to academic institutions, as was similarly the case with other banned literature. In those years—a period when official anti-Semitic propaganda was on the rise—Hertz's book may well have been the sole postwar source of reliable information on the Jews in old Poland. For many years its circle of readers was exceedingly narrow. It was only in the Solidarity period and during the relaxation of political restraints in Poland that Hertz and his work began to be discussed openly in a number of periodicals dealing with cultural and social issues. Universities in Warsaw, Kraków, Lublin, and Wrocław saw master's and doctoral dissertations launched on Jewish subjects, including those Hertz singled out in *Jews In Polish Culture*. Time will tell whether this is to be a lasting trend and what consequences it will yield. Yet one thing is indisputable—that Poland, where at present there are nearly no Jews, is unique in possessing innumerable archival sources without which it is inconceivable to attempt any serious study of the history and culture of the Jews from their earliest settlement along the Vistula to their extermination during the second world war.

Introduction

This book appears at a time when Jews and the "Jewish question" are once again being spoken of, though not necessarily written about, in Poland. Or, to put it another way, when once again there are confirmed instances of a growing wave of anti-Semitism. The Jews of Poland, as a great national and cultural community, a numerous social group, are now part of the past. Only scattered individuals remain, who for the most part are unconnected to that old community, having never identified with it, and who are now usually hidden behind the mask of a new name. But the old "question" still exists, and it is clear that hostility is shown toward these individuals as Jews.

Such persistent hostility illustrates one of this book's theses, that antagonism to certain people, defined in the case at hand as anti-Semitism, is not dependent on their numbers, their objective role, or their "alienness." It is not the few Jews in Poland who are the source of the anti-Semitism but certain deep and wide-ranging diseases that eat away at the society in which those Jews live. Jews become only a convenient means to facilitate the polarization of certain feelings and reactions. Even if there were not a single Jew in Poland today or if no Jew were playing the slightest part in Polish life, it is likely that some forms of anti-Semitism would still exist. The living would be replaced by their own ghosts. In Poland the traditions of anti-Semitism have left such deep traces that the Jew as symbol could suffice entirely.

Immediately after the war, anti-Semitism in Poland found its rationalization in the role that people of Jewish origin had played in the Communist party and in the machinery of the Polish government. This book discusses the circumstances that caused the Polish Jews to furnish communism with many outstanding leaders. It also discusses how they furnished leaders to movements foreign or hostile to communism. And it attempts to explain why it was specifically from the world of the Jews that so many nonconformists emerged to challenge generally accepted rules and philosophies. This Jewish nonconformism, which before the war gave rise to the expression "commie Jew," naturally persisted after the war. In communist Poland, state dignitaries of Jewish origin were the remnants of the old nonconforming Jewish intelligentsia, which had sought in communism a way to protest, an ideal of justice, and the fulfillment of their idealistic dreams. That in time some of these people were doomed to experience painful disappointment or to become opportunists is another matter entirely.

But in today's Poland, apart from the traditional and still very powerful anti-Semitism that arises from the bottom of society, an increasingly pronounced new form of anti-Semitism has appeared, one that comes from the top, or rather from outside Poland's borders, from the Soviet Union. Now it is no longer the "commie Jew" but "Jew revisionism." Moscow has undertaken a programmatic struggle against Jewish revisionists and is imposing that program on its Polish pupils. Just as the Jews were formerly accused of leftist subversiveness, today they are accused of rightist subversiveness.

The "commie Jew" and "Jew revisionism"! The phrases appear diametrically opposed, but in reality they are identical. In both cases the same thing is at issue. There is no doubt that individuals of Jewish origin are playing an outstanding role among the "revisionists" in Poland. Their names are well known and we can dispense with them here. The point is that the same path that once brought those people to communism is now leading them to revisionism. That path is a hatred of conformism, a passion for thought and criticism, and a striving for justice. Here too the Jews are the "yeast" creating ferment and anxiety.

Of all the threats to communism, revisionism is perhaps the greatest, because it comes from within, a revolt of mind and feeling against the hypocrisy and falseness of official doctrine. Communism is now dead as a philosophic system, but it remains a useful tool in the hands of those who rule a significant portion of our world. It is a canonized doctrine that cannot bear free and critical thought. The revisionists are attempting to think. In fact, revisionism is now acting like the child in Hans Christian Andersen's fairy tale: with increasing clarity it declares that the king is naked. There is nothing surprising in official communism's fear of revisionism and its attack against it. Revisionism is an internal danger, treason in the ranks.

In this battle anti-Semitism can be exploited to do the same job for communism as it did for czarism and other related systems in that part of Europe: the masses can be counted on to receive it well.

Anti-Semitism is especially menacing in today's Poland. Poland's future and the future of its culture are to an enormous degree connected with whether or not revisionism is held up to view as a force splitting official doctrine from within. Each success for revisionism means a step forward on the road to the liberation of minds, a step toward creative and cultural freedom. Individuals of Jewish origin, numbered among the "revisionists," are in the first ranks of those fighting for the future of

Polish culture. In attacking them, anti-Semitism is attacking those who spread the creative ferment that is splitting the shell of hypocritical communist conformism.

This book was written with those who are fighting for the future of Polish culture in mind. And it was also written with a thought to all those Poles whose stance is so very important in determining whether Moscow will be victorious or defeated in its battle with revisionism.

Jews no longer exist as a community in Poland. Anti-Semitism has, however, remained. And it is no less dangerous today than when the Polish-Jewish community, many million strong, lived, worked, created, and suffered in Poland. In certain respects it may well be even more ominous.

[1961]

The Sabbath Candles Have Gone Out

I

There are no Jews in Poland now. The remaining handful are but a reminder of the community of many millions that lived in Poland before the war. That community was eradicated and will never return. In one of the last stories he wrote before his death, the distinguished Jewish writer Joseph Opatoshu[1] provides an image of a small Polish town in the years to come. It was formerly a Jewish town, but in the period Opatoshu describes, there are no longer any Jews. All that remains is a dim memory of the strange people who once lived there. Of the town's present inhabitants only one, a gray-haired old man, saw those Jews as a child and still remembers something of them. In Opatoshu's story, the young people of the town, having by chance learned of its former inhabitants, try to find out from the old man who those people were, what happened to them, why they perished. Thus begins the legend of those who had ceased even to be ghosts, and the legend seems to bring them to life again.

It is a very beautiful story. Its basic idea is the certainty that Poland will never be able to forget her Jews, that they will live on, if only in a legend that is painful, tragic, and not to be torn from Polish reality.

"The most terrible genocide in human history, the massacre of several million Jews in Poland, which was chosen by Hitler as the place of execution, the blood and ashes of those victims which have permeated Polish soil, constitute an essential bond which has fused Poland and the Jewish people, and from which it is not in our power to free ourselves." So wrote Maria Czapska[2] in 1957 (*Kultura*, June 1957, p. 53). Her words are full of truth. But is it only the blood and ashes of the victims that will become the true bond joining Poland and the Jewish people? My impression is that this will not be the only bond but that, with the passing of time, the evidence of other bonds will become increasingly visible. Willingly or unwillingly, Poland will never be able to forget the Jews.

For a thousand years Jews had been one of the important elements in Polish life. From the beginning of Polish history the presence of Jews and their part in society can be observed. We encounter them among the first to record the founding of the Polish state, they coined money for the first Piasts, and with each successive century their presence grew increasingly marked and widespread.[3] They were a part of Polish reality for a thousand years. They were viewed in a variety of ways—with ill will more often than with good, and sometimes with hostility and condemnation. They were, however, an integral part of Polish life and somehow left their mark on that life as a whole. With disfavor Stefan Żeromski (1893–1925) called them "native foreigners," forgetting that this definition could be applied to others besides the Jews. Whether they were foreigners or not is an open question; in any case, they were natives.

They were also an important physical and spiritual component of the Polish landscape. And after the departure of the Jews that landscape had to change at once, perhaps spiritually even more than physically. How beautifully Antoni Słonimski wrote about the changes in those small Polish towns:

> Gone now are those little towns where the shoemaker was a poet,
> The watchmaker a philosopher, the barber a troubadour.
> Gone now are those little towns where the wind joined
> Biblical songs with Polish tunes and Slavic rue,
> Where old Jews in orchards in the shade of cherry trees
> Lamented for the holy walls of Jerusalem.
> Gone now are those little towns, though the poetic mists,
> The moons, winds, ponds, and stars above them
> Have recorded in the blood of centuries the tragic tales,
> The histories of the two saddest nations on earth.[4]

The Jewish chapter in Polish history is closed. But it will be preserved, and that which has been written can never be effaced; it will be echoed in the chapters to come, to be written by future generations.

How did that chapter come to be closed? What did it contain? What was the true role of the Jews in Polish life? Only now, when there are no longer any Jews in Poland, can these questions be given objective and exhaustive answers.

This is an enormous task, one requiring an immense collective effort. For a long time the greatest difficulties here will be those stemming from bias, small-mindedness, and, frequently, cowardice. In Polish society the Jewish question has always had its own specific emotional coloration, which did and still does carry over into the world of scholarship. The Jews were discussed and a great deal was written about them, but did any non-Jew make an honest and impartial attempt to study and understand Jewish subjects? How many Poles knew Yiddish or Hebrew and could thus acquire firsthand knowledge of Jewish affairs? It is bizarre: in Poland, where everyone was "concerned" with the Jewish question, the number of non-Jews who knew the language used by three million citizens of the republic could be counted on the fingers of one hand. The authors of long dissertations on Jewish subjects knew nothing about the problems and dynamics of Jewish life and did not trouble to find out.

As a result, leaving aside source materials and works by Jews themselves, one is astonished and dismayed by the poverty of the Polish contribution in this area. The excellent work done by Maria Piechotka and Kazimierz Piechotka on wooden synagogues appeared only recently and is the first serious and important work on any Jewish subject undertaken by non-Jews.[5]

The Piechotkas' book is, thus far, an isolated instance. The Polish Academy of Sciences published two volumes of a monumental history of Poland.[6] One would think that such a gigantic work would treat the history of the Jews extensively; but the information about Jews is confined to a few pages and is buried in the context of a larger socioeconomic discussion. A dozen sentences or so are devoted to the culture of the Polish Jews.

Things were even worse before the war. Of course Jewish historians were working then, and we have them to thank for a number of very valuable works. There is Bersohn's famous *Dyplomatariusz*.[7] Bałaban wrote a history of the Jews in Poland and several excellent monographs on Jewish groups in various localities, including Kraków and Lvov. There were many more such monographs. Jacob Shatzky began a massive work on the Jews of Warsaw but, unfortunately, did not complete it; and Philip Friedman published an exhaustive monograph on the Jews of Łódź. There are works by Schipper, Mahler, Ringelblum, and many others. In art history, Jewish folklore, and related fields, the works of Bersohn and Regina Lilienthal, to name but two, remain scholarly contributions of lasting value.

Although these contributions will be invaluable to future historians, they treat the life of the Jewish community in Poland as a phenomenon in itself that, as a rule, eludes connection with Polish life as a whole. Of course, certain basic connections are noted. In his history of the Jews of Łódź, for example, and in the articles he published in the *Rocznik Łódzki* (Łódź Annals), Friedman provides an image of Jewish life against the background of the city's development as a whole. In his history of the Jews of Warsaw, Szacki treats the development of Warsaw broadly as a part of Poland's overall history. But his subject is Jewish society in itself, with its specific themes and problems. Here he does not see it, or does so only insufficiently, as a component of the greater whole.[8]

The same applies to works in strictly cultural areas. The Piechotkas were probably the first to observe that the architecture of Polish wooden synagogues was an outgrowth of trends that prevailed throughout Polish wooden architecture and can be properly understood only in that context. Jewish scholars, however, even the most outstanding among them, limited themselves to describing and analyzing themes and goals in Jewish society as if they were autonomous, without connection to more general trends. It is significant that perhaps the first and only person to understand the cultural connections between Jews and non-Jews and to treat them in depth was a non-Jew, Stanisław Vincenz.[9] Like no one before him, Vincenz was able to depict the cultural interaction between the Jews and the Hutzuls, the mountain people of the East Carpathians. Though he was neither a Jew nor a Hutzul, he was perhaps aided by his tremendously warm and close feeling for both groups.

With few exceptions, the work done by Poles on the history and role of the Polish Jews is negligible. Tadeusz Czacki's work on the Jews and Karaites is still of value,[10] but the later books of Teodor Jeske-Choiński and Antoni Łuszczewski-Marylski have no historical value. Only as sociological documents, as material in which certain attitudes and opinions on the part of non-Jews can be analyzed, do they possess any interest.

The same can be said of studies by such important scholars as Kutrzeba and Franciszek Bujak. These works, written for foreign consumption, were superficial, propagandistic in conception, and satisfied with cheap simplifications. They do not occupy a lasting place in the work of those important scholars.

A vast number of books, pamphlets, and articles on various aspects of the Jewish question in Poland are purely documentary in nature. This type of literature includes both anti-Semitic works and apologetic works written in defense of the Jews. There are some valuable items among them, including those by Eliza Orzeszkowa,[11] Leon Hollaenderski, and Ludwig Lubliner, which contain certain factual material that should be taken into account. But the overwhelming majority of those publications lack even documentary value.

Worst of all is that an enormous amount of basic material was destroyed and can never be reconstructed. The war and the Nazis have rendered the work of future scholars incredibly difficult. In many cases they will have to grope their way, making use of fragments of the basic materials, if even they have been preserved. Such work can be undertaken only by a large number of scholars and no conclusions can be reached quickly.

II

Nevertheless, such work must be undertaken: collecting and inventorying the material, analyzing it, and, finally, creating syntheses. And, happily, that work has begun, albeit on a still-modest scale. In Israel and the United States the work being done on the history of individual Jewish settlements in Poland is a promising sign.

Not only Jews but also Poles should take part in this great research. There is one area in particular in which Poles and Jews should pool their efforts—the question of the role played by Jews in the development of Polish culture, from folk culture to mainstream art and literature. Regardless of how this role will be evaluated, it was not inconsiderable. Before vanishing from the land, Polish Jews left behind a contribution to Polish culture that most likely will prove lasting. As if bidding Poland farewell, the Jews gave Polish poetry Julian Tuwim, whose name and work will forever be a part of that nation's culture.

And, conversely, the role that Polish culture played in the spiritual life of Polish Jews cannot be overlooked either. One of the significant aspects of the Piechotkas' book is that it clearly establishes that role, creating a point of departure for future research. Vincenz provided a similar point of departure in another area. Of course, it will be the Jewish scholars themselves who will have the most to say on this subject.

However, for this work to begin in earnest and on a large scale certain preliminary steps will have to be taken. In no other area of cultural inquiry will emotional factors be of such great significance as in the case of studying the role of Jews in Polish culture or the role of Polish culture in the history of the Jews. The Jews disappeared from Poland through annihilation, the monstrous murder of a great human community. This took place in Poland; and even though it was carried out by the German invaders, it did not move all Poles to horror, dismay, or even pity. This must be clearly stated. Many Poles experienced the annihilation of Polish Jewry as a colossal shock to their psyches. Many others, however, found Hitler's plan the "solution of the Jewish question," and the opinion that "Hitler did the dirty work for us" was not held in isolation in Poland. There were even those who did not think the work so very dirty.

It is self-evident that the psychic shock suffered by the Jews who survived was enormous. The postwar exodus of the remnants of Polish Jewry would no doubt have taken place even had no anti-Semitism still existed. "You can't live in a cemetery" was a remark I often heard from Jewish refugees from postwar Poland. The Jews who spent the war outside Poland said the same and had no desire to return.

But the psychic shock and the great variety of antagonistic attitudes associated with it were not solely the consequences of what occurred during the occupation and in the postwar period. The entire previous period was marked by "seeking the solution to the Jewish question in Poland" and had been full of wild emotion, obduracy, psychological trauma, and profoundly pathological states of mind. How durable these phenomena have proved was best shown in the famous questionnaire in *Kultura* on the subject of anti-Semitism in Poland.[12] The opinions expressed in the answers have immense documentary value, primarily concerning the prewar period. Those opinions are those of people whose views had long since been fixed, views accepted fully and unhesitatingly.

At the same time, the answers to the questionnaire displayed a visible desire to avoid both what had happened in Poland and the very problem itself. When reading many of those statements, one thinks of the well-remembered Polish expression "Keep silent beside this coffin," a classic example of evading responsibility, an example of cowardice and hypocrisy.[13] In certain troublesome situations in which murder is involved, it is better not to say anything about it—whether the victim is a president or an entire people.

Except that one cannot keep silent beside these coffins. There is no evading them. And it would be terrible if there could be. Silence indicates an inner poison that destroys the soul and body of those who do not wish or are afraid to speak.

Without taking those emotional attitudes into account or considering the psychological climate surrounding Polish Jews, there could be no question of a serious examination of the role of Jews in Polish culture and the role of Polish culture in the development of Polish Jewry. Here nothing can be passed over in silence; here everything must be said in full. That psychological climate, and the concepts, rationalizations, and attitudes bound up with it, all require conscientious and objective analysis. A conscientious and objective analysis means one free—as far as humanly possible—from the emotions that were and still are connected to this issue.

Accordingly, a fundamental aspect of the preliminary phase of this work will be a thorough analysis of these attitudes and the value judgments based on them that helped produce the psychological climate for the so-called Jewish question in Poland. An analysis of this sort will not remove the existing biases, traumas, and psychoses—and that will not be its purpose. But it will make it possible to understand them and thereby facilitate further research. It must be remembered that biases, traumas, and psychoses existed on both the Polish and the Jewish sides, even though they were different on each side and subject to different conditions. It is the elements that were common to both sides that are the most important.

One such basic element is the question of the Jews' difference, their alienness, their isolation. These concepts or phenomena are not identical in meaning. One can be different and not alien; one can be alien and not live in a state of isolation. And one can be isolated without being either different or even alien. If the Jews had only been different from Poles, then of course their cultural interaction would have been comprehensive and vital. If, on the other hand, they had been a foreign body in the Polish national community, then cultural cross-fertilization would have been either very limited or very specific, or, at best, occurring only in those cases where the "alienness" had weakened. Similarly, if the Jews had isolated themselves entirely from the rest of Polish society, then—regardless of whether they were "different" and "alien"—cultural osmosis would necessarily have been limited, and it is questionable whether such osmosis could have existed on any larger scale. These distinctions require precise examination and analysis.

"Difference," "alienness," and "isolation" are linked to another problem of cardinal importance in the psychological climate of the so-called Jewish question in Poland. This is the problem of antagonistic attitudes on both sides. On the one side, there was anti-Semitism, and on the other, the disfavor in which Jews held non-Jews. Anti-Semitism is of particularly great importance here, since it gave prewar Poland's spiritual atmosphere its distinct coloration and had a major influence on the postwar climate. This question requires objective analysis carried out *sine ira* while endeavoring to reach the very springs of human motivation.

A great deal has been written on the subject of anti-Semitism in general and Polish anti-Semitism in particular. The number of works of value is, however, negligible, while those without value or of exclusively sociological or documentary value make up the overwhelming majority. The problem is complex and many-sided, and no approach will succeed unless it proceeds from broader assumptions about social antagonism in general. Two major aspects of the problem present themselves. First, anti-Semitism is only one specific instance of social antagonism. The immense amount of scholarly work done in the United States concerning blacks makes it immeasurably easier to study other forms of social antagonism, including anti-Semitism. The basic mechanism that causes antagonisms to arise and function is not involved here, though of course each case is different. Second, anti-Semitism was different in each country where it existed and in various periods of history. In its historical assumptions, in its motives and rationalizations, and in its outward forms, German anti-Semitism was different from Polish, which in turn differed from Ukrainian or Lithuanian anti-Semitism.

Those two major considerations lead to a third of no lesser importance, which relates to the mechanism of cultural osmosis, especially in conditions as specific as those in Polish-Jewish cultural relations. The questions of whether such osmosis in fact occurred, under what conditions it took place, what directions it took, and what it led to, must all be scrutinized. And here we cannot avoid certain fundamental inquiries both of a theoretical and of an empirical nature.

These are the basic questions that must be posed at the very outset of an inquiry into the role of the Jews in Polish culture and the role of that culture in the history of the Jews. Let us attempt to find an approach to treating those questions, although we have no illusions that it will be possible to provide simple or easy answers. It is, however, important to begin somewhere. That is my principal concern here.

III

To what degree were the Jews "different" from the rest of the Polish population, to what extent did they constitute a "foreign body" within the Polish national community? How far did their isolation go?

The facts of "separateness," "alienness," total "isolation," and social, political, and cultural "autonomy" were always accepted as self-evident by both Jews and Poles. The understanding of these terms encompassed various motivations and rationalizations, and the practical conclusions drawn from them also varied, but the facts themselves were everywhere acknowledged as obvious. Even such objective scholars as Aleksander Brückner or Jan Stanisław Bystroń, on the rare occasions when they wrote about Jews, would, if they did not stress their alienness, in any case write of their differentness and lay great emphasis on the fact of Polish Jewry's cultural isolation. All others placed differentness, alienness, and isolation at the forefront of their considerations and conclusions.

Those inclined against Jews found in these "facts" sufficient grounds for antagonism. For the most part they thought that the differentness of Jews was so fundamental as to indicate an absolute and irrevocable alienness. They concluded that certain features of the Jews were so bound up with that differentness and alienness that Poles could not coexist with them. This was, clearly, a deeply pessimistic assessment of the possibility of Polish-Jewish coexistence. We encounter such views in Stanisław Staszic (1755–1826) and Wincenty Krasiński (1782–1858), views that culminated in prewar racism.

Early representatives of this position saw the source of the Jews' separateness, alienness, and perniciousness in their religious beliefs. This view was widespread and has lasted almost to the present. The Jewish religion and its basic institutions—the rabbinate and Talmudic law—are what made the Jews an element fundamentally different from everyone else, alien and self-isolating, and, at the same time, endowed them with social characteristics that have proved very injurious to the non-Jews around them. According to this position, these factors could not be overcome or eliminated. What then remained to do? On the one hand, the influence of Jewish religious institutions must be limited as much as possible, and on the other, the Jews must be isolated from the rest of the population. Staszic gave both ideas a clear formulation and provided a number of practical recommendations on how to eliminate the influence of the Talmud, break the power of the rabbis, and remove Jews from those areas of economic life where they had a corrosive effect on the non-Jewish population.

It is astonishing that so sober-minded a person as Staszic failed to observe that the responsibility for inducing village dwellers to drink was shared by the Jews and the Polish landed gentry and that the right to brew alcoholic beverages was much more the business of the gentry than of the Jews. It was not clear to him that the Jews were just one cog in the gentry farm system and that the Jews' attributes—which Staszic naively ascribed to religious factors and the influence of the Talmud—had been conditioned by their economic functions within the confines of that system. Staszic's attitude toward the Jewish question was like that of a serf who saw the source of his misfortune in the tool, not in the one who fashioned the tool and was using it.

Staszic's basic assessment of the source and the nature of the Jews' separateness and alienness prevailed during the next century. Its spirit was present in the rationalizations expounded by those who, like Staszic, were basically ill disposed to Jews. What was inimical in Jews flowed from their religion. Such views can still be encountered in Stanisław Szczepanski.[14] Gradually, however, it came to be believed that the Jewish religion itself was only a reflection of the negative attributes of Jews as a specific, unique human community, unlike any other. Andrzej Niemojewski wrote an entire book arguing that the Talmud is only a reflection of the Jewish soul, that not only are the Jews its making but also, more important, the Talmud is their making.[15] Niemojewski also connected the Jewish religion and the socially negative features of the Jews.

Niemojewski's views presaged the coming of a new concept. In the twentieth century it became increasingly obvious that religious factors were ceasing to be predominant in Jewish life. In the period between the wars, especially in the larger urban areas, the influence of the rabbis was waning and trends toward secularization grew increasingly among Polish Jews. There was also an increasing number of Jews who had never even picked up the Talmud. Of course, one could speak of the constant influence of the Talmud's ethics, the traditions kept even by those Jews who had broken with their religion, the Talmud, and the rabbis. Such things were in fact said, but they sounded less convincing than they had in the time of Staszic and Krasiński. New rationalizations for anti-Semitism were needed.

Such rationalizations arose in various forms. Generally speaking, they could be reduced to a shared belief in the constitutional separateness of Jews, their basic alienness in any human milieu and under all conditions. Racism became the most extreme form those rationalizations took. People who held that position did not necessarily treat their own religious life with any great seriousness. They had more respect for concepts they regarded as scientific. Racism, in its various forms and formulations, was a concept capable of being treated as scientific.

Unlike Germany's, Poland's prewar racism never had a uniform, explicit formulation. Indeed, when speaking of Polish racism, we tend to mean various concepts whose common attribute was the view that Jews were organically and by definition alien to and different from Poles. Very often this idea took the form of a nationalistic, romantic mysticism, typical, for example, of Stanisław Chołoniewski and many other representatives of Polish anti-Semitism. In that view Jewish spirituality was not only organically different from Polish spirituality but also hostile and inimical to it. Hence the necessity of isolating the Jews to prevent destructive Jewish influences from penetrating Polish life. Such concepts were undoubtedly rooted in romanticism, and more in German romanticism than in Polish. Echoes of Fichte and Hegel were incomparably greater here than those of Joachim Lelewel and his school.[16] Moreover, as far as Jews were concerned, Lelewel would never have subscribed to such views.

Racism, like communist Marxism, belongs to a large group of magical world views, both sociological and historicophilosophical. In the racist view, the mechanism of cultural influence is reduced to a division of all values into the "pure" and the "impure," the former ascribed to the culture and spirituality of one's own group, the latter to the culture and spirituality of others. And especially to certain of these others. The pure undergoes defilement when it comes into contact with the impure. Hence the necessity of isolating the pure from the impure, of taking preventive measures against the Jews. Racism in any form is an extremely interesting subject of research for anyone who wants to understand the role of magic in the life of humanity. In this case the scholar's peace of mind will be disturbed by the realization that this magic proved in practice to be considerably less innocent than many other forms of magic and that its result was the agony and annihilation of millions of human beings. In every respect it is infinitely easier to investigate such magic on the terrain of the United States, for example, where its effect on relations between blacks and whites has been the subject of extensive and fruitful study.

Organic separateness resulting from religion and organic separateness resulting from spiritual and racial differences are the two extreme types of rationalizations for antagonism toward Jews. Between them was a whole mass of other rationalizations, either those connecting religion with race, or those introducing additional elements, but enumerating them would add nothing new or essential to our discussion.

The purpose here is not to present a history of or a systematization of the various concepts of anti-Semitism. That work has not yet been done but should be. Formulated objectively with the use of the entire apparatus of scientific inquiry, it would have enormous value both for the history of ideologies and—perhaps most important—for sociology and cultural anthropology. In few areas of myth-making were the magical elements as explicit and prevalent as in anti-Semitism.

For us, however, it will suffice to state the most general of facts: that there existed attitudes and rationalizations that posited an absolute, organic difference or alienness of the Jews that could not be overcome. Such attitudes and rationalizations implicitly or explicitly assumed that alienness must lead to antagonism. The basis of this assumption was the commonly held belief that antagonism to an alien is the natural product of the objective existence of alienness and of the way that alienness is felt by those who are not alien, those who are "kindred." Such antagonism can lead either to the complete elimination of the aliens or—if the former proves unattainable in practice—to their isolation so that they cannot injure those who are "kindred." In the case of the Jews their difference and their alienness were thought to be obvious. The only distinctions made were in characterizing the difference and alienness and in ascribing a source to them.

IV

The fact of the Jews' differentness and even their alienness was accepted in Poland not only by those who were unfriendly or hostile to Jews. Even those who were friendly accepted these notions as facts. And this included the Jews themselves.

Neither Mateusz Butrymowicz, Czacki, nor Walerian Łukasiński denied the fact of the Jews' separateness or disputed that the Jews in Poland constituted a community apart, one isolated from the Polish community.[17] Orzeszkowa and the other writers and social activists who, in a humanitarian spirit, sought a solution to the Jewish problem did not deny that fact either. And this was also true of the Jews themselves, both the assimilators and the nationalists. All of these people, however, were guided by different motivations and drew different practical conclusions from those of people like Staszic and Krasiński. They too pointed out the features peculiar to the Jews' economic activities and appraised them negatively. Finally, they too saw the source of those anomalies in Jewish religious life.

Unlike Staszic and Krasiński, however, these people of goodwill were optimists. Representatives of the Age of Enlightenment, rationalists, they believed that ignorance was the source of evil, that the march of education would do away with Jewish religious "superstitions," and that the Jews would both assimilate with the rest of the citizens and themselves become good Poles and productive members of society. Some of them, like Czacki, insightfully perceived the connections between the features specific to Polish Jews and Poland's entire economic and cultural situation. Others, like Łukasiński, saw great possibilities for the entire country's future in the Polish Jews and thought that a policy of spreading education and equal rights would best serve the cause of securing and developing those possibilities. For those with that point of view the Jewish problem was one of the basic issues in Poland's life as a nation, one of those issues that had to and could be successfully resolved through patient, persistent work in the fields of education and socioeconomic reform.

Moreover, they believed that signs of progress could already be seen. In his epistolary novel *Lejbe and Siora*, Julian Ursyn Niemcewicz[18] depicted how, influenced by education, the younger generation of Jews was changing the way it had lived thus far, how its mentality was being transformed, and how Jews were turning into good citizens and Poles.

That novel has been forgotten today. It is weak as literature, and the author's viewpoint is naive. But it remains interesting as a document of the time and as the expression of a great humanist's convictions. It also had an important influence on the emancipationist trends among Jewish youth of the time. Written many years later, Hilary Nussbaum's book *Leon and Lajb* was clearly influenced by Niemcewicz's novel.

In time these ideas were taken on by positivism, which also in this regard showed itself to be an heir to the Age of Enlightenment.[19] We see the tradition of Czacki and Łukasiński and Niemcewicz in what Orzeszkowa wrote in her brochure on the Jewish question and in the way she treated Jewish problems in her novel *Meir Ezofowicz*. What is evil is the Jews' ignorance, which is bound up with their religious beliefs. It is the rule of ignorant, fanatical rabbis that is evil. The only cure is education. Fortunately, according to Orzeszkowa, new trends are already appearing in the younger generation of Jews, a powerful drive toward freeing themselves from the yoke of superstition imposed by rabbinism. A hand should be held out to that young generation. Here is the promise of a better future and a road leading to the solution of the Jewish problem.

Assimilationist tendencies were very explicit among Jews in the epoch in which Orzeszkowa lived and wrote. There was also a good-sized group of Polish-Jewish intellectuals who shared her views. Many of her closest friends were people of that group, the poet and novelist Leopold Meyet, for one. That these tendencies and such people existed was, for Orzeszkowa and for many Poles of her time, the best guarantee that, through education and the granting of equal rights, Poland would acquire large numbers of valuable and devoted citizens.

More than the writers of the early nineteenth century, Orzeszkowa was also able to accentuate the historical bonds between Polish Jews and Poland. Writing after the January Uprising of 1863, in which Jews had acted admirably, Orzeszkowa was able to show how Jews had acquitted themselves as patriots and citizens. She also reached further back into history to affirm that in earlier times as well Jews had devotedly served the fatherland. The legend recounted in *Meir Ezofowicz*—a legend, incidentally, not without historical basis—was nothing other than an attempt by the great writer at ennobling Polish Jews, an attempt at their historical rehabilitation.

This introduces an important factor, one generally foreign to writers at the beginning of the nineteenth century. While affirming the separateness of the Jews and their isolation, Orzeszkowa at the same time questioned their alienness. If the Jews have become alien, that is a temporary phenomenon, arising from anomalies in both Polish and Jewish life. But the Jews were not always alien. Even now their alienness is more a matter of appearances, artificially strengthened by the rabbis' superstitions on the one side and by anti-Semites on the other. The Jews as a whole are connected to Poland, are an integral part of it, and have their own Polish historical traditions.

Other writers of the positivist era—Maria Konopnicka, Karol Szymanowski, and Aleksander Swiętochowski and Bolesław Prus in earlier periods—were close to Orzeszkowa's views. For them as well the essential problem was the ignorance of the Jewish masses, their dependence on the rabbis and the code of Talmudic law. They also saw progress in education as the cure. And finally, like Orzeszkowa, they placed greater accent on the Polish Jews' difference than on their alienness. It was after all with pride that Konopnicka's character Mendel Gdański said of himself that he was a Danziger, nothing else but that. The Jews' historical and emotional connection to Poland was raised and disseminated in positivist literature and perpetuated, though to a lesser degree, in the literature of the next period.

Nevertheless, if difference and separateness were stressed more strongly than alienness, that still did not mean that the writers of the positivist period now felt fully kindred with Polish Jews. Separateness differed from alienness in the degree of distance from or proximity to Polishness. By laying greater stress on separateness than alienness, the positivists cut themselves off from anti-Semitism, an attitude of antagonism toward the Jews as alien. They also expressed their optimistic belief that the Jews would undergo "kindredification," that the differences between them and the Poles would be effaced and what was alien about Jews would disappear. They were also encouraged, and their beliefs fortified, by the progress in linguistic and cultural assimilation among Jews.

However, regardless of whether separateness or alienness received the greatest stress, there was an acknowledged lack of "kindredness" or at least a lack of complete and undoubted "kindredness." Aside from assimilationist individuals and groups, apart from those "Poles of the Mosaic faith" (many of whom, besides, were quick to change their religion), the great mass of Jews were not Poles and in many fundamental respects differed greatly from Poles. There was still something essentially alien about them—and that idea is found even in Orzeszkowa. These notions were never clearly defined, the demarcation lines never clearly marked—they were sensed intuitively.

The source from which the distinguishing features of Polish Jewry were supposed to flow was still Jewish religious life and its institutions.

In other words, ignorance was the source. It was only later that the structural anomalies in Jewish economic and professional life began to be viewed as not solely the necessary result of the Talmud and the rule of the rabbis.

V

If we pass from the Polish to the Jewish side, we encounter similar valuations about the Jewish question. On the Jewish side too there were differences in understanding certain phenomena and trends, but the way separateness, alienness, and isolation were viewed is the same as we have noted among the Polish writers.

Just as a fundamental divergence had arisen between the positions of Staszic and Łukasiński, no lesser differences existed between the Jewish assimilationists and the Jewish nationalists.

The views of the assimilationists were in complete accord with the position represented by Czacki, Łukasiński, and Orzeszkowa. The assimilationists also accepted the separateness or even the alienness of Jews and saw the source of those features in Jewish religious life and its institutions. They shared the belief that education and full participation as citizens were the only way to resolve this difficult problem.

Without denying the fact of alienness, the assimilationists, of course, placed their principal emphasis on separateness. Like Orzeszkowa, the assimilators, starting with Jan Czyński,[20] Hollaenderski, and Lubliner, cited the historical tradition of connection between the Jews and Poland. Hollaenderski, in his valuable book *Les Israélites de Pologne*, and Lubliner in his *Des Juifs en Pologne* reached into the past, eager to extract all evidence of civic and patriotic stances by Polish Jews. It was a question of finding historical evidence that would legitimize the Jews in the eyes of Polish society and justify accepting them into the national community. Each group that assimilates into another seeks that sort of legitimacy. The United States—the great melting pot—provides many examples in this regard. In America Kościuszko and Pułaski, Steuben and Lafayette performed the same function that Esterka, Ezofowicz, Szmul Zbytkower, Berek Joselewicz, and others did for Polish Jews.[21] As in the case of immigrant groups seeking assimilation in America, these figures became the patrons of Polish Jewry and were its guides on the road to assimilation and symbols of identification with Polishness. By their lives and activities, both Hollaenderski and Lubliner gave proof that they were good Poles. After 1831 both were forced to emigrate and were actively engaged in political activity abroad. Lubliner was a close friend of Lelewel's.

Czyński the Frankist and Hollaenderski and Lubliner, who kept their old religion, all shared the view that Polish Jews were "sunk in superstition" and were thereby alienated from Polish life, economically unproductive, and deficient in civic virtue. The source of the problem was ignorance, superstition, the Talmud, the rule of the rabbis. Hollaenderski, who knew considerably more about Jewish life than contemporaneous Polish authors, was unsparing in his depiction of Jewish superstition and the rule of the Kehillah and rabbis. Czyński and Lubliner were no less critical. But, at the same time, all were optimists. What they saw primarily were positive facts, the stirring of new trends, the emergence of good citizens, dedicated Poles. Lubliner especially saw a wonderful promise for the future. Education, the struggle against ignorance, that is the road to the future. A great deal will depend on the work done by prominent figures among the Jews themselves, but they must have considerable help from the Polish side. Such help is in Poland's interest and could not be more vital to her future. Hostility toward Jews and age-old bias will not resolve this difficult problem, but goodwill, brotherhood, and genuine equality will.

The next generation of assimilationists held faithfully to the views of their predecessors. This was a generation formed of people who themselves (or their parents) had come out of the ghetto and who owed their advancement in society to the education they had obtained, at times with great effort, and to their break with traditional customs. They were convinced that their experience could serve as a model for the Jewish masses to achieve emancipation. When those masses became linguistically and culturally Polonized and their religious life reformed, the economic structure would be transformed and the Jews would become Poles of Mosaic religion, an integral part of the Polish national community. Freed of Talmudic influence, the Jewish religion would become a deistic system, more ethical than religious, one based on the Bible and the teachings of the great Jewish moralists, of whom Maimonides was mentioned particularly often. Taken together this meant a complete reversion to the ideas of the Age of Enlightenment. In this formulation Mosaism became a religion of reason.

In Poland these views found their best expression in a small book by Hilary Nussbaum entitled *Leon and Lajb: A Social-Religious Study*, which appeared in Warsaw in 1883. It is a dialogue between two Jews, Leon, an assimilationist, and Lajb, an orthodox Jew. Each is a man of great knowledge: Leon of secular knowledge (though he is not ignorant of the Talmud) and Lajb of traditional, religious knowledge. Lajb's ideal is to deepen that knowledge as much as possible, to go to Palestine, and there, in the land of his forefathers, to achieve the highest degree of wisdom. He is not a Zionist; for him Palestine's meaning is exclusively religious. Leon, on the other hand, considers Lajb's ideals antisocial and profoundly detrimental. The Jew's place is in Poland, among Poles. He should engage in productive labor and serve the country that is his fatherland.

Their dialogue touches on all areas of the Jewish question as it was viewed at the time. Leon is victorious. Lajb admits that his views were wrong and contrary to the spirit of the time; he renounces Palestine, he renounces the Talmud, and he resolves to become a good citizen of his country. Although the book is naive and its form artificial, it had enormous programmatic and educational significance and, in that respect, is a valuable document of the era. It expresses the optimistic belief that the separateness of the Jews can be overcome and that the assimilation of the Jewish masses is only a matter of work and time.

Various other publications of the assimilationist camp possessed the same spirit. The weekly magazine *Izraelita* (The Israelite), for example, for half a century (1866–1908) engaged in persistent educational activity and undoubtedly played a very important role in forming the new generation of assimilated Polish Jews. It also paid careful attention to women and had many women readers.

The aim of *Izraelita* was to turn the Jews of Poland into citizens and Poles. No easy task. The mass of Jews whom the magazine attempted to reach were indifferent or even hostile to it. Anti-Semitic feelings increased in Polish society after the Polish uprising of 1863 and grew increasingly stronger with each decade. Although *Izraelita* could count on support from many prominent figures among both Jews and Poles, that support was not always able to balance the hostility felt by the masses. In addition, the so-called progressive circles—especially the socialists—were very critical of the magazine's slant. Problems with censorship also affected the magazine. The editors of *Izraelita*, like all their colleagues in the press of the Russian section of Poland, had to weigh every word to avoid conflicts with the censors.

The very name the founders of the magazine chose was indicative of its platform. An "Israelite" is not a Jew with a capital J, meaning a member of a distinct national community. "Israelite" indicates a religion and an ancestry, but not national separateness. An Israelite was meant to be a Pole of a certain religion and ancestry but no less a Pole for it. Elsewhere in Western Europe the Alliance Israélite Universelle and the Israelitische Gemeinde expressed the same intentions that the Polish assimilationists did. It is significant that Hollaenderski entitled his famous book *Les Israélites de Pologne*, whereas Lubliner wrote about the "Jews."

As mentioned earlier, the magazine's main period of activity coincided with a growing wave of anti-Semitism in the Congress Kingdom of Poland.[22] In Warsaw in 1881 there was an attempt to organize a pogrom against the Jews in which the Russian police played a leading part.[23] *Izraelita* thus had to place great emphasis on apologetics, demonstrating to non-Jews that anti-Semitism was groundless, harmful to Poland, and incapable of providing a solution to the problem. The magazine frequently based its line of reasoning on examples from the West and the equality the Jews had attained there. Curiously, from time to time it printed articles about American Jews, arguing that the complete equality that the Jews had attained in the United States had led them to identify with the whole of American society and to become good citizens.

These were, of course, apologetics well served by historical argument. *Izraelita* made constant reference to those chapters in the history of the Polish Jews that attested to their patriotism and dedication to Poland. Clearly, given the censorship operative at the time, only suggestions, parables, or examples from the history of other nations could be used in such material. But certain things slipped by, and the reader of that time knew how to read between the lines.

The magazine diligently noted all signs of citizenlike action by Jews. The establishing of a new hospital funded by a Jewish industrialist, of a school, a nursery, a home for the aged—all this was discussed in detail. All attempts at restructuring economic relations among Polish Jews were noted and discussed with similar or even greater diligence. *Izraelita* wrote a great deal about attempts to settle Jews in the countryside as farmers and about Baron Maurice Hirsch's project,[24] Posner's Kuchary, and so forth.

The magazine devoted a great deal of attention to religious matters. It was well disposed toward efforts at reforming Judaism in Germany and France. It did, however, accuse American Reform Judaism of having lost its Jewish nature entirely, but the criticism was rather mild. *Izraelita* printed articles about the Jewish moralists and supported the translation of Jewish prayer books and sacred writings into Polish. When the celebrated preacher Dr. Jakub Cylkow began to publish his translations of the Old Testament into Polish along with his own commentaries, his venture received highly favorable support from *Izraelita*.[25]

The magazine's contributors sincerely believed that antagonism toward the Jews would decline as the Jews adapted themselves to the rest of society and their separateness and alienness disappeared. They were convinced that education and economic progress would lead to a solution of existing problems and an elimination of existing antagonisms. In this they were in perfect agreement with Lubliner and Hollaenderski as well as with Łukasiński, Czacki, and Niemcewicz. All those people believed that separateness and alienness were the exclusive causes for the existence of the Jewish question in Poland, and that this separateness and alienness were the results of ignorance and of the peculiar features of Jewish religious life.

VI

Toward the end of the nineteenth century a new factor appeared on the scene of Jewish life in Poland—people who advocated a national Jewish renaissance. They believed that the Jews were not only a religious group with definite traditions and ancestry but also a national community with its own language and culture, a community all its own and different from the other national communities.

Ideologues of this sort were also found in other countries, particularly in Russia and, to a lesser degree, in Germany. The rise in anti-Semitism in that part of the world no doubt played an important role in the emergence of such aspirations, but so did the general nationalistic trends that had begun to appear everywhere at that time. In several ethnic groups, until then of interest mainly to ethnologists, tendencies toward national rebirth arose, aspirations to accentuate their separateness among the world's nations. At this time such tendencies grew increasingly strong among Ukrainians, Belorussians, Lithuanians, Latvians, and others, as well as in other parts of Europe and the rest of the world. Jewish national emancipation was a particular current within the stream of mass national emancipation movements, one that was fated to become a mighty river. These processes took place in similar fashion everywhere, and their mechanisms everywhere displayed the same pattern.

Every such attempt at defining one's own national identity must from the outset lay great emphasis on one's own difference from other national groups. The ideologues of Ukrainianism—Mykhailo Drahomanov, Ivan Franko, Volodymyr Antonovich, Mykhailo Hrushevsky, and others—accentuated forcefully that Ukrainians were not Russians or Little Russians, that the Ukrainian language was not a dialect of a Pan-Russian tongue, and that the Ukraine had its own distinct historical and cultural identity. At the same time, they laid equal emphasis on the distinction between Ukrainianism and Polishness. The same attitudes are easily observable in other national groups undergoing an awakening.

It was no different with the Jews. Their case was made easier by their having always been a distinct linguistic, cultural, and religious community. The need was to demonstrate that this community was at the same time a national community or, in any case, that it contained all the makings of such a community.

Consequently, it is understandable that the advocates of national Jewish emancipation were most emphatic in affirming the separateness or difference of Jews from non-Jews and quite frequently did not shrink from emphasizing the alienness of Jews vis-à-vis the greater society. They were also hostile toward the assimilationists, whom they saw as renegades to the Jewish cause. It was of no significance that they themselves had often come from milieus that were entirely assimilated, and that some of them had gained some command of Yiddish or Hebrew only late in life. This was often true of the ideologues of other nationalistic groups as well. Some of the Jewish ideologues—Stanisław Mendelson, to name but one—had formerly taken an active part in the Polish political movement, in which at times they had played important leading roles. Mendelson was, after all, one of the leading figures in the Polish Socialist party. Some, like Vladimir Medem, one of the creators of the Bund, had little in common with Jewishness, even in terms of religion. Theodor Herzl, the creator of Zionism, himself came from a milieu that was entirely assimilated. But, to repeat, the history of all other national emancipation movements can furnish similar examples. It is enough to point to the Ukrainians and Lithuanians and, in our own times, to colonial peoples.

The ideologues of Jewish national rebirth systematically tried to demonstrate the separateness of the Jews. Jewish historians such as Simon Dubnov were in agreement with the majority of Polish historians that the Polish Jews had always constituted an isolated community whose contacts with the surrounding world were sporadic. The Jews owed this to their religious institutions. Jewish nationalists agreed with the assimilationists and non-Jews that the Jewish religion was the source of the Jews' separateness, but they differed in their assessment of the role that religion should play. Even those who were completely agnostic and critical of traditional religious institutions believed that fidelity to those institutions had saved the Jews from extinction as a nation. And for that reason even those most critically inclined toward religion had a high regard for its function in preserving national identity. In that they were not much different from those Poles who saw Catholicism as a mainstay in preserving Polishness.

Some of the Jewish ideologues went as far as regarding the Jews as a physical-anthropological group in itself, thereby preparing an argument for the racism that was to come. Consequently, theories like Ludwik Gumplowicz's on the non-Jewish origin of the Eastern European Jews were categorically rejected.[26] Gumplowicz's theory of the Khazars was, not without reason, viewed as an effort to justify the necessity of assimilation. If Jews are not actually Jews, it makes no sense for them to insist on their separateness. Understandably, in assimilated circles the Khazar theory enjoyed great success.

The Zionists in particular were willing to refer to the Jews' alienness in the diaspora. Thus the theorists of Zionism accepted anti-Semitism as having some basis. As long as the Jews were in the diaspora and constituted a foreign body in it, there would be anti-Semitism, which is a form of antagonism toward the alien. Thus the only solution was the mass emigration of Jews to their own land, the creation of a new Jewish homeland. As we know, even Herzl himself was not certain which country was to be chosen for that homeland. Uganda was seriously looked into as a possibility and had its adherents for a long while.

The Zionists' position was thus similar to that of the anti-Semites. Both spoke of the organic separateness of the Jews and of their alienness. Although they differed fundamentally in their evaluation of the role of the Jews and their historic significance, their intellectual premises were the same, and they did not differ greatly in their conclusions. Here we mention only parenthetically that Gumplowicz's philosophy of history had its influence on the advocates of Polish anti-Semitism who belonged to the "League" and the National Democrats.[27]

The non-Zionist Jewish nationalists did not go that far. Most important were the Bundists, who stood for a national Jewish renaissance within the countries where they were settled. Their slogan was cultural autonomy, which would both ensure the Jews' national and cultural development and make possible their coexistence with the larger society. Given that position, not alienness but difference, more in the cultural national than the political sense, was stressed. But even this difference did not deny the possibility of sharing certain fundamental values and ideals. The Bundists were socialists, collaborated closely with the socialist parties in the lands of the diaspora, and rejected chauvinistic nationalism. The Zionists frequently accused them of assimilationism. It is symptomatic that in Poland the anti-Semitic camp was more hostile toward ideologues of the Bundist sort than toward the Zionists. This was not at all a matter of chance.

All the positions of the nationalistic Jews agreed with the idea that Jews were different from Poles, constituted a distinctly separate cultural and national community, and had their own specific interests. The Zionists laid full emphasis on alienness, the Bundists on differentness and separateness, but both ascribed the fact of Jewish survival to their age-old isolation from the surrounding community. Unlike the Poles and the assimilationists, they viewed that isolation as an extremely positive phenomenon.

VII

There was, however, one position that put considerably greater accent on the kindredness of the Polish Jews than on their separateness or alienness. This position did not deny Jewish separateness in matters of language, religion, and custom but made the point that the Jews, for all their separateness, were an integral part of Polish life, within it and not at a remove from it. This position acknowledged that Jews had a part in Polish culture and assessed their contribution favorably.

We encounter this position primarily in literature and sometimes in historical writing. It is to be found among both Poles and Jews.

The idea of the Jews' kindredness found its most beautiful expression in Mickiewicz. There is no question—as Abraham Duker has shown—that the poet's views on the Jews were sometimes inconsistent, and ambivalent attitudes can be found even in *Pan Tadeusz* (Mr. Tadeusz). Nevertheless, in its final formulation Mickiewicz's concept is consistent and explicit. Israel constitutes an integral part of the Polish community. It was providence that called Poles and Jews to coexist and to bear witness to certain eternal truths. Israel is the "older brother" who is spiritually and physically bound up with Poland and her destiny.

Mickiewicz's idea of kindredness found its fullest expression in the figure of Jankiel. Let us observe what a major role Jankiel plays in *Pan Tadeusz*, a moral, political, and even military role. Jankiel is the one who reconciles those who are at odds, who is the link between the various elements of the world depicted in *Pan Tadeusz*. He is respected by both the followers of Soplica and those of the Count. He is Robak's confidential agent, a political and military emissary. And at the same time, he does not cease to be a Jew. He keeps the Jewish faith and customs, he is a *podrabinek* (an assistant to a rabbi), and he performs a traditional economic activity of Jews in Poland—he is an innkeeper. A Jew, he also has the "reputation of a good Pole"; he is a patriot, fervently and sincerely devoted to the Polish cause. "The dear old Jew loved the fatherland like a Pole."

In Jankiel's actions Mickiewicz brilliantly caught some of the culture-creating functions that were the lot of Polish Jews. Jankiel is the source from which certain cultural values—primarily musical ones—are dispersed throughout Lithuania. It is because of him that the mazurkas and the *kolomyjkas* become common property. He is credited with being the first to bring General Jan Henryk Dąbrowski's mazurka to Lithuania.[28] It is amazing how accurate Mickiewicz was in assessing the role of Jewish village musicians in forming and spreading Polish musical folklore. This is an aspect of *Pan Tadeusz* that has been given relatively little attention, but, unquestionably, the poem contains a trove of observations and perceptions about the culture-creating role of Polish Jews. We will discuss this at greater length later on.

Jankiel is "different" in religion, custom, occupation, and dress. But at the same time his difference is contained within his kindredness, which is something considerably broader and more essential. It does not bother Mickiewicz that this kindredness encompassed a variety of attitudes and relationships. This is variety in unity, variety that enriches and develops the unity. In this, as on many other points, Mickiewicz proved a significantly deeper observer and thinker than many professional sociologists and ethnologists.

The theme of the Polish Jews' kindredness appears in other, lesser Polish writers as well. Władysław Syrokomla used a Wilno bookseller as a character to raise again the issue of the Jews' cultural functions. Syrokomla's bookseller is also a Jankiel but a tragic and solitary one. He is a Jew who brings Polish books to people in thatched cottages and saves important remnants of the past from oblivion. Much later, the eminent Polish-Jewish historian Shatzky would write a beautiful piece on the role and activities of those small dealers in old books who made such a great contribution in disseminating Polish values and cultural traditions. Those second-hand antiquarian book dealers were immortalized in prose by the novelist and journalist Ksawery Pruszyński and the historian and bibliographer Karol Estreicher.

As conceived by their creators, none of these characters is alien. They are different and other but, like Mendel Gdański, they feel deeply bound to Poland and play a positive role in Polish life.

This way of treating the nature and role of the Polish Jew is also found in Jewish fiction, primarily in the work of Opatoshu.

Joseph Opatoshu was a Jewish writer who wrote in Yiddish on Jewish themes. He was a Jew both as a man and as a writer. Spiritually bound with Jewry, its past and traditions, he also believed in its future. He was a Jewish nationalist, and the slogans of the assimilationists were foreign to him.

But at the same time Opatoshu was deeply bound to Poland. He owed a great deal to Polish culture, a debt of which he was fully aware. He was interested in Polish affairs until the end of his life, and far from Poland, in New York City, he collected Polish books and kept up relations with Polish writers.

In his novel *In the Polish Woods*, devoted to the January (1863) Uprising, the idea of the Jews' bond to Poland is worked out with great clarity. Jews are not Poles, they are Jews. They have their own culture, their own aspirations, and their own affairs. But they are Polish Jews. Things Polish are not alien to them. While maintaining their separateness they are part of Poland as something greater and more general. Here too there is variety in unity.

To my knowledge, aside from artistic literature, this sort of view was represented only in Jacob Shatzky. He was an interesting figure. A native of Warsaw, a graduate of the Jagiellonian University, an admirer of the poet, novelist, and playwright Tadeusz Miciński, he was in Piłsudski's Legions.[29] He took part in the fighting, was wounded and decorated. After the war he worked for a short time in the Ministry of Foreign Affairs. In 1923 he left Poland for America, where he lived until his death in 1956.

Shatzky was a Jewish nationalist. Most of his work was written in Yiddish, a language of which he had as excellent a command as he did of Polish. His multivolume history of the Jews of Warsaw, which unfortunately was never completed, was written in Yiddish. Jewish affairs were his life; he identified with them; they gave his life its meaning.

Not many Poles could be found with a knowledge of Polish life, culture, literature, and history as expert as Jacob Shatzky's. His knowledge of Polish history was astonishing. He was a great connoisseur of Polish literature: his affections always remained true to his youth, when he wrote literary criticism for Wilhelm Feldman's magazine *Krytyka* (Criticism). The literature of Young Poland always retained a special charm for him.[30]

In Shatzky's historicophilosophical concept, the Polish Jews were not alien. They were Jews, they were different, but in terms of the great scope of Polish life, they were kindred. Shatzky thought it tragic that the Jews' kindredness, one that existed objectively, was not only unacknowledged but also denied, undone, rejected. It was rejected by anti-Semitism and denied by extreme Jewish nationalism. Anti-Semitism was one of the reasons that Shatzky left Poland. And more than once Jewish chauvinism was to cause him problems in America.

We can discuss these trends, concepts, and valuations only in a most sketchy form. But we must begin with such ideological concepts, especially because they did not exist in a void but had some connection to the attitudes and valuations shared by a great mass of people.

In summing up those concepts, we must accept that the overwhelming majority included a notion of separateness that embraced a variety of value judgments, ranging from a simple statement of difference all the way to utter alienness and hostility. The latter clearly predominated in the period between the wars. During the years of the occupation this hostility became one of the most important elements—though by no means the only one—in the spiritual climate in which the annihilation of Polish Jewry occurred.

The Kindred and the Alien I

The belief that Jews are alien or at least different, other, held sway among those ideologues and writers who, from the beginning of the nineteenth century, devoted their attention to the Jewish question in Poland. Those were the views of the intellectual elite, thinking people, writers. To what degree did those views correspond to the attitudes, opinions, and feelings of the broadest social masses, Polish and Jewish?

One would probably be correct in accepting that, to a considerable degree, the reflections of the ideologues and the opinions of society at large were in accord. Those ideologies were not pure speculation, divorced from life. They were based on certain facts, certain collective experiences. As is usually the case, they were a rationalization of the larger society's feelings. They provided those feelings with some formulation, some logical expression, some grounds. On the other hand, directly or indirectly, they influenced those feelings and sought a rational outlet for them.

However, there is never perfect harmony between the ideologues and the attitudes of the larger human community. Every ideology, by the very fact of its being a rationalization, must contain an element of simplification, reduction; it must be a form of logical shorthand. An ideology strives to avoid internal contradictions and—though it rarely succeeds—attempts to be as uniform and consistent as possible. At least on the surface, as external expression. Only scrupulous analysis can extract the ideologists' internal contradictions and factual errors.

What we usually define as a community's attitudes and feelings, its reactions, opinions, and moods, is a different matter, although here too rationalizations play an important role. Each of us seeks some logical or pseudological basis for our beliefs. Such justifications are nearly always stereotyped formulations, taken from tradition or borrowed from professional ideologues, from those whom we consider authorities. Most frequently we take such rationalizations on faith, caring little about checking their logical or empirical basis. The important thing is that they provide us with a sense of certainty in our opinions and in our relations with other people. A similar role is also played by those philosophies of life that we often consider to be the wisdom of the common people.

All the rationalizations we use constantly in our daily lives do nothing to eliminate the various contradictions in the attitudes of both individuals and entire communities. Even when man attempts to give a rational form to his motives or actions, he remains a creature of emotions, full of contradictory feelings and reactions. Only rarely is he aware of those contradictions. His relation to other people, to himself, and to the entire world of values is distinctly ambivalent. And at the same time, magical factors play no less a role today in the thoughts and actions of man than they did in the lives of our remote ancestors. The only difference is in the forms they take, the external expression, the stereotyped rationalizations. As far as the latter are concerned, many of them have preserved their freshness for centuries or even millennia.

We must bear these factors in mind when examining human behavior. For they are, to some degree, decisive in human relations and have fundamental significance in the attitude of each of us toward those among us whom we consider different. Regardless of the rationalizations we use, the factors determining behavior usually have little in common with sober observation and logical thought.

We must remain mindful of these phenomena when examining the place of the Jews in Poland and their role in Polish culture, as must anyone who studies the relations between ethnic and cultural groups in any country, in any epoch. Polish-Jewish relations, though conditioned by features peculiar to Polish life, did contain certain basic, universal elements that can be observed in one form or another throughout the world.

II

Each of us is different from others in some respect. There are all sorts of objective differences in appearance, behavior, demeanor, language, conviction, and so on. However, many of those differences do not impinge on our attention, or, if they do, they register as something quite ordinary, natural. When registering such differences we do not in the least ascribe the quality of alienness to those in whom we notice those differences. Within a family, among brothers and sisters, there can be great external and internal differences. Nonetheless, perfect harmony, mutual attachments, and love can reign. In the area of the erotic it is precisely differences and contrasts that can provide the greatest attraction. It is the differences in appearance and character that can create a point of departure for strong human bonds.

Thus perceiving difference is by no means identical with perceiving alienness. Someone can be different from me but still be kindred. It is, however, another matter when we feel that someone is alien. In that case, as a rule, we claim that this alien person is in one or many respects different from us and that that difference is so basic and striking that it results in a sense of alienness arising in us toward that person.

These attitudes and assessments are extremely common, common to each of us. Sometimes we rationalize them; most frequently we accept them as obvious, requiring no justification. X is fundamentally different from me and for that reason I must fear him as alien.

This difference can be keenly felt as something utterly incompatible with what we consider specifically characteristic of ourselves. Moreover, we can perceive a threat to ourselves in that difference, a danger to our own existence and to what we consider of special value. X can be so greatly different that his existence threatens my own, that there is no room for the two of us to be together. In that case, difference will be the basis for a sense not only of alienness but of hostility as well. To such an alien we are unfriendly and antagonistic.

A certain, albeit small, amount of antagonistic behavior characterizes the way we relate to anyone we perceive as alien, even when our relation to him is devoid of any emotional coloration, when we are indifferent. That very indifference attests to a lack of trust, a certain dose of ill will. In order to trust someone fully, we must cease to consider him alien. That does not mean that we must always and unreservedly trust those whom we consider kindred. But someone who is alien to us, by the very fact that he is alien, causes us to feel a sense of distance, uncertainty, mistrust. And that can easily turn into open antagonism, hostility.

Wherever hostile attitudes are prominent in human relations, alienness exists. At times the feeling of alienness gives rise to hostility, but sometimes hostility gives rise to the feeling of alienness. When family members, married couples, lovers, or friends quarrel seriously, they become alien to each other. We often speak of people who have become "alienated" from our life or our milieu.

Let us remember, however, that a sense of alienness does not necessarily have to be accompanied by open antagonism. The amount of antagonism in a chance encounter with someone alien to us, resulting from a lack of trust or uncertainty, can be very small. More likely it results in a lack of interest in that alien person and his affairs, to indifference on our part, to neutrality in our opinion of him. A Guatemalan is alien to a Pole. But he is not the object of the Pole's ill will. A Pole can be perfectly indifferent to a Guatemalan. After all, what does a Pole know about a Guatemalan? He is entirely outside the reach of the Pole's life experience. A name, a symbol, a shadow. In our daily life the great majority of "aliens" are only shadows, symbols, figures which—if we encounter them directly at all—pass by us without engaging our attention and quickly fade from memory.

In reality, however, this problem is not as simple as might appear from our presentation of it so far. Like everything human, these interactions are full of contradiction, inconsistency, and—when it is a question of their refraction in people's minds—ambivalence.

Let us begin with difference. In order to state that X is different from me, I must first notice that difference. In other words, there must be a difference that impinges on my attention in a sufficiently strong and convincing manner. What kind of difference must it be, what causes it to impinge on me, in what circumstances does it occur?

Here every formula is a disappointment, no fixed criterion can be applied. For "objective" difference and "subjective" difference bear no resemblance to each other.

As our point of departure let us consider differences in external appearance, which should strike us most strongly and immediately. In regard to physical appearance people differ greatly: X is tall and blond, Y is short and dark haired, Z is fat and red haired, N is thin and bald. We see those differences, are aware of them, talk about them. But are they always felt as differences? What I mean is: X is aware that in appearance he differs from Y, Z, and N, but he does not ascribe any essential significance to that difference and does not feel it as difference. "Difference" does not always mean the same thing. A difference can be simultaneously perceived and utterly ignored; it can just go unseen. If X, Y, Z, and N are friends, members of the same family, part of the same close community, they will ignore differences in appearance. Instead, only that which binds them together will be noticed.

Fine, someone will say, but in this example it is a question of people of the same race, people whose physical differences fall within a range of certain basic features that indicate they are of the same race. Thus, right from the start we are unable to avoid the problem of race. Especially when we live in an epoch in which seas of blood have flowed in the name of the race. And even though everything that needed saying on the subject of the errors and absurdities of racial theories has already been said, we must devote a few remarks to that subject here.

III

"Race" is a schematic construct used by anthropologists to classify the physical types of the creature called *Homo sapiens*. A racial type indicates a concurrence of certain anatomical features in a person. The question of selection of such features is itself a subject for discussion. For the purposes of classification one may take the concurrence or recurrence of certain features. Moreover, we know that a "pure" racial type is a theoretical fiction. In practice—let us accept that this occurred as the result of crossbreeding over millennia—various combinations of anthropological features were created. In certain populations those combinations can be more distinct, in others less distinct. However, they are never as distinct as in artificially produced strains of dogs, cats, or horses, for example.

Anthropology knows no Jewish "race." Nor any Semitic "race." "Semitic" indicates a group of languages only. To speak of a Semitic race is the same as speaking of the race of those who speak English. The Jews are everywhere a combination of various racial elements, and among Polish Jews the "Nordic" type was by no means a rarity. In Poland so-called Armenoid and Mediterranean features were considered typically Jewish, and it was such features that people usually had in mind when speaking of the Jewish "type." In the American melting pot, where those features are common among Italians, Hispanics, Greeks, Armenians, Arabs, and others, no one ascribes them specifically to Jews.

All attempts at determining a uniform Jewish racial type—even the Jews themselves have set out on these dangerous waters—were peremptorily rejected by serious science. That, of course, had no influence on social mythology, which treated the Jewish "race" extremely seriously. How seriously, places like Majdanek and Bełżec best testify.

For a long time attempts were made to determine the connections between physical "races" and the mental, social, and cultural features of human beings. A large number of pseudoscientific theories and political philosophies arose in that context. Science, however, knows no such connections. At most it was observed that certain mental inclinations were more distinct in one anthropological type than another. But here we are speaking of generalizations, more hypothetical than categorical in nature. Scientifically speaking, racism is an absurdity that has no basis in objective fact. It is another matter entirely that this absurdity became an expression of faith for millions of people and became the source of suffering and extinction for millions of others. Man's madness is boundless, and rational thought and reliable knowledge rarely have any significant influence on human beings' attitudes and actions.

Nevertheless, we must accept that conspicuous anthropological features are the basis on which we differentiate among human beings and define them as different from and alien to us. Skin color is one particularly eye-catching feature. In this case one even speaks of "natural" differences, ones subject to no doubt, obvious to everyone.

The problem of skin color is of fundamental significance in countries like the United States, South Africa, and all the African colonies, where it is one of the most important bases for differentiating among people. And it is precisely in those countries that this is considered a "natural" differentiation, one stemming from the very nature of things. Various theological doctrines and philosophical theories rationalize and defend the naturalness of such differentiations. "If God hadn't wanted it that way, he wouldn't have created blacks and made them the way they are" is a none-too-logical but highly authoritative doctrine popular in the American South. But what is the reality of that "naturalness"?

My friends' son kept having trouble with one of his schoolmates. He was constantly complaining to his mother—Bruce is this and that, Bruce did something nasty to me today. Bruce's nastiness was talked about for years on end. Then by chance, and not from her son, the mother learned that Bruce was black. Herself free of prejudice, she delicately asked her son about it. He shrugged his shoulders. "Yes, he's black. So what?" And thus, paying no attention to Bruce's skin color, he returned to the subject of his nastiness.

It was obvious that Bruce's skin color did not register in the white boy's mind. In any case, he had close friends who were black. It could not be otherwise in a New York school—and all that happened in New York, not in the South. My young friend's reaction did not mean that he did not "objectively" notice skin color, or the hair and eye color, complexion, or height and weight of other boys with light or dark skin. But those things did not register "subjectively," did not serve as the basis for any classification, pigeonholing, differentiation. There was no question here of "natural repugnance" for an alien race, as the racists so eloquently put it.

The example given here has been confirmed in all studies without exception that were done on American children throughout the country, the South included. A child does not register the fact of racial difference, does not notice it. That comes later under the influence of the adult environment when, maturing and entering life, the child adopts the value system mandatory in a given civilization. If that system is based on differentiating among people according to skin color, differences in appearance will immediately be perceived and become the basis for appropriate social classifications.

This will not happen, however, if the prevailing value system does not recognize such differentiations or if they are very weak. In that case existing and objectively noticed external differences will not be perceived subjectively as something essential, strongly intrusive, and entailing fundamental practical consequences.

Such is the case for example in many Latin American republics, including even Brazil. No doubt, there too a certain racial snobbery exists, especially in the "higher" classes with aristocratic, Spanish traditions. Peru is another example. But among the broad masses of society, where racial mixing has been going on for centuries, racial differences are not registered and do not have important social consequences.

The same can be said of a whole series of great civilizations in which differences of skin color were not perceived. I have the impression that they are not perceived in Portugal, for example, and they are not strongly perceived in France. In the past they were not perceived at all in the world of Islam. In the entire history of that civilization we find no instances of racial discrimination, no evidence that racial differences were even perceived. The followers of Allah and his prophet belong to the same community regardless of differences in outward appearance.

Everything argues that those differences were also not registered in the late Roman Empire, when it comprised people of all races and all appearances. People with black skin were among Romans with the highest standing, and it is only by implication that we assume that their skin was black or very dark. And again, by implication, we can assume it probable that Tertullian and St. Augustine did not have white skin. Contemporaries do not seem to have paid much attention to the bishop of Hippo's appearance.

The question of skin color and of "racial" appearance in general becomes especially interesting in the context of what is called "passing." In the United States this refers to mulattoes in whom original black features have been erased to the degree that they can begin to pass for white. But passing can be related to other cases as well. In Poland, Germany, and Hungary one could also speak of passing in relation to people of Jewish origin whose "non-Aryanness" was known to no one. Those people had "Aryan" surnames, were Christians, and seemed no different from others in speech, custom, and appearance. And they kept the "taint" of their origin—if they were even aware of it—a well-hidden secret. The Nuremberg laws revealed that there were many such people.

Sinclair Lewis built his novel *Kingsblood Royal* around the problem of passing. Rummaging through old family papers, the hero of the novel accidentally discovers that one of his ancestors was black. And so he is not white but mulatto, colored. He could have kept that secret hidden, but does not wish to deceive others or himself. The truth about his ancestor reveals another truth to him: he suddenly feels his own inward "negritude." He tells his family the secret, causing a terrible shock. They beseech him to keep the truth of his origin to himself. They even threaten him, but he will not yield. His family renounces him, his friends abandon him, he loses his position in society, and he is alienated from the world of the whites. He crosses over into the world of the blacks and there finds something of a place for himself.

Unquestionably, the novel is built on certain oversimplifications. Even in the South people tried to ignore passing, which has been occurring for many generations. But that is not the heart of the problem Lewis posed. The point is that as soon as the community learns of the hero's ancestry, it immediately perceives black features—physical and inward—in him. And more: he starts to notice these features himself. Since he is of black ancestry, he must satisfy the expectations one has of blacks. He must be different from whites; he must have definite anthropological features, definite mental features, and a definite way of behaving. Those things were not registered, not perceived, before his secret was revealed. And there is no doubt that, objectively, they do not exist. That black ancestor was his great-grandfather, and it is unlikely that he could have bequeathed to his descendants any anthropological traits that would depart from those of the European Mediterranean type, for example. The differences that begin to be perceived were the subjective contribution of the environment, which began to classify a black accordingly. And the newly created "black" immediately assumed a way of acting and behaving toward whites and blacks that was in keeping with the pattern for blacks in the United States.

Analogous phenomena and attitudes are well known in the cases of Jews passing in Poland and in many other countries in Eastern and Western Europe. As long as X's Jewish ancestry remained a secret, no Jewish traits were perceived in him. However, from the moment it ceased to be a secret, differences in racial appearance and peculiarities of language, mentality, and customs began to be perceived. In such cases people as a rule would say: "Aha, he's a Jew. I'm not surprised. I always suspected there was something fishy about him." And saying this, those people truly believed that they had always found something fishy about X.

We must state this very plainly: the subjective factor, the socio-psychological factor, is of decisive importance in our perception and evaluation of differences in outward appearance, even when they occur objectively. In many cases such differences are seen by the eyes but not by the mind. They are not registered as something essential, something that could serve as the basis for social differentiation, social categorization or classification. But, at the same time, differences which either objectively do not exist or which in other conditions would not impinge on the mind are perceived and evaluated. They are perceived when, as a result of certain socially accepted assumptions, it is expected that they must exist and leave their marks.

One could say much more on this subject. In reality, a number of variations occur here, uncertainty toward and mistrust of one's own perceptions are operative. However, basically the behavioral mechanism is uniform: differences are perceived when mandatory conventions and community beliefs demand that they be perceived. They are perceived when they should be or when it is expected that they should come into sight.

IV

Differences, however, can be other than outward in nature. There can also be inner, spiritual differences expressed in a person's behavior, thought, and feeling—in other words, cultural differences.

It is clear that differences of this sort have impinged forcefully on people's minds in all epochs and all civilizations. In modern times, with the development of modern nationalism, they have become one of the most important bases for differentiating among people. Language, religion, the institutions of public life, traditions, customs, way of life—all these impinge on our minds with great force and become a point of departure for differentiation and classification.

Often those cultural differences are connected with outward differences. The belief that people of another language, nationality, and culture are also different in appearance is part of the common stereotype of the foreigner. People who speak Italian are lively and dark haired, the French gesture, Russians have Mongolian features, the English are cold and self-possessed, and so on. These are typical clichés which we have always used and still use, not doubting them. Certain anthropological features and certain behavioral patterns that occur frequently in certain civilizations can give those clichés an empirical or pseudorational basis. The model for cultivating an English gentleman, truly traditional in England, was of enormous importance in creating the stereotype of the Englishman among people of other countries. But it remains true that not every Englishman is a gentleman, not every Italian is lively and dark haired, not every Frenchman gestures, and not every Russian has Mongolian features.

In all encounters with people of another language, nation, or—more broadly speaking—culture, we expect them to agree with our image of them, and if some deviations occur, we either ignore them or interpret them accordingly, reducing them to the accepted pattern.

However, regardless of the form of our clichés, the important point is that differences in language, country, nationality, and culture constitute the basic criteria by which we differentiate among people. On that basis we classify people and posit the basic differences operative among them.

In practice, however, things are not all that simple. Cultural differentiation can be derived from a variety of criteria that are not in the least in harmony with each other. Indeed, they can be in open contradiction.

Let us begin with language as a criterion. The Swiss speak four languages, and in Switzerland linguistic difference is not identical with differences in nationality and state. There is no doubt that the Swiss constitute a united people in a united state, with powerful, shared historical and cultural traditions. The people of India use dozens of different languages, not to mention local dialects. But still the young Indian nation state is a fact. Both in Switzerland and in India, and in many other countries, people speaking another language are not considered different. On the other hand, the English, the Americans, and the Irish speak the same language, although they all feel different from each other. Within the same national linguistic group, differences in dialect can be so substantial as to greatly impede communication. The Chinese are a sufficient example of this. However, the perception of those differences does not necessarily lead to value judgments that become a basis for classifying people. The perception of differences in dialect can, for example, be connected with class differentiations in which linguistic peculiarities indicate membership in a higher or lower class. In that case, however, it is a question of social value judgments of an entirely different sort.

We are moving further and further away from the romantic mystical conception of a homogeneous national culture which played an enormous role in the development of nationalistic trends and in time degenerated into racism and primitive socialist realism. Today we are well aware that within every national group there exists a multitude of specific cultures connected with class, region, profession, and so on. And they do not necessarily fit into the framework of the traditional literary culture which we recognize as the official national culture. The latter is most frequently the product of centuries of activity of the upper, literary classes, who made their world of values into an official, representative system recognized as typical of a given nation. At times that official culture had a powerful influence on folk or local cultures but did not dominate them, did not enclose them entirely. In reality, every national culture is a multiplicity to which writers, and in recent times propagandists and journalists, strive to lend a homogeneous appearance.

At the same time it is increasingly difficult to define what constitutes the peculiarity of a specific national culture, regardless of whether it is a question of "official," regional, or class culture. The most important cultural patterns are universal and filter into various civilizations and peoples. And that has always been the case.

Humanity's great religions created powerful systems of universal values. Christianity created a great world civilization. Islamic and Buddhist civilizations do not restrict themselves to one locale. Judaism filtered into various civilizations—not only into Jewish civilization—and impregnated them. The culture of the knights, the middle class, and the peasants was universal in nature. Obviously, in different countries, depending on local and historical conditions, those cultures took on the appropriate coloration. But their fundamental nature was in accord. The culture of the Polish peasant has features strikingly in common with the peasant cultures of an entire mass of other nations. When at one time in America Margaret Mead's work initiated an examination of what was called the *national character* of specific countries, the criticism was leveled, and not without grounds, that what Mead's school considered specific to a cultural group in one country could also be seen as specific to analogous groups in other countries.

This does not mean that we must reject the idea of the existence of national cultures as the particular historical products of definite national communities. Such a position would be absurd. Nations exist and a cultural community constitutes their raison d'être. The point, however, is that none of those national cultures is a metaphysical monolith and that none of them is entirely specific or unique to only one national community.

Nevertheless, in practical life we are rarely conscious of those factors. We accept the myth that national cultures are unified and unique. Romantic mysticism delineates our opinions and decides our behavior. We have a cliché for our own national culture and clichés for other national cultures, and in accordance with them we shape our definitions of people. A person we define as a Frenchman *must* represent a culture different from ours and by virtue of this must be different from us. This we expect from him; this we a priori assume. It is not the objective factor that is important here but our subjective assessment based on the value system in which, and by which, we live.

Objectively existing external circumstances, which under given conditions can especially impinge on our minds, are also important here. In countries that are more homogeneous in religion, belonging to a dissident sect attracts a great deal of attention and easily becomes the basis for differentiation. The relationship to non-Muslims in many Arab countries today is but one example. In Catholic countries, Protestants were different, and in Protestant countries, Catholics were. It was only relatively recently that the English reconciled themselves to the existence of "Papists." All this, however, disappears or diminishes when membership in a religion ceases to play a decisive role in the life of a society or when a country—the United States, for example—is a conglomeration of religions. In such cases, even if some differentiation on the basis of religion remains in force—which does happen in the United States—it becomes an element in certain more general conventions of social life and has, relatively, a small influence on the affairs of the entire national community.

Differences in custom can be extremely important in differentiating among people. In matters of custom we are traditionalists, even when we ourselves are not strictly faithful to those customs. A custom at variance with our own jars and disturbs us. And it does not matter whether that custom is, objectively speaking, very important. The role of cuisine is well known. In Anglo-Saxon countries the French are still "frog eaters" or even simply "frogs." That French delicacy—markedly at odds with the dietary customs of other nations—often evokes shock and disgust. Poles sometimes refer to Germans as "sausage eaters"—or rather they did in the old, idyllic times. That the sausage became part of Polish cuisine, where it assumed a respected place, is another matter. Examples of differentiations based on customs in eating could be adduced without end. For Poles, garlic became almost synonymous with Jew, no matter how widely that illustrious plant is used over the world. But, obviously, rational reflection and observation are not the important factors here. The essential factor was that there were certain patterns of what should, and should not, be eaten. A person who eats something that should not be eaten is different from us, even alien.

The objective nature of cultural differentiations cannot be doubted. It is a fact. Moreover, regardless of universal similarities, those differentiations are numerous and deep, comprehensive and variegated. That in many cases they represent values that cannot be enclosed within the framework of some single, specific system has no great significance in practice. In every human community—national, religious, class, local, professional, and so on—they are felt as something unique and peculiar to a given place and tradition. The point, however, is that these objective cultural differentiations are not necessarily applied as criteria in differentiating among people—criteria that are clear, precisely defined in terms of content, and properly ordered. Thus we have a clear parallel with the sphere of anthropological or purely external differentiations. In both cases, objective differences need not be a basis for subjective perception and evaluation. Moreover, in the area of cultural differentiation the same attitudes and reactions can be observed as those we discussed on the subject of passing.

The discovery that someone is of an ancestry different from one's own leads to ascribing to that person the cultural features that correspond to our stereotype of the culture to which he *should* belong. This is a familiar phenomenon in Polish-Jewish or Polish-Ukrainian relations. To his amazement, a Polish musician learns by chance that a woman colleague he greatly admires is of Jewish descent. "You're Jewish? Then you don't like Chopin, you like Anton Rubinstein?" "Why?" asks the pianist in surprise. "Well, because Chopin is alien to the Jewish soul." This conversation, which actually took place and was reported to me, is a perfect example of cultural classification based on a stereotype accepted a priori and the expectation that reality must accord with it. Millions of Poles still believe that only a Pole can perform Chopin well. This is believed by people who could not tell a waltz by Chopin from one by Strauss but are still convinced that only a Polish pianist can "enter into" Chopin. The discovery that X is of an ancestry which in my mind is connected to a definite cultural pattern causes me immediately to place X within that framework and to expect X to behave according to the rules required by that pattern. It is irrelevant that in the given instance X adores Chopin and performs his music very well. X *should* not be able to have "that feel" for Chopin.

At every step, in all epochs, countries, and civilizations, we can encounter similar opinions and behavior. An American woman whom I know experienced genuine shock when she met some Polish intellectuals. In the part of the United States where she came from there were no Poles apart from a handful of railroad workers. There was absolutely no place for an intellectual in her image of a Pole. That woman, an intellectual herself and trained in scientific thought, was quickly able to disregard the Polish stereotype she had acquired in her native town. But it took a certain effort on her part. People with her intelligence and scientific training are never in great supply. Most frequently, a traditional stereotype—as a rule having strong emotional coloration—is unwavering and defines a new acquaintance, regardless of his objective qualities.

V

Not everyone whom we consider different from us is defined by us as alien. But in defining someone as alien, we are proclaiming him to be different. Alienness implies difference.

"We and You," "Us and Them," "Ours and Yours," "Kindred and Alien"—that division has always run through humanity. It is from this angle that in our daily life, in our philosophies and our historical or sociological theories, we classify the people we encounter directly or indirectly, the people we hear about, think about. That division is basic to all civilizations and all stages of history.

Aliens are not kindred. Our relationship to them need not always be openly antagonistic: it can be neutral; it can take on a friendly coloration; and in certain cases it can even be friendly. However, it is never marked with that intimacy, closeness, or trust that marks our relationship with those who are kindred. There is always some distance, which, most frequently, comes with a modicum of mistrust. In every instance, categorization is unwavering: the alien is not kindred.

However, moving from this general categorizing to specific attitudes and behavior is not a simple matter. In practice the division of people into the kindred and the alien is not rigid or unambiguous. And the closer we move from general theories to the specific facts of life, the more we are struck by the fluidity and ambiguity of that basic categorization.

Someone is different for some reason, in view of something. The same is true of the alien. Someone is alien because of something, and that something always forms the basis of our definition of the alien. An alien is someone who is not our relative; an alien is a person of another nationality or religion, a person whose kind of work or relaxation is different from ours. Someone who lives in another city, another house, another street is alien. There are innumerable circumstances that can serve as a basis for drawing the "Us and Them" line, for defining people as alien. There is always a negative element at play: a person who is not like us is alien; or, a person we are not like is alien.

Let us note that the definition of the alien as someone who is not like us is not based on a stable and unchanging system of criteria. The alien is always someone who is different from us in certain features that we ascribe to ourselves and our own, but those features are not fixed once and for all but undergo constant change.

In an isolated settlement anyone who comes from the outside, who was not born there or who does not have close and numerous relatives there, is alien. Even if such a newcomer lives there for decades, he may always be considered as alien and be treated with a certain reserve and mistrust. Sometimes, even to the end of a long life, he will be thought of as someone who "doesn't belong." Apart from not being "local," this person need not differ in language, religion, custom, appearance, beliefs, or culture. He will, however, remain alien. He lacks the one feature that those born there consider essential: he is not from there, not a native.

In any human group—not necessarily territorial or isolated—anyone who is not "from there" can be alien. For a gang of adolescents who play together, the children from the next street over can be alien, even those from the next building. Anyone is alien who does not belong to my club or group of friends, who does not go to my school. Anyone is alien whom I do not know personally or know only slightly. In our daily human relations, we are constantly defining people as alien or kindred in the most varied situations and combinations.

A large number of important social and legal institutions depend on ritual to "kindredize" aliens, to initiate them into our group. Rites of initiation in primitive civilizations, baptism and confirmation in religious life, the initiation ritual among Freemasons, the procedure of naturalization of new citizens, the parties that a newcomer must give for his neighbors in many places in America—these are all examples of the universally mandatory rituals of "kindredization." Those rituals occur in the most varied situations, in all civilizations, in all possible ceremonial forms. Their decline in a group signifies that the group's bonds are weakening and that human relations are becoming largely random.

Always and everywhere one is alien *in relation to something.* Someone who is alien to me in one set of circumstances can cease to be so in another. Someone who lives in another part of town can be alien to me since he is not my neighbor. But at the same time that someone can be kindred if he happens to be my brother, friend, or a member of my social group. Always and everywhere we relate to other people as both alien and kindred *at the same time.* X can be the person closest to me, but at the same time he can also be alien and an intruder in my professional or family life. Precisely from a good friend do we expect no intrusion in matters that do not concern him or our friendship.

This leads to ambivalent valuations and attitudes, which in certain specific situations can be of enormous social significance. To a white plantation owner in the American South his black slave was both alien and kindred. He was alien as a black, as a person of a despised race, as a slave; he was kindred as a part of plantation life, as property, as a trusted person, even as a friend, an element in the slaveowner's value system. Instances of intimacy and warmth between white master and black slave were not rare in the southern states. To a Polish nobleman his villein might be a *cham*—a cad, a cur, a boor—and there might be a gulf separating them, but at the same time that villein could be close to him, so close that no gulf existed. In each case the level on which their encounters took place was decisive. On one level those two men were alien, on another, kindred and close. But innumerable levels exist on which we encounter our fellow men.

These are very important points since, as we shall discuss in detail later, the kindred-alien type of relationship was of fundamental importance for the situation of the Jews in Poland. They were alien on one level, kindred on another, part of a system of valuations and feelings that is mandatory everywhere, in all civilizations.

Let us add that "the alien" and "the kindred" are historical categories. There were times when to a Venetian, a Genoan was not only alien but also a mortal enemy. There were aliens and "age-old" enemies galore in Germany, Italy, and all countries where there was a highly developed particularism—dynastic, political, or simply of custom. Over time these things undergo change, and today it is highly doubtful whether a Venetian and a Genoan would react to each other as did their distant forebears.

On the other hand, as a result of one circumstance or another, a feeling of alienness and hostility can arise where it has not existed before or where it was weak. The class struggle in the nineteenth century was an expression of a newly emerging sense of hostility for the alien, and also of a sense of alienness in general that had been unknown in the world of patriarchal-patronal relations. The organized workers and the entrepreneurs became alien to each other to a degree unknown to the society of masters and journeymen.

Alienness can occur or intensify even in cases in which the so-called objective differences undergo a considerable reduction. There is no doubt that the antagonism between blacks and whites in the American South increased considerably after emancipation, even though the objective cultural and social differences between both groups had begun to diminish. And there is no doubt that in Poland—and outside Poland as well—anti-Semitism erupted with particular force in the period when the Jews had begun to adapt fully to their environment. Of course, those objective facts had no bearing on the mass of rationalizations created at the time, rationalizations that laid full emphasis on the alienness of the group that was the target of antagonism.

The categories of the kindred and the alien belong to the world of cultural values. We judge people to be kindred or alien in relation to certain value systems by which we live. Kindred is someone we place within those systems or within one of them, someone who "belongs" there; anyone whom we believe "not to belong" is alien. Objective observation and reflection, objective evaluation, are of minimal importance here or are of no importance at all. It is our subjective judgments, as a rule socially and historically conditioned, that are decisive.

Our entire lives, our behavior, actions, thoughts, feelings, are marked out by the value systems that we accept as our own. They are socially and historically conditioned: they were passed on to us by the traditions in which we were brought up; they result from our participation in various social groups and their aspirations. And since a person, particularly today, participates in a multitude of social groups, various value systems cross-fertilize within him.

These systems do not always harmonize with each other. In contemporary civilizations that is rather the exception. We live in a world full of conflict, a world of many divisions, and this is reflected in conflicts among the value systems within each one of us. And it also results in an increased ambivalence in our attitudes and valuations.

Those value systems determine our relationship to other people. In accordance with how we see them, those people can be fitted into the value systems we think of as ours, and they are then kindred; or if they cannot be, they then become alien to us. But since we accept various value systems, can rarely harmonize them, and for that reason are ourselves most often in a state of inner conflict, the same people can be both alien and kindred. It all depends on the level on which we encounter them and on the kind of values delimiting that level and our behavior. White and black, non-Jew and Jew, French and German, club member and nonmember, neighbor and nonneighbor, and so on—all these divisions can indicate completely different types of feeling and valuation depending on the kind of social contact in the given case.

We must repeat that the kindred and the alien are psychosocial categories, historically conditioned and resulting from changing collective experiences. They are not something absolute that exists independently of our feelings. They can be felt by us very strongly, but that does not mean that they must be grounded in facts independent of our minds. A kindred person is one whom we consider so for certain reasons. And an alien person is one whom we consider so for certain reasons. These valuations of ours are constantly undergoing change and, moreover, can coexist depending on the level of our encounters with others.

VI

The categories of kindred and alien are filled with emotional content. Our feeling relation to someone kindred to us is very different from our feeling relation to someone who is alien. We are friendly to the former, mistrustful or hostile to the latter. Declaring someone to be alien causes feelings in us that range from cold indifference to heated antagonism.

That someone is alien to us does not mean that we must feel decidedly antagonistic toward him. If our relationship to someone is marked by antagonism, however, there is no doubt that we will feel that person to be alien. The element of alienness is of fundamental importance in all antagonistic attitudes.

The problem of antagonism toward aliens is among the most studied in the literature of contemporary sociology and history. And no wonder. Antagonism to aliens has been one of the most powerful engines in the history of man. In our epoch, the age of great national and class conflicts, that problem has weighed especially heavily on mankind, and so a great deal of attention and work has been devoted to it. In Poland Florian Znaniecki and his disciple Józef Chałasiński's works made a valuable contribution in that area. In America the study of interracial conflict has produced a treasure trove of materials and studies of immense value.

We cannot discuss the findings of those studies and deliberations in detail here; we can only highlight their basic features.

Antagonism toward the alien is conditioned by the conviction that the alien represents values that are a negation of our own, a threat to them and thereby a threat to ourselves as well. Here the alien is a symbol of danger. Moreover, the alien can be treated as the cause or source of our misfortunes. Since he represents something threatening to us, he must be threatening and harmful in fact and thereby responsible for our setbacks. It is a matter of indifference that the sources of our misfortunes may lie elsewhere. The objective causes of those misfortunes can be highly varied and complicated. They can be unknown or only partially known to us. We do, however, know that some such causes must exist.

Everything that we want to see as the source of our misfortunes is concentrated in the alien. The alien then becomes the "scapegoat" for our misfortunes; he is responsible for them and for that reason should be punished. In every national mythology we meet such a concept of the alien, which in practice is most often focused on a specific alien. Roman Dmowski persistently argued that the Germans and the Jews bore the responsibility for Poland's misfortunes. In time the Jews dislodged the Germans in his thought. Every nation has its Dmowskis and concepts of that sort. Only the person of the alien changes. With full conviction Mikhail Nikiforovich Katkov declared that the Poles and their malicious intrigues were the source of Russia's misfortunes.[1]

An alien is an intruder among us. He encroaches on our life; he introduces values that are not in accord with ours, that contradict them and, for that reason, menace us. It is difficult for us to tolerate an alien in our midst, for he is an agent of disharmony and disarray. And if—as is the case to a remarkable degree in our civilization—we ourselves are in a state of disharmony and disarray within the compass of the values we profess, the alien becomes all the more threatening and disturbing. If an environment that is coherent and stable rejects the alien, it never treats him as hysterically as an environment that is inwardly disturbed and uncertain about its own values. It was not a matter of chance that our era has been marked by the most dramatic and fanatic manifestations of hatred toward aliens. This is an era of terrible social and cultural sickness. The growth of anti-Semitism and the forms that it took in many European countries were symptoms of the profound illness of entire communities and an entire civilization.

Antagonism to the alien has always been a great driving force in history. Only its intensity and forms have varied. Epochs of great socio-psychological illness were marked by instances of alienation, the birth of new antagonisms and the aggravation of old ones, and the brutality of the forms of conflict. Human communities in a state of deep inner conflict, uncertain of their own values and disturbed by their own weakness, regarded with all the greater alarm those who might introduce new values threatening the old. Whether those aliens really bore some new and different values was given no thought. Alien-enemies, bearers of corruption, were seen everywhere.

When studying antagonism toward blacks in the American South, Gunnar Myrdal demonstrated convincingly that that antagonism was a symptom of the profound moral and social crisis that had befallen white society in that part of the United States. Instead of speaking of a "black problem" here, it would have been more correct to speak of a "white problem." Myrdal's observations can be applied to all other countries and civilizations. Anti-Semitism spoke more about the Polish, German, or Ukrainian "problem" than about the Jewish one. There the Jews—

themselves a sick community—made for a rather chance and external circumstance. Some antagonism toward the alien would have to have been generated even if there were no Jews at all. In other instances, Armenians and Parsis, Catholics and Protestants, the Chinese, half-breeds of every sort, and so on, filled the role of the Jews and with similar results. During Katkov's time in Russia such a role was assigned to the Poles. It is another matter that in each of these cases the choice of the alien-enemy was not purely random. The group that was the target of antagonism occupied a definite social position and performed definite functions which created the conditions favoring antagonism toward them and provided a convenient basis for rationalization. It does not follow, however, that this choice of an enemy proceeded from sober, logical premises and was the result of clear-minded observation. Objectively speaking, aliens whom we consider enemies need not necessarily be either aliens or enemies. In the American South hostility toward blacks increased during the period when blacks were becoming increasingly like whites and had fully accepted white values and aspirations. The more American a black became, the more alien and hostile he was felt to be by white Southerners. The same, and to no less a degree, can be said of Jews. Anti-Semitism assumed its most acute forms when the assimilation of Jews to non-Jews, speaking objectively, had become an unquestionable fact.

But this is not a world where the rules of scientific thought are binding. This is a world of values, feelings, definitions based on emotion. This is the human world. And human beings, in their constant attempt to rationalize their feelings and actions, do not cease to be nonrational.

This nonrationality of man is also expressed in the ambivalence of our attitudes toward the alien-enemy. What we have already said of the many levels in our evaluations of people as aliens applies equally to antagonistic attitudes. The same white Southerner who is hostile toward a black in one situation can be entirely friendly to him in another. The joke about the Polish squire who hated all Jews with the exception of his broker, his lawyer, his doctor, his banker, and so on, illustrates a similar phenomenon in Polish-Jewish relations. Of course, the polarization of hatred can go so far as to leave no room either for such exceptions or for an ambivalent relationship toward a specific person. Even in cases of the most extreme polarization, cases of the most systematic and uncompromising hatred of the alien, one can encounter examples of ambivalent valuation and behavior, probably rarely conscious.

There are known cases—unfortunately, very few—of full-fledged Nazis who, while unhesitatingly annihilating Jews or Poles, helped or even saved them in certain situations when it was a question of people they knew personally and for whom they had some liking. In the history of the most fanatical antagonisms—nationalistic, religious, or class—one encounters similar examples of duality in feeling and behavior. Anti-Semites making exceptions for certain Jews, white Southerners with real affection for "their own" blacks, Turks who aided certain Armenians, the English Protestants in the seventeenth century who saved certain Catholics, are some of the innumerable examples to be found in all countries, civilizations, and epochs. In many instances people have felt friendship toward those whom they in principle considered mortal enemies and wished to destroy.

VII

All these considerations, which are very general and rather theoretical, are of fundamental importance to our problem: the role of the Jews in Polish culture. The attitudes and valuations forming the climate for the Jewish question in Poland ran the gamut from feeling the Jews as different to feeling them as alien and enemies. That climate underwent change. There were periods when the sense of differentness predominated and there were those when alienness and hostility were paramount. But in each period different valuations crossed with each other, leading to ambivalent and alogical attitudes. And, finally, as we shall discuss later, in all these periods those attitudes and valuations were mixed with others in which the kindredness of the Jews predominated.

Cognitive and rational factors, however, always occupied a secondary position. And all those who, like Staszic, accused the Jews of inducing the peasants to drinking, who accused them of usury, and, finally, those who saw a mortal danger to the community in the Jews' moral principles did not meditate overmuch on the objective conditions in which certain peculiarities of the Jews could or had to be formed. There was not even an inquiry into whether or to what degree these charges were grounded in objective facts. Wawrzyniec Surowiecki provides an astonishing exception here. A contemporary of Staszic, Surowiecki, like no one before him and few after, understood the meaning of the objective economic and social functions fulfilled by Polish Jews and insightfully analyzed the conditions under which they lived. But Surowiecki did not have a major influence on his contemporaries, and over time that eminent thinker was forgotten. It was only recently that Aleksander Gella revived Surowiecki in his excellent monograph *Wawrzyniec Surowiecki* (Wrocław, 1958), arguing convincingly that he was a figure of great stature. We will return to Surowiecki's ideas at a later point.

But Surowiecki was exceptional and quickly ignored. The stereotypes, however, remained binding. Only a few years before the outbreak of the Second World War did clear-minded studies indicate that Jewish usury was significantly less onerous than that of non-Jews, that the well-to-do peasants were the greatest "bloodsuckers" in the Polish countryside, and that in a country as poor and backward as Poland credit had to have some features of usury, that is, it had to be very expensive.

Neither Polish anti-Semitism nor Polish philo-Semitism was or could be a coherent system free of logical contradiction and based on solid knowledge. They were rationalizations of certain emotions, feelings, and valuations. Nevertheless, anti-Semitism and philo-Semitism, even though the latter has not been a frequent phenomenon in the twentieth century, were facts themselves and had an enormous influence on the totality of human life. In practical terms, it cannot be said to be a matter of indifference whether Jews were judged by sober reflection, based on a comprehensive and thorough knowledge of reality, or by emotions patched with rationalizations of one sort or another. Obviously it was not. But what was essential was that certain valuations and attitudes existed, that they made use of definite rationalizations, and that all this entailed explicit, practical consequences. And those consequences were decisive in creating the climate for the entire problem, for the tragic affair that bore the name "the Jewish question."

We now come to further considerations more concrete in nature. We must examine the objective conditions under which the Jewish question was formed in Poland. This is a highly complex issue, but our point of departure will be the Jews' isolation, their exclusion from the rest of Polish society. Our approach will be based on one fundamental fact—that the Jews in Poland constituted a caste. In our discussion we will not be able to avoid certain fundamental deliberations on the subject of caste organization in general.

Caste

I

Throughout their centuries in Poland, until their destruction, the Jews formed a caste. Caste is a broader notion than ghetto, which denotes a closed territorial unit. A caste, on the other hand, includes the whole of the greater group in a given area, regardless of where its individual members are located. The Polish Jews, who lived mainly within local ghettos, in their entirety constituted a caste. This was not the only caste in Polish society. However, no other group—except the Gypsies—had such characteristic and conspicuous caste features as the Jews. Over the centuries, profound changes took place within that caste. Its functions and role in the life of Polish society as a whole also underwent changes. Nevertheless, the Jews did not cease to be a caste, even in the period when the slogan of struggling against the caste system had begun to prevail among them.

The caste system is not confined to such social systems as that of the Indians or the ancient Egyptians. In one form or another it emerges in various systems, in various civilizations, countries, and epochs. It can be encountered even in the most highly developed industrial systems and in social democracies. In the United States, and especially in the South, blacks are a conspicuous example of a caste group. In old Poland the class system, including the landed nobility, the middle class, and the peasantry, had many features essential for a caste system. In somewhat altered form the remnants of that system survived until recent times, even until the present.

A caste is a closed group. Every member of it was born in the caste and dies in the caste. It is difficult, usually impossible, for an individual to leave the caste. At times, leaving takes the form of flight from the caste and is connected with attempts, not always successful, to erase any traces of caste background. Participation in the caste requires absolute acceptance of a number of rules that delimit the very fact of the caste's existence. These are religious, legal, linguistic, moral, and professional rules—most generally put, these rules are cultural. A member of a caste must adapt his whole life, his behavior, thoughts, and feelings, to the rules of the caste. Those rules are accepted both by the caste itself and by the larger environment in which the caste and its members reside. Both the caste and that environment expect each member to behave as the rules require. This entails the observation of a specific etiquette which usually pedantically defines all the details of a way of life.

For example, the caste's rules determine how its members dress. A member of the caste should use his own language; and if he uses the language of the larger environment, he should employ a caste-marked grammar, accent, and vocabulary. A member of a caste is bound by certain rules concerning diet, residence, medicine, and so forth. When rifts begin to appear in a caste system, when it turns from a legal and moral institution into one that is only moral, its rules lose their force and there are frequent deviations. However, until recently in Poland it was thought appropriate for a Jew, even one who spoke Polish, to "Jewify" the language, to use grammar, expressions, an accent and inflections that accorded with the accepted image of the Jew. Analogous linguistic demands are still placed on blacks in the American South. In addition, in Poland a Jew who "dressed like a European" was known—as rumor had it—to dress especially garishly, thereby betraying his "Jewish" taste. In America one speaks of "black" taste. We should note that to a large degree those opinions have a basis in fact. The Jews in Poland, the blacks in America, and various caste groups in other countries display a certain aggressive quality in their dress and behavior. This has deep psychological roots, which we cannot analyze here.

From these examples of the kinds of detail regulated by caste, we move on to more fundamental things. The caste is not necessarily a group whose organization, behavior, and place in the national community are defined in law. Of course, in the class system in Poland the caste nature of each social group had its basis in legal regulations. The entire organization of the Jews as a caste, including their internal autonomy, the *Kahal* (Kehillah) system, their relations with other groups, and so forth, was defined by written law. Even today in the United States some southern states have laws—for example, forbidding mixed marriage, mandating segregation in public places—that impose caste regulations on the black population. Nevertheless, a caste system can also exist and develop even when it has no legal basis. The caste system existed in Poland in the period between the two wars, even though it was not imposed by law and there were no laws that, formally speaking, would have upheld it. Isolated instances aside, in today's world the caste system is more a matter of custom and certain prevailing social values. Those social regulations, although without formal legal sanction, can possess a power no less than that of the strictest legal provisions. The

Jews in Poland were well aware of that and the blacks in America are no less so.

Very often a caste is an economic organization, because certain economic activities reside within the model of the caste and the way its members act. In India and ancient Egypt the economic nature of the castes was quite pronounced and, of course, had the sanction of religion and law. But the same can be true where no such sanctions exist or where they are not rigorously applied. In Poland in every century definite occupations and economic functions were attached to the Jewish caste. Even in prewar times, the Polish people saw the Jew in a gabardine (or even without one) as a "merchant" or "peddler." Such activities were to be expected from a Jew in a gabardine, for they were in keeping with the generally accepted image of the Jew. Besides, through the centuries in Poland and elsewhere definite economic functions determined, or partially determined, the image of the noble, burgher, peasant, or Gypsy. This remained so even when class distinctions began to be blurred or when a separation of economic function and class membership began to occur. In the case of the Jews this image lasted to the end. Although in reality increasingly frequent instances of departure from that image complicated the picture and produced far-reaching social consequences, the image itself was not shaken. The "merchant" and the "peddler" had been utterly fixed in the model of the Jewish caste.

Furthermore, a caste is a cultural organization. Specific cultural features mark the caste and distinguish it from the cultures of other groups in a given society. This can even be said of American blacks, who, although participating as a whole in the general American culture and a product of it, have preserved certain social, mental, and moral features created by the very fact of caste life. In Poland, in the case of the Jews, that sort of cultural specificity was very far advanced.

Every caste is marked by mores, customs, and morals peculiar to it alone, its own philosophies, its own way of life, stemming from the very existence of the caste. In the Polish class system, as in others as well, the same could also be said of the nobility, the burghers, and the peasants. Each group had its own cultural and moral features, its own specific way of life, its own specific system of values. Thus caste elements are introduced into the class system. A nobleman lived, thought, and acted in the way suitable for the nobility. His way of life, thought, and action set him apart from representatives of the other classes and assigned him a definite place in the society as a whole. Naturally, his assuming that place was determined by a series of basic circumstances, birth chief among them.

The Jews were a cultural group par excellence. They were a religious and linguistic group. They had definite historical traditions. They had created their own literature, philosophy, and art. They had their own legal and legal-moral system. All those elements went into composing the model of a Jew. In only a few caste systems do we meet such a full and comprehensive cultural organization as that of the Jews. The caste system in India furnishes the most analogies in this regard.

It does not follow that all Jews were the same within their own caste. No caste is ever uniform. Even within the most rigid caste system, differentiations of every sort appear, subgroups emerge, and internal conflicts arise. Without ceasing to be a caste, American blacks demonstrate, as does all of American society, differentiation in class, profession, region, religion, degree of education, and so on. Similar differentiations existed among the Jews as well. The gap between the *kahal* aristocracy and the small-town poor was great.[1] And it was no smaller between the rabbinical, intellectual elite and the ignorant masses. In later periods, when breaches had begun to appear in the caste system and when all of collective life had begun to change, those differentiations became increasingly marked.

A caste occupies a definite place in a given nation's general society. This fact is one of the essential aspects of the caste system. One specific rung on the ladder of the social hierarchy is assigned to it. Caste members are subject to definitions strictly determining their behavior and attitudes both in and out of the caste. A Jew was a Jew and that said everything about him, at the same time assigning him his place in Polish life as a whole. Just as saying that a black is a black assigns him his place in American or South African life or in that of the colonial countries. In Poland the same could be said of the noble, the peasant, the burgher, and the Gypsy.

In old Poland the social hierarchy was marked by a division into upper and lower strata. The nobility as a whole was the upper class constituting a privileged group. The peasants, burghers, and Jews belonged to the lower classes and were of a "low" or "base" order. But here too value judgments were not uniform, and in particular instances this division was not rigid. Various shifts occurred and ambivalent opinions were common. Only the Gypsies, both as a group and as individuals, were always at the bottom of the ladder, and ambivalent attitudes toward them were the exception. Such exceptions were evident in those rare instances in which a Gypsy appeared as an acknowledged authority, for example in coppersmithing, folk remedies, or horse-trading.

These are the most general observations on the Polish Jews as a caste. Now we must move to a more detailed analysis of the caste system in which the Polish Jews dwelt for centuries.

II

For the purposes of our discussion there is no point in treating the historical conditions that helped form the caste system in Poland and the role of the Jews in it. Similarly, it is of little importance to what degree that system was imposed on the Jews from without and to what degree they themselves were instrumental in its formation and in perpetuating their role in it. Undoubtedly, it was imposed on them, and undoubtedly the Jews themselves not only accepted it but also made it stronger and deeper. This is a universal phenomenon, observable wherever castes exist. In Poland, and throughout the world, the caste system grew out of a specific historical context, was accepted as self-evident by all the people concerned, and was, almost to our own times, considered both normal and proper. Polish Jews had found a place for themselves in it and, once again, almost to our own times, made no attempt to destroy that system. On the contrary, they attempted to fortify it. The nobility, the burghers, and the peasants did the same within their own class-caste organization.

Poland's entire historical development—and in this it was neither exceptional nor isolated—the entire system of socioeconomic and cultural relations, and, finally, everything that traditionally formed the stuff of Jewish life both in Poland and out of Poland, all caused the Jewish masses to be closed within the rigid framework of a caste organization. Let us accept it as a historical fact and not enter into shallow and fruitless arguments about why it happened, whether it had to have happened, or who is responsible for it. Let us add that a great deal has been written on this subject and that none of it seems in the least worthy of mention, especially because it was written from the perspective of moral or political bias. Anti-Semites have heaped the entire responsibility for the caste organization onto the Jews; the Jews and their non-Jewish defenders, onto the Christian environment.

A Jew was born a Jew and died a Jew. This did not mean that individuals, or even groups, could not leave the caste. Escape was accomplished mainly by a change of religion. For centuries that was the only way out. In the age of the republic of the gentry, law and custom favored conversion. A neophyte was looked upon favorably, found powerful protectors who were often his godparents, and was ennobled and thereby accepted into the upper caste. Undoubtedly, that was not, speaking in terms of custom, acceptance without reservations. But such moral reservations were part of every case of ennoblement. The *homo novus* was looked upon somewhat condescendingly, with little respect, but that would fade with time; and the second or third generation would be completely assimilated into the mass of nobles and treated by them as one of their own. It was only considerably later, in the twentieth century, that the "ugly" origin of many Polish noble families began to be mentioned. In the eighteenth century Frankism brought a rather large group of *homines novi* into the ranks of Polish nobles.[2] In the nineteenth century leaving the caste by changing religion became a common phenomenon. However, because of the large number of converts, the attitude of Christians to them became less favorable and, in time, even unfriendly.

From the second half of the nineteenth century on there were attempts to leave the caste without changing religion, marking the start of the so-called era of assimilation. Assimilation consisted in rejecting the rules of the caste and acquiring the rules and ways of the world outside. In the initial period the Christian environment viewed such attempts favorably. The best minds of the time supported assimilation and encouraged it as a mass phenomenon. The situation changed when the tendency to liberate oneself from the rules of the caste had become more common, not only among individual Jews but among the broader masses as well. In Christian circles the attitude formed that the caste framework should be preserved, even in respect to Jews who were unquestionably assimilated. Anti-Semitism was the most important element in that attitude. Yet we encounter something analogous in other civilizations as well. The mores of the white world in the American South strive to maintain the black caste, even though that caste is in a state of disintegration and blacks, by their way of life, their morals, their economic activities, and so on, clearly deny its existence.

Every case of leaving the caste—either by changing religion or by assimilating without changing religion—had one thing in common: the person leaving implicitly accepted the fact of the caste's existence. The goal was always to leave the caste, flee from it, not to combat or destroy it. It was implicitly or explicitly acknowledged that the caste not only existed but also had legitimate reasons to exist. Assimilationists may well have opposed the caste system, but their primary concern was to find themselves outside the caste and to be joined by the largest possible number of other "refugees." It was unimportant that, especially in later years, converts and assimilationists continued to be treated as members of the caste when, to a certain degree, they had formed a new one. Assimilation was not a struggle to eliminate the caste as such but merely to leave it. It was thought that through mass exodus the caste would gradually dwindle and finally disappear. That was the most optimistic aspect of assimilation. It was only considerably later that broader emancipationist tendencies aimed at overthrowing the caste system and transforming the former caste into a national group stirred within the caste itself.

The converts and assimilationists—people who had left the caste—were judged unfavorably by those who had remained. The converts were considered renegades who had, in the most radical and unqualified manner, rejected the premises on which the caste was based and to which it owed its existence. And thus hostility toward the *meches*[3] was justified. But the assimilationists who had remained true to the religion of their forefathers were also viewed unfavorably. They too were apostates, people whose lives were a denial of the caste's rules, its customs, its beliefs, and its philosophy. In time, however, when secular currents began to penetrate the caste more extensively, the attitude toward the assimilationists grew ambivalent. It became a source of pride within the caste itself that among the assimilated were many people of wealth and education, people who were known and respected in the larger world. True, these people were apostates. But they had achieved something, one could be proud of them, they were living proof of the forces hidden within the caste's masses. Such ambivalence can be observed in all other related social processes. Here again, groups in the United States, both blacks and the various ethnic immigrants, provide many instructive examples.

If we ignore cases of individuals or groups leaving the caste, however, it remains true that the Jew was born and died a Jew. That is, he was born and died in a caste. From cradle to grave his life was determined by the fact of belonging to a caste group.

We will not concern ourselves here with describing in full the substance of Jewish ghetto life. The literature on its ethos, customs, beliefs, pedagogical methods, and so on is enormous. In Polish, the works of Regina Lilienthal on Jewish children and Jewish holidays (*Dziecko Żydowskie* [Kraków, 1927]) are still indispensable. Our concern here is with other aspects of the caste nature of the lives of Polish Jews.

In the first place, in every situation a Jew appeared as a member and representative of the caste. A non-Jew could easily determine when he was dealing with a Jew by the latter's appearance. Clothing, the long beards of the men, the wigs of the married women, facial features, the way the person spoke Polish, gestures, various details about behavior—all this allowed for quick classification. That classification included an emotional attitude toward the person, placed him in a definite professional and cultural group, made him an element in a specific value system, and ascribed certain mental traits to him. As a rule, this classification also contained a factor of judgment. X is a Jew, hence this and that is true of him, thereby he adheres to such and such a world of values which I judge in a certain way.

There is no doubt that, especially after the first half of the nineteenth century, definitions of this sort encountered difficulties. X did not always correspond to the accepted model. The Jew could no longer be told from the non-Jew by his dress, his facial features, his speech, or his behavior. He might not even be different in the economic activities he performed. He could be a doctor, a lawyer, a technician, even a squire. He did not, objectively speaking, correspond to the model on which the definition had been based. This could cause a certain anxiety, uncertainty, disillusionment. X is not the way he *should* be. However, the knowledge that X was a Jew usually proved decisive. Because he was a Jew, he must accord with the image. Certain interpretations of X's appearance and behavior were made, often unconsciously, with the goal of identifying X with the image of the Jew. He has (or, more precisely, must have) Jewish features, both physical and spiritual; there are traces of an accent in the way he speaks (or it would be taken amiss that his Polish was *too* correct); there is something about the way he behaves that betrays his Jewishness. It made no difference whether any of that was actually true objectively. Subjectively it had been perceived and registered. The interpretive mechanism demanded that traits be found to identify X with the image.

That sort of mechanism is at work always and everywhere, in all cases of interpersonal contact in which there is a need for definition and categorization. And that need is our inseparable companion for life. We are constantly defining people of other nationalities, other religions, other social classes, other professions, other social or recreational groups, other sections of our city. It can be a Jew or a Frenchman, a Russian or an American; it can be a doctor or a chauffeur, a Catholic or a Protestant, a shoemaker or a professor, a Parisian or a Lodzite. In each case we use abstractions and reduce living people to fit them. We look at those people through the stereotypes of our definitions and see them in the masks that collective experience and tradition have placed on them. The Jews did not regard the "goyim" any differently. However, the fact that the Jews formed a caste, that they constituted a clearly distinguishable group that, both in its entirety and as a collection of individuals, was subject to especially rigid definitions, caused the interpretations to be especially sharply focused. Like the American black, the Gypsy, or even the Polish peasant, the Jew had to correspond rigorously to what was expected of him.

In a particularly difficult case, when X departed entirely from the image, knowledge of his Jewish origin would prove decisive. In the absence of such knowledge, passing would occur and X was not defined as a Jew. What was supposed to prove his Jewishness no longer existed. It would, however, be perceived immediately either if X himself avowed that he was of Jewish origin or if that fact emerged by some other means. The interpretive apparatus would be set in motion, and X would be categorized and evaluated accordingly.

III

The interpretive apparatus went further. The definition of a Jew embraced a world of beliefs and moral, political, and legal principles; it embraced the world of economic activities and allotted to the Jew definite functions and tasks in that world. This created a comprehensive stereotype, one that had been systematized and conditioned by emotions.

This stereotype was the fruit of long historical experience. Like all the experiences of human collectives, those which produced the stereotype of the Jew were not based on objective observations and rational analyses. They were fragmentary, random; they made use of easy generalizations, abounded in internal contradictions, and were emotionally conditioned. The stereotypes were pure abstractions. But they were facts, they were reality. And regardless of what would remain of them after filtration through sober, logical analysis, they were historical truth, the "wisdom of nations," a tradition that indicated the direction and nature of interpersonal relations.

Under the stereotype, the Jew was a person not only of another faith, language, and tradition, but also of another morality. He was scheming and evasive. He thought only about his own profit and sought to cheat Christians. He had all the features that folklore everywhere in a precapitalist economy endowed upon every merchant. In Poland, where merchants, especially small merchants, were nearly exclusively Jews, those features were ascribed to the entire caste.

Such generalizing also had its basis in the Jews' distinctly different religion and customs. Their religious rules and customs, unknown, mysterious, evoked anxiety and suspicion. That under the conditions of precapitalist and early capitalist economy—and in Poland those conditions lasted nearly until our own times—small business inevitably had its own specific characteristics, which in Poland were ascribed exclusively to Jews, made it easy to connect such characteristics with Jewish customs and religion. Similarly, in other countries the specific characteristics of small business are ascribed to the customs and religions of the Chinese, Armenians, Parsis, and so on. Only after the Second World War, when no Jews were left in Poland but business conditions remained the same, was it possible to observe that the non-Jewish merchants, who "jumped" to fill the places left by the Jews, immediately assumed all the latter's characteristics. This was excellently demonstrated by the historian and literary critic Kazimierz Wyka in an essay published right after the war in *Twórczość* (Creative Work).[4]

The stereotype defined the Jews' economic makeup, and, of course, the caste as a whole functioned as an economic group. In reality, though, the caste's economic functions were more highly varied than allowed by the stereotype. The stereotypical attitude, for example, underestimated or even ignored the role of Jewish craftsmen. On the other hand, it overestimated the role of Jewish usurers. In Polish folklore, the Jew is tantamount to a merchant or rather a trader, a broad notion that included all forms of economic brokering. Up until 1939, a Jew in a gabardine was addressed as "Merchant." That even carried over to Jews who, objectively speaking, had left the caste and did not carry out the economic functions proper to it. The determination that X was a Jew entailed ascribing to him, no matter what his profession, "merchant" characteristics and the mentality that in Poland was considered typical of merchants. Because X was a Jew, his only thought must be for profit, his own self-interest; he must be a speculator; and so forth.

It must be borne in mind that a dislike of trade occupations prevailed in Poland. The country's economic backwardness and the nobles' traditions had created an atmosphere of contempt for trade as a profession. It was an economic activity given very low value, and people who pursued it were not respected. In Poland it would fall to the lot of the caste occupying a low place in the social hierarchy. In addition, the Jews had had centuries of experience and tradition in that area. They were the only group in Poland predestined to act as the brokers and distributors of economic goods, to take on the tasks for which the others were not prepared or for which they had contempt.

The relation of a non-Jew to a Jew was marked by the prevailing stereotype. Irrespective of how a Jew was deemed in a particular case, favorably or not, he was expected to comply with the requirements of the stereotype and to act the way a Jew should. In practice those expectations were not generally disappointed. It is a universal characteristic of caste systems that caste members accept the rules imposed by people outside the caste and follow them. Whether at issue are the local populations in the colonial countries, the American or South African blacks, the peasants in old Poland, or, finally, the Jews, caste members everywhere accept the ritual that the outside world requires be strictly observed in relation to it.

It is not difficult to observe a common pattern in all cases of this peculiar etiquette. In more ways than one, the behavior of a Jew toward a Christian is reminiscent of the traditional behavior of a black toward a white in the United States or the Union of South Africa, or the behavior of a native toward a European in the colonial countries. Outwardly, submissiveness, flattery, and obedience are required. Inwardly, a highly developed mistrust and insincerity prevail. The principle of a double standard of morality, so insightfully and comprehensively studied by American observers of black attitudes, is obligatory at every step. I must behave as the other expects me to. I must be obsequious to him, acquiesce to him, stress my inferiority to him. But at the same time I know this is a mask that conceals other feelings. I must also always be prepared for the possibility that the other, even though he seems friendly, considers me a member of the caste, despises me, and may at any moment make me feel it. Thus I can never trust him, can never fully believe in his goodwill, and must constantly expect that he will act toward me in keeping with the pattern.

Such distrust is especially strong among those who wish to leave the caste or, objectively speaking, have already left it. The shadow of the caste forever dogs their heels. Their peculiar oversensitivity, touchiness, and constant mental tension stem from the fear that they will still be treated as members of the caste. This is all the more painful to me because I am *no longer* a member of the caste, do not wish to consider myself one, and want to flee as far as possible from the caste. But do others see me like that? Aren't they still treating me like a man belonging to the caste? And aren't they letting me know it? Constant uncertainty, constant suspicion.

This is that Jewish oversensitivity that so often has been spoken of in the past and persists in the present. And, undoubtedly, such oversensitivity exists. The belief that "all Poles are anti-Semites," or that "every Christian despises the Jews," is as widespread among Jews as are similar beliefs among blacks about the attitude of whites, or among natives in colonial countries about the attitudes of Europeans. The Polish peasant, speaking through Wyspiański's character Czepiec, expressed the same view about the relation of the lords to himself. Among Jews "oversensitivity" led to defining every non-Jew as an anti-Semite and set in motion an entire interpretive apparatus analyzing every detail of the non-Jew's behavior. In America I have often heard Jewish immigrants from Eastern and Central Europe say that here, at least, they do not have to think that others are treating them as Jews. In the American situation those defining and interpretive attitudes atrophy or else their effect weakens rapidly. To a great degree this explains why Jews in America, without ceasing to be Jews, become Americanized so rapidly and identify so easily with America.

That oversensitivity, the constant mistrust, the compulsion forever to apply the proper interpretations, all this has a far-reaching influence on the psychology of people in a caste and leads to emotional disturbances. This situation is intensified when people from outside relate to the caste not only with contempt but also with mockery. As a result, the caste becomes an object of ridicule both for those who are not members of it and for those who are. This creates a self-mocking relationship, a derision of one's own role, a special malice toward one's own characteristics and defects. *Shmontses,* a special type of Jewish humor, developed against that background. We find an entirely analogous form of *shmontses* in the folklore of American blacks. As black America undergoes emancipation, it wages war against that type of humor, which in today's America is considered highly improper. And so it is atrophying. It has been years since Hollywood films used "Negro gags."

The obligation to apply the appropriate etiquette in relations with the outside world creates a double standard of morality. That sort of double standard exists everywhere there is a caste system. Since the world around me demands that I behave in keeping with its definition of my person and role, I must behave in that way *to protect myself.* Those considerations of self-protection also cause me to apply to the outside world criteria and moral rules different from those I apply to myself and to those close to me. Of course, in individual cases, this attitude is not rigid. To people from the outside world whom I trust and value I can apply the moral rules I would apply to myself and those I care for. Apart from those cases I should not fall into exaggerated honesty. This is not required of me, and I would not be believed if I were honest. On the other hand, the rules of honesty should be binding on me in relation to Jews, although that does not always prove practicable. But dishonesty toward a Jew would encounter the caste's condemnation, which would not be the case if a non-Jew were involved. Small business in Poland was marked by that double standard, which was born of the caste system. Although its origin was ascribed to the Jewish mentality, the Talmud, racial traits, and so on, it was in reality the product of the caste system and its mentality. It is interesting that Jews in the United States, free of the caste framework, enjoy a high regard as businessmen.

IV

Wherever a caste system exists, it is connected to a rigid set of social judgments consolidated by tradition. The caste is the subject of definite value judgments which have an enormous influence on the life of society.

In the Polish class system the nobility formed an upper, privileged caste with charisma. A nobleman was a descendant of Japheth; better blood flowed in his veins; he was of a higher quality in every respect. The folklore of the nobility produced its own anthropology in which racist elements played a major role.

Everything not of the nobility was inferior. The peasant was descended from Ham (in the anthropology of the fundamentalist American South Ham is the forefather of the blacks) and was not only socially but anthropologically of a lower order. The Jew, of course, was descended from Shem. The nobility's anthropology took too little interest in the burgher to find a proper genealogy for him, but, obviously, he too was inferior.

This "anthropology" was closely connected with the "sociology" accepted by the world of the nobility. This sociology consisted of concise definitions applied to the "inferior orders" of Polish society: the peasant was a *cham*, the burgher a *łyk*, the Jew a *parch*.[5] *Cham*, *łyk*, and *parch* made up the value system in which the Polish nobleman enclosed the nonnoble classes. These terms designated rigid social groups that were placed in a definite sociopolitical, economic, and cultural framework. Each group was subject to distinct, and contemptuous, value judgments.

As long as the caste system in Poland was deeply rooted and accepted as self-evident and natural, those terms and their meaning were in general use without reservations. The peasant was resigned to being a *cham*, the burgher to being a *łyk*, and the Jew to being a *parch*. Each group treated its own caste as something obvious, and each was resigned to the place the system had enjoined for it. Naturally, revolts did sometimes occur, more often individual than collective. The greatest resistance was shown by the middle class, especially the more wealthy among them, in whom the traditions of the old patriciate and memories of their past importance remained alive until the end of the republic. The peasant and the Jew—two groups with especially clear-cut caste traits—fully accepted the definitions of *cham* and *parch*.

These definitions and judgments were not only applied in relations between nobles and nonnobles. They also expressed relations between the lower classes. For the burgher too the peasant was a *cham* and the Jew a *parch*. The peasant saw the Jew as a *parch* and the Jew saw the peasant as a *cham*.

It must be pointed out here that such definitions did not necessarily express keen social antagonisms, did not necessarily attest to the existence of deeper intergroup conflicts, and were not in the least a sign of hatred. They did, of course, express one group's contempt for another. But in the conditions of a caste system such judgments could be perfectly well contained within a framework of peaceful and tension-free relations.

The fact that the Jew was called a *parch* by the peasant did not have to be a sign of anti-Semitism, if by anti-Semitism we mean an openly expressed antagonism toward Jews. When calling a Jew a *parch*, a peasant—or, for that matter, a nobleman or a burgher—was defining the place of the Jewish caste, passing a value judgment on that caste, and fixing its position in the entire structure of collective life. That judgment may not have been flattering, but it was not a sign of hostility. Similarly, a nobleman, when calling a peasant a *cham*, was positioning him socially, evaluating him as a member of a definite caste, but was not necessarily hostile toward him. Taken together, all this confirmed the existence of the castes and placed each of them within the framework of the whole.

Just as the peasant was resigned to being a *cham*, the Jew accepted being a *parch*. A black in the American South to this day may use the word *nigger* in relation to another black. That word when addressed to a black by a white is distinctly offensive. Similarly, a Polish Jew would sometimes call another Jew a *parch*, even when he had begun to feel offended if addressed this way by a Christian. When a Jew used this word in reference to another Jew, it was solely a term of disapproval of the way that person had behaved. Analogously, the words *cham* and *łyk* acquired a much broader application from the second half of the nineteenth century on. In each case the word began to be severed from its caste basis and became simply a term of abuse. But in the way it was used and to whom it was addressed there were still some traces of its former caste basis. A *cham* did not have to be a peasant but could be any person, regardless of origin, who acted not as a nobleman would but as a peasant might. *Parch*, almost never applied to non-Jews, indicated behavior that accorded with the traditional image of the caste Jew. This is precisely what an American black means when calling another black a nigger.

It was difficult to determine whether, in the system of values of noble Poland, the Jewish caste occupied the lowest place in the social hierarchy or whether the peasants did. In practice those assessments tended to be ambivalent and dependent on the situation and the type of relations involved. In certain situations and for certain considerations, the Jew could be ranked higher than the peasant, in other situations and for other considerations, he could be ranked lower. The important thing was that the Jew, the peasant, and the burgher were all significantly lower than the noble. In general, however, the Jewish caste was placed very low.

The contempt for the Jewish caste is especially striking when we shift to the assessments the groups of the "lower order" applied to each other. Here too there are certain analogies with the relations that developed in the American South between blacks and "white trash." Something similar is also observed in some colonial countries in relations between "pure-blood" natives and half-breeds.

For the Polish burgher or peasant the Jew was definitely a *parch*, something worse, lower, laughable. If, for example, a Jew appeared in a minstrel comedy or folk show, it was as a rule as a comic figure worthy of derision. His language was ridiculed, as were his dress, customs, and occupation. He was a coward who lived in eternal fear. He was greedy and dishonest and was nearly always severely punished for it. In the folk image of the Jew religious factors played an important role. The Jew bore responsibility for the sufferings and death of Jesus, and he was obdurate and blind in persisting in his religious errors. No doubt the influence of the clergy was strong here.

The derided Jew is an important motif in Polish folklore. It is not difficult to see that the true object of the derision is the caste and its characteristics. Its separateness, its customs, its activities make the caste highly comical. Comical also is the conceit of a Jew who thinks himself better than someone else but who is only a *parch*. The comedy here is not very different from what the noble felt about the peasant and the peasant about the noble. To a great degree the humor stemmed from the disparity between the behavior of a member of another group and the image considered proper for that group.

Once again it must be strongly emphasized that it would be difficult to speak of anti-Semitism here in the sense that word acquired later on. Of course, anti-Jewish riots did erupt in the cities from time to time, and among the peasants things sometimes went as far as open displays of hatred for the Jews. But, if we omit the Ukraine in the seventeenth and eighteenth centuries, these were not very serious events. They had their own socioeconomic basis that was connected with broader historical processes. This was particularly true for the Ukraine, where the slaughter of the Jews was a fragment in a great popular revolt and went along with the slaughter of Polish nobles. There the Jews were the victims of a general upheaval directed against the entire socioeconomic and political order in that part of the republic. And because the Jews constituted a part of that order, they were killed in enormous numbers on a par with the nobles. Events never became that extreme in Poland proper.

Anti-Semitism is a concept that rationalizes a specific form of intergroup conflict. It introduces a definition of the Jew as an enemy who should be hated and combated. Such rationalizations began to appear in Poland only in the second half of the nineteenth century and ultimately crystallized in the twentieth. They could not be said to have existed in earlier periods. The attitude toward Jews—contemptuous, ill disposed, derisive—was not the attitude toward enemies who are responsible for our misfortunes and who should be destroyed. There the Jew was simply an element in a larger system, which beside the "lords" also contained the *łyks*, the *chams*, and the *parchs*.

V

It is obvious that the Jews for their part also formed their own definitions and stereotypes of the social world within whose confines they found themselves. This came primarily in the broadest definition of the non-Jew, the Christian, the "goy." In similar fashion the American black created a definition of the "white man," and so did the natives for the Europeans in the colonial countries. Those never were and never are flattering definitions. They were made for internal consumption and were not used openly in contacts with the outside world. They expressed the defensive posture a lower caste assumed toward the higher castes.

A "goy" was different from a Jew. In the social system as a whole he occupied a position considerably higher, but as a human being he was considerably inferior to the Jew. His beliefs, way of life, value system, economic activity, all departed from the norms that the Jew thought proper; and for that reason he was inferior and laughable. If Christian folklore created a comic Jewish type, Jewish folklore in turn created a type of the comical and stupid goy.

A goy's comicality would be especially apparent when he undertook an activity in which the Jews excelled. A *goyishe kop* (goy brain) could be seen primarily in business and in those activities that required some economic experience. There the goy was a fool, and in his jokes the Jew would take revenge for his own humiliation.

A goy can never be trusted. It is difficult to foresee how he will behave toward a Jew or what might come into his head. One has to be constantly on guard and to pay careful attention so as not to do anything that might incur his disfavor. The goy has his own image of the Jew and the Jew should behave accordingly. Obviously, one could not be sincere with a goy. The mask of submission and humility must be worn at all times. Since Jews are amusing to goys, a Jew should be deliberately amusing, emphasizing his comic aspects by his behavior.

This does not mean that the goy was supposed to be hated or considered an enemy. "Anti-goyism"—if that expression can be used as a counterpart of anti-Semitism—came very late as an attitude and emerged in connection with the Jewish emancipationist movements at the end of the nineteenth century and the beginning of the twentieth. As the goy held the Jew in contempt but did not necessarily hate him, so did the Jew hold the goy in contempt but did not necessarily hate him. Remaining a member of the caste, the Jew accepted it as self-evident that the goy was such as he was and that he could not be viewed or related to otherwise. The Jew's attitude toward the goy did not indicate a revolt against the caste system. It was exclusively a defensive attitude against the consequences of life in a caste.

There were, however, clear distinctions made within the general stereotype of the goy. Of course, a goy was always a goy irrespective of the place he occupied in the social system. A goy was outside the Jewish caste, and thus his attitude toward a Jew was uniform. Nevertheless, every goy had his own social position in the world of the goys and that could not help influencing the way the Jews related to him.

From the nobles the Jew had taken over the assessment of a peasant as *cham* and a burgher as *łyk*. Economically, and even culturally, the Polish Jew was most closely connected with the nobility. The economic functions he performed were to a great degree an offshoot of the economic system of the nobles. Without being aware of it, the Polish Jew identified with the world of the nobility when making his social and cultural assessments. Hence in the eyes of a Jew the peasant was a *cham*.

But another important factor enters the picture here. The Jewish ethos sets wisdom and knowledge as its highest good. In Judaism, as opposed to Protestant Puritanism, wealth is not a value in and of itself or an outward sign of charisma, but a means for achieving wisdom and knowledge. With the exception of the Chinese, perhaps no other culture has placed so high a value on knowledge as traditional Jewish culture. The type of knowledge is less important. What matters is that it be knowledge. In the Jewish world a rich uneducated man had a considerably lower standing than a poor wise man. It is striking that this fundamental characteristic of the Jewish ethos was completely ignored in the stereotypes created by the outside world, which always ascribed to the Jews the attitude that material wealth was the highest value. This was the obvious result of the economic functions traditionally performed by the Jewish caste.

The goy whom the Jew knew and encountered most frequently in daily life did not value knowledge. On the contrary, he was uneducated, ignorant, and usually illiterate. Hence the Jew's contempt for the peasant, who in the Jew's eyes was twice a *cham*, once as a peasant so defined by the world of the nobility, and again as a stupid, ignorant creature to whom knowledge was alien. To an immense degree that image was transferred onto the burgher, who was not only a *łyk* but also an ignoramus, and onto a great portion of the nobility as well. With the exception of very well educated individuals whom the Jews treated with genuine respect, every goy was a *cham*. It should be emphasized that in the folklore of Polish Jews one also encounters numerous signs of esteem for wise non-Jews who were defenders and friends of Jews.

Of course attitudes are never formed logically and without contradiction. The Jew had a twofold view of the goy: the goy was a creature of a higher order even if he was a peasant; but he was also a stupid goy, a *cham*, a lower creature deserving of contempt. Outside the caste the first definition was obligatory, within the caste the second. Although logically speaking these attitudes were highly ambivalent and even contradictory, they coexisted perfectly.

Similar attitudes were reflected in the double standard of morality of which we have already spoken. The Jew considered himself a representative of the chosen people. Unlike the American black, unlike the majority of the natives in colonial countries, and unlike the Polish peasant, the Jew had a highly developed sense of his own cultural importance, his own charisma. In the history of the world there are not many ethnic groups, especially caste groups, in which the sense of the importance of their spiritual culture—the concentration of the most momentous elements of life in that culture—played such a role as it did among the Jews. Perhaps only in China, and to some degree in India, can we find similar examples. The Jews, moreover, were conscious that they owed their endurance and historical continuity to their culture, primarily to their written tradition. The Jews were the people of Writ, the people of the Book. The goys with whom the Jews came into contact, the few exceptions aside, had neither that sort of tradition nor that attitude toward Writ and Book. And thus they deserved contempt.

Because it was incontrovertible that the goy stood above the Jew in the social hierarchy, that contempt could never be expressed. One had to submit. But could there be anything wrong with knowing how to take advantage of the goy's stupidity? Such attitudes are not a rarity among Chinese merchants outside of China. This kind of thinking provides an even stronger basis for a double standard of morality, which in fact every caste system produces.

VI

A caste is a closed group. As an entity it is cut off culturally, morally, and economically from the other groups in the national society. But is it *isolated* from them? It would be difficult to call it so. Both the caste as a whole and its individual members maintain constant relations with other groups and their members. And such relations necessarily entail some interaction and mutual influence. Absolute isolation is out of the question.

Today we are well aware that the rigorous caste system in the United States did not prevent mutual influence between blacks and whites. As a result, by the time of emancipation the American black had taken on a whole series of white cultural elements and southern whites had taken on more than a little from blacks. And here we speak of a community whose original bonds and cultural traditions had been violently severed and which had to start all over in creating a culture for itself. It took from the whites' culture but at the same time gave back to the whites something of its own plantation experience.

As a place, the Jewish ghetto was isolated. The Jews as a whole had their own world, formed an autonomous unit, and in a great many respects were separated from others. But to some degree in old Poland this could also be said of the noblemen, the burghers, and the peasants. The Jews' degree of isolation must have been particularly great if only because of their cultural individuality, which was more specific than that of the Polish nobility or Polish peasants. But there was constant contact among nobles, burghers, and peasants, and there was constant contact between Jews and Christians. Those contacts were many-sided and varied.

Basically speaking, a tremendous distance existed between a Christian and a Jew. Both sides strove to maintain that distance, each for its own reasons. In religious, political, social, or cultural life, Christians and Jews did not meet. The same was true for the distance between a lord and a *cham* or a *łyk*. There too each side kept to its allotted sphere.

There were, however, areas and situations in which that distance shrank or even disappeared. In plantation America the distance between the white plantation owner and his black slave was colossal. But at the same time the black nanny and the black butler entered the life of white people, both as a social institution of considerable significance and as living human beings whose influence on the affairs of the white plantation owners was comprehensive and profound. The black nanny and the black house servant were intimates, counselors, friends, and at times in daily life true tyrants. The black as friend, confidant, and counselor became part of the South's tradition, an element of the local culture. The white master's attitude toward his slaves could be full of warmth, attachment, and the greatest possible goodwill. And in many cases the black slave was ready to devote his life to the master and his family. In the American South, the traditional ties between the families of former masters and former slaves have survived today. Similar examples can be found in all countries and civilizations where a caste system has formed. The member of a lower caste is still a member of a lower caste, and a great distance is maintained between him and the world outside the caste; but at the same time, in certain definite situations and in regard to certain specific relationships, that distance disappears and is transformed into closeness.

The case of the Jews in Poland was no different. One of the most important circumstances determining the Polish Jews' character as a caste was the definite economic functions they performed. The overwhelming majority of them were merchants, middlemen, and tradesmen. Those functions were organically connected to the entire economic system of gentry Poland and were the offshoot of a farm, villein economy that was only slightly industrialized. The claim, popular from the end of the nineteenth century on, that the Jews had kept the Polish economy on its low level was absurd. The truth was that the Polish economy kept the Jews at a low level, just as it did all the other groups in the Polish collectivity.

In performing their economic functions, the Jews entered into constant and comprehensive relations with non-Jews. These were not always and not necessarily limited to the purely economic level. In a great many cases they went considerably further and deeper.

Until nearly the end of the nineteenth century, a significant part of the Jewish population on Polish territory lived in the countryside or in small towns that were closely connected to the countryside and were in fact still a part of the farm economy. The exception was the section of Poland partitioned by the Prussians, where the small Jewish population was distinctly urban. But in both the other partitioned sections the Jewish tenant, innkeeper, publican, middleman, and fruit farmer constituted an important cog in the machine of the farm economy. A large portion of commercial credit and administrative functions had been turned over to the Jews. In addition, they played a significant role in small towns as grain merchants, suppliers of goods of every sort, tailors, shoemakers, and so on. In Galicia especially one may add that the local doctors and lawyers, from the end of the nineteenth century on, were increasingly of Jewish origin.

As they used to say, "The squire couldn't do without the Jews." The historical circumstances that brought about such a state of affairs are not important for our purposes. The specific conditions of Poland's economic development made the Jews the sole element that could have become that cog in the machine of the nobles' farm economy. When that economy began to disintegrate, it was the noble landowner along with his Jew who were the victims.

It must be constantly emphasized that there was a strong and comprehensive connection between the Polish Jews and the Polish nobility. Without exaggeration the former can be called the product of the latter. They were connected by economics, but not only by economics. As we shall see, cultural bonds existed as well. It is no accident that anti-Semitism did not find strong support among the landowners, even between the wars, when that class was already in a state of greatly advanced decline. In that period, many individuals with famous aristocratic names were friendly toward the Jews.

Without ceasing to be a member of his caste, the Jew had numerous and varied relations with the world of landowning nobility, relations not devoid of intimacy and warmth. The Polish novel of that period, up through Maria Dąbrowska, provides innumerable examples of close, warm relations between manor and Jew. At times that closeness was passed on from one generation to the next, creating a tradition of patronage between the landowning family and "our Jews." In such cases the Jew ceased to be a *parch* and became a *żydek*, a "little Jew," one of their own, who could be trusted and whom they considered a part of their own world.

This detail of terminology is worth some attention. Use of the word *żydek* or the feminine *żydóweczka* indicated an acceptance of the Jew, his inclusion in the nobility's own world of values, their own reality. Of course, the "little Jew" was also a member of the caste from which the nobility kept a great distance. But at the same time, the "little Jew" was considered close, one of their own. In a fit of temper the noble might abuse the Jew by calling him a *parch*, but that did not alter the basic relationship. The relation between a white master and his beloved and trusted slave in plantation America was not dissimilar.

It was not only the Jews in the countryside and the small towns who were drawn in this manner into the world of the landowning nobility. After all, until the second half of the nineteenth century, the economy of even the larger Polish cities was to one degree or another an offshoot of the farm economy. The Polish Jew in the big cities—which were in reality only extended small towns—gravitated toward the farm in one way or another and adapted his economic activities to fit its needs.

The landowning nobility's folklore had no lack of warmth for *żydeks* (though not necessarily for Jews). For its part, Jewish folklore betrayed no lack of friendship and affection for kindly lords, and there was a tradition of loyalty to friendly patrons. The term "good goy" was as common among Jews as "little Jew" was among Poles.

Thus one cannot speak of the Jews' "isolation" in Poland. Of course, as a caste they were within a closed system and formed a world of their own. But at the same time, as individuals and in smaller groups, they were in constant contact with the world outside the caste, constituted an integral part of that world, and played an important role in it. Those contacts were frequent, numerous, many-sided, and emotionally colored. As part of the Polish landowning nobility's world of values, the Jew, or rather the *żydek*, had a value. This is what created the channels for cultural interaction. Although these channels were delimited by the entire system of social and economic relations regulating the farming nobility, interaction did occur and, as we shall discuss at some length, was important.

The world of the landowning nobility also created the basis and framework for contacts between Jews and peasants. The peasants and the Jews constituted different elements in the farm system. Within the limits of that system peasants and Jews had continual contact—in the inn, the marketplace, and various other situations of rural life. The Jew was a tradesman, itinerant peddler, source of credit. Very often he was also an intermediary between the peasant and the lord or the lord's representative in dealings with the peasant. None of this made him alien to the peasant. Undoubtedly, in cases of acute social conflict the Jews were victimized because they were identified with the manor, as happened in the Ukraine in the seventeenth century and later on during the Koliïvshchyna.[6] But those were special situations. Normally, in the manor and peasant hut alike, the Jew was thought of as "our little Jew," who was known and could be trusted. In full accord with the nobility, the peasants could treat the Jewish caste as a whole as *parchs* but excepted *żydeks*, those whom they encountered constantly.

Several observers of the Polish peasant village have stressed the authoritative role played by Jews in the village community. In his book *Cudzoziemcy w Galicji 1787–1841* (Foreigners in Galicia 1787–1841 [Kraków, 1902]), Stanisław Schnür-Pepłowski cites the observations of Ernest Kortum concerning the Galician Jews at the end of the eighteenth and the beginning of the nineteenth centuries. In his book *Ueber Judenthum und Juden*, Kortum wrote: "The peasant, treated as an inferior by the squire, sees the Jew as his only friend. He speaks frankly with the Jew, listens to his advice, accepts his help, and avails himself of his influence'' (p. 50). Other observers pointed to similar relations, even in considerably later periods. Writing in 1937 in *Wiadomości Literackie* (Literary News, no. 40) about her wanderings through Polesie, Wanda Wasilewska stated that the Polesian peasant treated the local Jew as the man he trusted and turned to him as an intermediary in relations with the state authorities.

The contacts linking Jews and burghers were the weakest. There was a clash of economic interests here. In consequence the level of encounter was narrow, and the connections infrequent and rather antagonistic when compared with the connections between Jews and nobles or peasants.

VII

Let us sum up the argument made to this point. The Jews in noble Poland formed a caste. The caste organization arose in the Middle Ages, was maintained and developed throughout the history of the noble republic, and survived its fall. In reality, the caste character of the life of Polish Jews existed—though in a form that became increasingly a relic of the past—until 1939. Then came the annihilation. The caste of the Polish Jews was contained within the framework of the larger social system that characterized the historical development of the Polish people.

The caste was of decisive importance for the identity of the Polish Jews and for their position in the Polish collective. The distinguishing features of Polish Jews can never be understood without taking their caste nature into account. And because everywhere, in every civilization, in every national society, throughout the world, a caste develops its own specific characteristics and interpersonal relations, the history and role of Polish Jews will never be fully understood if treated as something exclusive to Jews or exclusive to Polish Jews. Of course, in Poland the situation of the Jews assumed its own local coloring and was an offshoot of the entire development of Polish civilization. But its assumptions and basic manifestations placed it in much broader categories. These assumptions and manifestations have not been understood or taken into account by most historians or commentators. The anti-Semitic writers did not understand them, and in keeping with their program, they neither could nor wished to. Jewish writers representing Jewish nationalism did not take them into account either. And they were overlooked by the few Polish and Jewish scholars who attempted to approach these questions seriously.

Further, we have seen that a caste, despite being separate and self-enclosed, is not isolated from collective life as a whole. The caste is in and of the larger society, especially when it performs well-defined and important economic functions. As a result, there were constant, strong, and comprehensive contacts between Jews and non-Jews in Poland.

Those contacts, occurring throughout the thousand-year history of Polish Jewry, had profound cultural consequences for both sides. Whether they became Poles or maintained their separateness, Jews brought something to Polish culture and absorbed something from it.

Those Who Leave the Caste I

A caste is a closed group. It is closed "from within" as a cultural, moral, religious, and legal entity. And it is closed "from without" by the outside world's relation to it, by the place that world assigns it, and by the role it forces the caste to play. It is very difficult, often impossible for an individual to leave the caste.

A peculiarity of the Jewish caste's position in old Poland was that, in individual cases, no basic obstacles to leaving were posed "from without"; on the contrary, existing circumstances favored individuals' leaving the caste. In old Poland this could only occur in one way: through baptism, changing religion. Catholic Poland smiled on proselytes from the Jewish world. The Lithuanian Statute cleared the way for converts to enter the class of the nobility. In practice, in the Crown a Jew who was baptized would acquire noble status.[1] Of course, those instances were not frequent but neither were they as rare as is usually assumed. In his *Neofici polscy* (Polish Converts), though an incomplete, biased, and carelessly written book, Teodor Jeske-Choiński cites a substantial number of Jewish families who were ennobled in the eighteenth century after changing their religion; and he was able to examine only a portion of church documents, and not for all of the republic.

As opposed to the situation in Western Europe, forced conversion was rare in Poland. On the whole, conversion among Polish Jews was voluntary. It presented an exceptionally great opportunity not only to abandon a caste held in contempt but also to join the privileged caste. If there is a tendency in Poland to exaggerate the country's liberal traditions, they can rightly be cited in the case of Catholic proselytizing among Jews.

There is no evidence that the nobility's attitude toward ennobled converts was any worse than that toward others recently ennobled. It may even have been better, a phenomenon undoubtedly springing from religious sentiments. A convert was living proof of the triumph of the Catholic faith and was thus deserving of special benevolence.

Nevertheless, the convert, like all those recently ennobled, was a parvenu, a *homo novus*, who could not be entirely accepted by noble society at once. A certain social distance persisted, though in time it disappeared. Professional heraldists, whose accuracy in tracing genealogies was at times quite dubious, may also have aided the new nobles in establishing themselves. But ennoblement usually entailed permission to assume a coat of arms, which helped greatly in erasing the past.

On their side, the new nobles would display a certain timidity toward their new fellow nobles. Frankist families associated with each other and intermarried, at least for the first two or three generations. That sort of clannishness, issuing from the converts themselves, was understandable. In similar situations analogous attitudes can be observed throughout the world. The *homines novi* did not feel confident in their new milieu. They felt freer in their own, where they were bound to others by similar experiences, by memories of the past, by certain traditions, and, sometimes, by a sense of obligation toward their former coreligionists. The latter was especially striking in the case of Czyński. All this would be effaced in the generations to follow. The descendants of *homines novi* would cease to fit that description.

Even after the fall of the noble republic, conversion continued to play a similar role. Of course, changing religion ceased to lead to ennoblement in the legal sense of the word, but it still meant leaving a caste held in contempt and entering one held in esteem. Over the course of time it began to mean leaving caste in general, becoming part of a more or less casteless milieu. The number of such cases grew steadily, assuming greater proportions with each year. Jewish conversion, both to Catholicism and to Protestantism, was a quantitatively significant phenomenon at the end of the nineteenth and the beginning of the twentieth centuries. By that time, however, new factors had emerged that influenced the changing of the tradition as it had existed until then.

Most important, the attitude of non-Jews toward converts took a turn for the worse. The time of steadily growing anti-Semitism had come. One of the most important aspects of any sort of anti-Semitism is the striving by the non-Jewish milieu to maintain the castelike character of the Jewish community. The fact that rationalizations accusing the Jews of alienness and separatism are used in the process has no meaning. In Poland, as similarly in other countries, antagonism toward Jews increased in proportion to the rise of anticaste tendencies among Jews. As anti-Semitism grew more acute, it strove to confer caste status also on those Jews who had left the caste. A convert began to be treated as one who remained a Jew even after changing his religion. Ultimately, this led to racism for which the criterion of religion had no meaning.

At the same time, other avenues for escape had appeared among Jews. As the general secularization of life progressed, the religious factor ceased to play the decisive role in changing one's circumstances. People began aspiring to leave the caste without necessarily changing their religion. It was not changing religion that would lead an individual to emancipation; it was changing his culture and his entire way of life. That was the social meaning of assimilation. Leaving the caste became possible through cultural transformation.

Both the Jew who got baptized and the Jew who assimilated while keeping his religion sought a way out of the caste for themselves as individuals. They were not fighting against the caste per se; they were fighting against their own place in it. In fact they were affirming the existence of the caste. They accepted its existence but did not want to be part of it themselves. There is no doubt that the assimilationists desired and strove for the end of the caste. However, they imagined that end as the result of a mass exodus of individuals. In the history of black America, "lily Negroes" and "Uncle Tomism" are examples of similar tendencies.

From the end of the nineteenth century on, a growing desire spread among Polish Jews to eliminate the caste system itself while maintaining their national-cultural separateness. That was the beginning of emancipation movements within Polish Jewry. These tendencies were the counterpart of emancipationist and nationalistic mass movements that had begun to stir throughout the world.

II

Let us begin with the question of leaving the caste by changing religion. We have said that law and custom in noble Poland, although not forcing conversion, were highly favorable to it. There were strong social incentives to impel Jews to change their religion and thus their entire circumstances of life. We have also observed that cases of Jewish conversion were neither isolated nor exceptional. But relative to the entire mass of Jews in Poland, the number of converts was not large. We cannot determine the number of Jewish families who changed religion during the thousand years that Jews lived in Poland; we cannot even determine the number in the eighteenth century, the era of Frankism. Probably, all told, there were hundreds of families or perhaps a few thousand. In any case, the Jewish mass remained faithful to their religion, customs, and caste.

This was because the Jews were a group closed "from within." Their character as a caste was primarily the result of their singular religion, customs, language, culture, and economic function. Of fundamental importance here was religion, which—as few other of the world's religions—determined the ethos of the group, its identity, and the identity of each of its members. Judaism is an integral religious system. It brings the sacral into all, even the smallest details of collective and individual life. It is not only a system of religious beliefs but also an order based on a strict and comprehensive rule of action. An Orthodox Jew fulfills the regulations of that rule in everything he does. The rule is embodied in a highly rationalized form. Judaism itself is a rational system, even when it crosses over into mysticism, as it does in Hasidism. The regulations for behavior are based on an interpretation of the Writings, an interpretation that is unusually detailed and pedantic and to which entire generations of scholars have devoted their lives.

At the same time Judaism is a legal-religious system. Among the world's religions only the Roman religion can be compared with Judaism in this regard, but Judaism went even further, creating an all-inclusive system of legal-religious regulations. The legal elements of

Christianity—especially copious in Catholicism—owe their origin both to Judaism and to Roman law. The content came from the former, and the form from the latter.

These unique attributes of Judaism enabled the Jews to survive in the diaspora. No other cultural group has manifested similar durability. The old Oriental civilizations, in China and India, are as old as the Jews and display no less continuity in historical tradition; but they never knew diaspora. Even the Armenians, whose fate to some extent suggests analogies with that of the Jews, received some support from those Armenians who were not in diaspora. Even so, they were not able to preserve their cultural uniqueness to the degree that the Jews did.

All of these religious, legal, and cultural properties made up the substance of Jewish life in the caste. And these properties constituted the principal internal obstacle for those who wished to abandon the caste. Cases of extreme cynicism aside, each instance of a Jew's changing his religion was accompanied by an inward shock of enormous dimensions. For anyone with a religious nature, a change of faith is an immeasurably difficult and serious decision, a deep spiritual crisis. The great converts, including St. Augustine and Cardinal Newman, have all acknowledged this. For Jewish converts the decision was exceptionally difficult and the spiritual crisis exceptionally severe because Judaism was an entire system of life. Here conversion meant renouncing all previously held values, a complete transformation.

It also meant a radical break with one's old milieu. Socially speaking, there is no question that, by taking an individual out of the caste, conversion also meant a break with the old milieu. But that break also entailed utter condemnation by the old milieu. A convert had not only abandoned his caste but had also renounced it, renounced its ideals, its spiritual essence, its very raison d'être. He was an apostate and a traitor. Jewish folklore offers ample proof that Jewish popular opinion was incomparably more severe toward the *meches*, the converts, than toward the goys. Traces of that attitude still remain, even in America and Israel. People who stress their connection with Jewishness but are Christian by religion encounter considerable suspicion, even from Jews who are entirely agnostic.

Of course, in many cases the converts ignored their former coreligionists' reactions. They would seek support from their new coreligionists, which inevitably hastened the loss of their old connections with Jewishness. There were no Marranos in Poland. However, it was not always easy to gain entry to the new milieu, and it became increasingly difficult by the end of the nineteenth century. The new milieu displayed a growing resistance to absorbing newcomers from the Jewish caste. Hence the converts more or less formed a milieu of their own, as for a time had been the case with the Frankists. Later on, in the twentieth century, the phenomenon of converts sticking together was quite common, at least for the first or second generation. However, the spread of "mixed" marriages accelerated the new integration. We can speak of such marriages only in passing here, although in and of themselves they were a very interesting phenomenon.

Ostracism by the old milieu and the new milieu's distrust—relatively brief at first but, later on, increasingly great and long lasting—were only social consequences of the fundamental decision to change religion, become baptized, and renounce one's former beliefs and rules for living. That decision was probably less difficult after the first half of the nineteenth century, when religious indifference was on the rise and baptism itself only the final stage in moving away from Judaism. In many cases baptism had lost its religious meaning and was only an outward expression of advanced assimilation, the last phase in leaving the caste. The conversion of Jews, so common among the intelligentsia at the end of the nineteenth century, was losing its religious meaning and was primarily a means of identifying socially and culturally with the non-Jewish world.

But even then the decision was not always easy. Even people who were indifferent to religion had kept certain traditions, certain attachments, if only in the form of loyalty to their parents or grandparents. "I'm being baptized for the sake of my children's future, I would never do it otherwise" was a common expression in those milieus.

The situation had been different in periods of intense religious life. In the seventeenth and eighteenth centuries changing religion was a difficult and serious decision for a Jew, so cases of conversion were infrequent. The law and prevailing mores offered attractive opportunities to a convert: baptism led to ennoblement and entailed a tremendous rise in status. In old Poland law and mores could afford that generosity: the number of Jews who availed themselves of it was relatively small.

III

The Jews constituted a caste held in contempt. In the "outside world" the Jew was a *parch*. He tried to be a *żydek* though he did not always succeed. All that changed, however, when he moved from relations with the outside world to life within his own community.

The Polish Jew felt that he was a member of a great religious community, the inheritor of rich historical and cultural traditions. But, above all, he felt that he was a member of a charismatic group, a participant in that charisma. There are not many communities in the world whose sense of collective and individual charisma is developed to the degree it is among Jews.

The Jews were the "chosen people," the people of the Covenant with God. Charisma could be maintained by faithfully keeping the commandments of the Covenant. The Covenant itself had the form of a legal convention whose observance required an unusual exactitude and conscientiousness. That a Jew was born a Jew and was thus a member of the chosen people made him a participant in the charisma, a chosen individual. This placed enormous obligations on the Jew but also lent him enormous distinction. In his daily prayers a Jew thanked God for creating him a Jew.

To abandon Jewry meant to renounce the charisma that, because of the Covenant, was the portion of every Jew. And thus not only was baptism apostasy or treason; it also meant defying the Covenant, abjuring charisma. In the eyes of an Orthodox Jew, anyone who without being baptized renounced the laws of the order was not much better than the *meches*. Changing language, changing "worldly" beliefs, acquiring a secular education, none of these was the key element in the indignant attitude of Orthodox Jews toward their coreligionists who were assimilating. The key and unforgivable element was the nonobservance of the basic rules of Judaism, rules that issued from the Covenant and that, on the part of the Jews, constituted its guarantee.

The divergence of roles was tremendous: a *parch* to the outside world and one of the elect within the caste. Centuries of such dualism had, as a rule, enabled the Jew to pass from one role to the other without great difficulty. Baptism could free the Jew from being stamped a *parch* but at the cost of losing a share in the charisma.

The dualism in the Jews' opinions and attitudes was, of course, no secret to the non-Jewish world. The latter's reactions to it were not friendly, but neither were they especially hostile. That dualism was often treated as comical. The *parch* who at the same time thought himself the bearer of charisma made for such a jarring contrast that he could only be a source of amusement. In Polish folklore (and not only Polish) and in bourgeois literature, the contrast between the Jew as *parch* and the Jew as one of the "elect" was often a source of ridicule. Echoes of this can be found, even in much later periods, in various types of low Jewish comedy (*shmontses*) and even in the works of such Jewish writers as Shalom Aleichem.

In the period of increased anti-Semitism, the dualism in the attitudes and behavior of the Jews lost its comic quality in the eyes of non-Jews and became one of the rationalizations for hostility, giving rise to accusations of hypocrisy, immorality, unscrupulousness in business, and so forth. Those accusations were at their strongest in the period when, objectively speaking, Jewish dualism had begun to wane.

IV

Although the decision to change religion was not an easy one even in the era of the noble republic, a certain number of Jews renounced their old values, were baptized, and forsook the caste. Was this entirely a question of opportunism, the desire to change one's social or economic position? It would be extremely interesting to study the mental processes that accompanied those conversions.

Unfortunately, we can say nothing about those early cases. We have no documents that would provide evidence about the spiritual path taken by the Jews who accepted baptism. None left behind any "confessions" of the sort made by St. Augustine. Fortunately, however, certain later materials relating to Frankism have been preserved. Frank himself and Frankism have been the subject of scholarly studies, among which Aleksander Kraushar's work *Frank i frankiści polscy* (Frank and the Polish Frankist) remains of serious value.

There is no question that Frankism was a highly specific phenomenon. It came late, at the end of the republic and the beginning of the nineteenth century. In a way, it was also a "movement" that comprised not just individuals but an entire group, perhaps not overly large but not small either. That group had its own leader, internal structure, common goals, and fate. On the other hand, the group manifested certain tendencies and attitudes that, according to all the evidence, were also symptomatic of earlier cases of individual conversion. The most important elements for us are the Frankists' motivations and the milieu they represented.

Frankism was a religious movement. It arose out of Jewish sectarianism, which culminated in Sabbatianism. Jewish sectarianism—in this respect no different from many sectarian movements in other religions—was the reaction of mysticism to the rationalism of Judaism. The idea of messianism played a fundamental role here.

Judaism is a messianic religion. It differs from Christianity in that Judaism still awaits the coming of the Messiah. Christianity itself had no shortage of sects that awaited another coming of the Savior. In Orthodox

Judaism the concept of the Messiah is political and legal in nature. It is also a nationalistic concept. Sectarian Judaism brought strong mystical elements to bear here. It also lent the figure of the Messiah substance and historical form by anticipating his coming in the near future, during the life of a given generation. It would be interesting to determine to what degree the Christian idea of the Messiah influenced the formation of messianism in Jewish sectarianism.

Frankism began as one of the messianic trends in Judaism. It was a protest against rabbinical schematization and sought answers to its questions in mysticism. In that respect, it did not differ from a whole series of predecessors. Jewish history has no shortage of individuals who assumed the role of the promised Messiah and were able to attract large numbers of the faithful. It was also no rarity for such movements to end by breaking with Judaism and converting to another religion.

We will not enter into the history of Frank and his movement here. What is important for us is that mystical messianic Jewish sectarianism, and protest against rabbinical legalism and rationalism, were points of departure for the Frankists' tendency to convert. Those people who ultimately found a place for themselves in Catholicism underwent a certain spiritual process, passed through a series of religious traumas. The motives that guided them were religious in nature.

It is probable that the converts of earlier periods were guided by similar motives. It would be extremely interesting to explore the extent to which the rise of mystical-sectarian trends in Judaism was matched by an increase in conversion. Most likely there was some correlation, and many of the converts came to Christianity through Hasidism and other forms of Judaistic mysticism.

What more do we know of the Frankists? What sort of people were they? In which of Polish Jewry's milieus did they originate? The fragmentary data that we possess enable us to form some image of the Polish Frankists. That image is certainly not exact, but it is probably close to the truth.

We can assume that in great measure the Frankists were recruited from among the well-to-do and even the wealthy. The claim, quite widespread among their opponents, that Frankism attracted people without social standing seems to be unfounded. The Frankists included merchants, leaseholders, independent tradesmen, and people connected to the courts of the magnates. Although a certain portion of his followers were poor, the data that have been preserved do not indicate that Frank had any greater influence among the poorest Jews.

Again despite the claims of their opponents, the Frankists cannot be called ignorant people. On the contrary, there is much to indicate that they were quite educated, not only in the sense of traditional religious education but also of secular, nontraditional knowledge. Many, though not all, spoke fluent Polish. Some could have known other languages as well. The level of secular education was usually even higher among the women.

On the whole they would have to be counted in the upper strata of the ghetto world. If they were not part of the *kahal* aristocracy, they were in any case a significant factor in their milieu. They were the rabbis' opposition. Only the more eminent people, those distinguished by wealth and education and thereby possessing a certain degree of authority, would allow themselves to belong to an opposition of that sort. There is also no doubt that they were linked economically to the world of the great magnates or gentry landowners. Among their godparents were people with distinguished names.

Frank himself was accused by his former coreligionists of being an ignorant man. But this accusation should be treated with caution. It is used universally in dogmatic disputes. Anyone with whom we do not agree is an ignorant man. In any case, both as a man and a mind Frank was a leader able to attract great numbers of people and gain authority.

The religious, the wealthy, the educated—this, most generally conceived, was probably the milieu from which Frankism emerged. We also have the right to assume that both the earlier and, to some degree, the later converts were people from the same milieu. This does not mean that there were no individual cases of conversion among the poor and the uneducated. However, even if such cases existed, the people were attracted by the example and the authority of those they considered their leaders.

The wealthier and more educated in the secular sense must have had more numerous and more comprehensive relations with the Christian world than did the ignorant mass of poor Jews. From other sources we know that wealthy Jews had innumerable opportunities for such contact. A wealthy Jew most often was an important component in the economic machinery of an estate belonging to a magnate or a richer noble. He was a leaseholder, a tenant, a banker, a supplier of all types of consumer goods. As a prospering tradesman, he would rely chiefly on the nobles, even the magnates, for his customers. In their contacts with the non-Jewish world, poor Jews dealt mainly with poor peasants. The financial elite of the Jews had access to the lords' manors, and although they kept the character of *parchs* or *żydeks*, they played a significant role. Such opportunities for contact meant the possibility of cultural influence.

We know some details about the daily lives of wealthy Jews in old Poland. Their houses and apartments bore traces of what their owners had seen in the manor houses. As is usually the case, it was the women who, less impeded than the men by the strict rules of religion, were the force behind the search for models in a "better" world. The descriptions we have of the "courts" of various rabbis and tsadeks are somewhat reminiscent of the magnates' courts both in atmosphere and in organization.

The conversions themselves are the best proof that influences from the Christian world were penetrating the Jewish one. Quantitatively speaking, that was not a significant or comprehensive penetration. Neophytism was sporadic; still, a certain penetration did take place and was not without significance. There could be no question of complete isolation. Had it existed, conversion would have been unknown in Poland.

We may now assume that in old Poland Jewish converts were recruited chiefly from among the more well-to-do and more educated, who, for those reasons, had constant contact with the non-Jewish world. We have now come to a point of major significance for the Jewish question in Poland.

V

A Jew could accept the divergence of his roles between the "outside world" where he was a *parch* and the "inside" where he was a bearer of charisma. However, that divergence became increasingly difficult to accept for people whose position within the caste was very high and who at the same time had achieved authority and standing outside it as well. It must be borne in mind that, outside the caste, ambivalent evaluations were applied to many Jews. Without ceasing to be *parchs*, they played an important part in the economy of the nobility, enjoyed the lords' trust, and often took on responsible and delicate missions for them. These conditions may well have caused such Jews to fall into a state of inner conflict. Within the caste they had a sense of their own power and importance, but outside the caste as well they performed objective functions that gave them a basis for developing a sense of power and importance. At the same time they did not cease to be *parchs*, members of a despised caste.

The emergence of the ability to compare one's own situation with that of others creates the condition necessary for the formation of attitudes leading either to individual advancement or to a mass emancipation movement. Only when that ability arises do the first cracks appear in a social structure based on accepting the self-evident, natural, and proper character of one's fate. The ability to make comparisons, becoming emboldened to make them, is proof that doubts have arisen about the necessary value of the existing order. If the individuals or groups making the comparisons have, as the result of historical changes, developed a sense of their own importance, dignity, and power, those comparisons start leading toward a belief in the possibility and necessity of carrying out fundamental changes in their social condition. This mechanism of social action is encountered in all epochs and civilizations.

The Jews were a group whose involvement in economic activities was exceptionally intense. In old Poland certain areas of economic life were exclusively, or nearly exclusively, allotted to Jews. To speak of Jewish monopolies is not unfounded here. They controlled commerce, banking (actually, usury), and certain trades. This created exceptionally good conditions for making fortunes. And although the Jewish masses undoubtedly lived in extreme poverty, the percentage of well-to-do and wealthy Jews was quite significant. We must, of course, be moderate in assessing the sizes of those fortunes, taking into account the country's general economic backwardness and low standard of living.

Max Weber pointed out that small dissident religious groups surrounded by an unfriendly and discriminatory environment have a tendency to display intense economic activity and create significant personal fortunes. Economic activity is one of the few careers open to them, and personal fortunes are a means both of self-protection and of compensation for social humiliation. Sects like the Mormons in America, the Parsis in India, and the Jews and Armenians in Europe and the Near East are examples of the tendency Weber described.

In a country as economically backward as Poland and where the nobles' ethos held "base" economic activities in contempt, the Jews, by force of circumstance, had to take the path they in fact took. They were the only element of some importance creating largish fortunes by means of trade and speculation. Although it is true that the nobles also engaged in highly speculative operations and even made fortunes (the usurer of the noble class was not uncommon), this was always done in tandem with a Jew.

The nonsacral portion of a Jew's life was filled with economic activity, which also encroached on family life. A Jew's market stand, his little store or small workshop, involved the entire family. A Jew and his family were absorbed in economic transactions, both when mere subsistence was involved, the most usual case, and when fortunes were being made. In all this the Jew displayed astonishing persistence, industry, and resourcefulness.

But, at the same time, economic goods never occupied a place of superior value or even of high value in the Jewish ethos. Probably few communities could be found in which economic values were so subordinated to noneconomic ones as among Jews.

Unlike among the Puritans, economic activity among Jews was not strictly sacral in nature, not a means of serving and rendering honor to God. Certain sacral rules applied also in the economic sphere as they did in all details of Jewish life, but this was entirely different from the Puritans' view of economic activity as a means of serving God.

Among Jews wealth was not proof of charisma, another difference from the Puritans. No doubt, God favored pious Jews and, when he so willed, could bless them with riches. But riches did not in themselves attest to the rich man's state of grace. There were bad Jews among the rich, and very saintly Jews, indisputably dear to God, among the poor.

The chief, the highest value for a Jew was knowledge, wisdom. Its acquisition was the most proper means of serving God, and its possession was visible proof of charisma. Compared with learning, wealth was of little significance. At best, it could be of use in facilitating the acquisition of wisdom. In freeing a man from daily cares, wealth allowed him to dedicate himself fully to learning.

The richest Jew meant little compared with the poorest rabbi famous for his knowledge and saintliness. It was the rich man's dream to have a philosopher in the family who would be able to devote himself entirely to his studies. Hence, it was common for rich men to give their daughters in marriage to poor but promising young students of wisdom and to support their sons-in-law for many years. The rich were unsparing of money when learning was concerned; they financed the building of synagogues, aided rabbis financially, and gave money for teaching and books.

This was, of course, sacred knowledge, whose basis was the study of and commentary on the sacred books and the writings of famous rabbis. It was strictly scholastic and scholastic-legal knowledge. It gave rise to a religious-legal system that delineated every detail of a pious Jew's behavior.

In an era of universal illiteracy, the Jews were the only social element in Poland that had a deep respect for books. It is not a matter of chance that the book trade, especially the antiquarian book trade, became nearly everywhere the domain of Jews. Books were goods close to the heart of the Jew, even if they had no connection to Jewish orthodoxy, language, faith, or culture. Books were books. Long centuries engendered a tradition of the book, of study, of striving for knowledge and wisdom. Apart from the Chinese, perhaps no other civilization created a cult of knowledge and the written word like that of the Jews.

It does not follow that wealth was without significance. It did have great significance, especially in relations with the outside world. It raised the Jew's position relative to the goy, it provided the Jew with a sense of his own importance and power vis-à-vis the outside world. A rich Jew ceased to be a *parch*, he ceased even to be a *żydek*, or at least he could feel that both categories were of less significance for him. Wealth created a new position, opened the way to new contacts, and provided a basis for making comparisons between one's own situation and that of others.

But also "inside," especially if it went along with knowledge and piety, wealth had its own significance. It could bring a person into the *kahal* aristocracy, make possible closer contacts with the rabbis, and convey social status. But it always had to go along with piety and knowledge. Jewish folklore pokes fun at presumptuous and conceited rich men who are ignoramuses. There are a great many mischievous stories indicating that, in the eyes of Jews, wealth in itself is not a reason for social prestige.

VI

Unquestionably, the knowledge that constituted the highest value in the Jewish world was sacral knowledge. But traditional Jewish knowledge was very broad and encompassed various areas of life. The Talmud was a legal system and also a book of the wisdom of life. It contained the most varied regulations and reflections constituting a sort of encyclopedia of knowledge. That was, of course, a specific sort of encyclopedia, one canonical in nature, exegetic, infinitely more magical than empirical or rational. Nevertheless, it was Knowledge with a capital K.

In practice, that knowledge often did not exclude the possibility of engaging in studies of some other kind. For example, the study of medicine fitted into the traditional model of the learned Jew. From the early Middle Ages on, Jews studied medicine, and the name of eminent Jewish physicians figure in the history of all the lands of the diaspora. They also treated goys, including the Polish kings. Jakub Izaak was Zygmunt I's court physician, Salomon Aszkenazy was Zygmunt August's, and Jonas Casal and Abraham of Troki treated Jan III. Jews could be found among the Polish magnates' court physicians, to mention only Nisanowicz, the Radziwiłłs' doctor. Tobies Kohn (1652–1729) was supposedly the first physician to provide a detailed description of the disease known as *plica polonica*. In the nineteenth and twentieth centuries, when Jewish life had begun to undergo secularization and when secular learning had become a highly valued means for achieving social advancement and for leaving the caste, the study of medicine possessed particular vitality among the Jews. For a Jewish family to have a son who was a doctor now had the same meaning as having a son who was a learned rabbi had had in former times. There is no lack of Jewish names among the Nobel laureates for medicine.

Jews were also attracted by various fields connected with medicine. There were Jewish pharmacists and chemists, or rather alchemists. In Poland the professions of doctor's assistant, barber surgeon, and bloodletter were for many years considered Jewish specialties. In practice, all this was often close to quackery, but to a lesser degree than the usual folk medicine, which was based entirely on magic and primitive empiricism.

From the fragmentary data at our disposal, we know that in Poland, by the end of the eighteenth and the beginning of the nineteenth centuries, there were Jewish doctors who could be termed fully qualified. Jews were among the military doctors during the November Uprising of 1831. Among the converts in the first half of the nineteenth century, Jeske-Choiński mentions the children of doctors who, obviously, must have received their training much earlier. We do not know exactly how or where. It may have been in the countries of Western Europe, where wealthier Jews had begun traveling to study. They were attracted by Mendelson's renown, as the life of Salomon Maimon clearly demonstrates. There is no indication that the Jewish physicians' medical qualifications were any lower than those of their Christian colleagues.

It can also be assumed that the necessities of life compelled many Jews to acquire practical knowledge of state law. Such knowledge would be very useful in business dealings with the outside world. In any case, there was an interest among Jews in secular and state law, and by the beginning of the nineteenth century we begin to encounter Jewish lawyers in Poland. In time law took its place beside medicine for ambitious young Jews as a means of achieving social advancement through education.

In one way or another, secular knowledge, non-Jewish knowledge, was infiltrating Jewish milieus, mainly those of the wealthy and the traditionally educated. Maimon's example demonstrates best that it was also reaching the poor, if only sporadically. Maimon's example also testifies that new philosophical ideas, far removed from the diaspora's age-old traditions, were entering the world of the Jews. In the seventeenth century, in distant Holland, those influences bore fruit in the work of Benedict Spinoza.

What we know of Maimon's spiritual development explains the road that could be or even had to be taken by young Jews who were subjected to the influence of ideas coming from without. The failure of attempts to reconcile or harmonize those ideas with traditional wisdom produced deep inner conflicts, a fundamental spiritual perplexity. There were also dramatic outward conflicts, which led, as they did in the case of Spinoza, to alienation from the Jewish community. All that, however, was conditioned by the importance of learning, knowledge, and wisdom in the Jewish ethos.

In the world surrounding the Jewish caste in Poland the knowledge acquired from books was not held in high esteem. Such knowledge was foreign to the mass of the peasantry, and among the nobility and even among the magnates there was no excess of educated people. That situation began to change during the reign of King Stanisław August Poniatowski and after the partitions but never developed into a cult of the book and knowledge that was characteristic of Jews. Polish aristocratic circles resented Fryderyk Skarbek for "lowering himself" to be a professor.[2] And much later on, Stanisław Tarnowski's scholarly career was viewed simply as the whim of a great lord.[3] This caused Tarnowski himself to suffer when Franz Joseph refused him the Golden Fleece.[4] It was only toward the end of the nineteenth century, when Poland developed an intellectual class, that a milieu emerged in which books and knowledge were highly valued.

Thus there was a distinct conflict between the ideals of the Jews and those of the non-Jews. The book belonged to the traditional image of the Jew, its absence to the traditional image of the goy.

Among educated Jews, particularly among those who possessed secular and practical knowledge, there must have been a sense of their own value which could not always be reconciled with their role as *parch* or *żydek*, especially when their knowledge and services were gladly used and their competence valued. In those instances the feeling of belonging to a caste would have been particularly painful and the temptation to abandon the caste very great. This explains why so many of the early converts were people with higher educational qualifications.

VII

We have devoted considerable attention to the problem of the early conversions, more than seems justified by the number of converts. It is my opinion, however, that the early conversions contained elements basic to the departures from the caste which came much later and which were much more numerous. Moreover, they contained *in nuce* elements that in time would be of major significance for the anticaste aspirations expressed in the national emancipation movement. That movement had to be preceded by individual assimilation, which in turn was preceded by individual conversion.

Socially speaking, individual conversion was an expression and consequence of the conflict between two cultures, two value systems. This conflict expressed itself in inward crises and religious experiences that were felt with great power. The making of comparisons between a person's own condition and that of others was the context that brought that conflict to the surface and led to the making of a decision. Making such comparisons was a symptom of a person's increasing sense of his own importance, which frequently went together with wealth and education. The final social consequence was the abandonment of caste and the transition to a new milieu. The legal system in noble Poland favored this process to an exceptional degree.

In the nineteenth century, after the fall of the republic, conversion of Jews became more and more frequent with each decade. Relying on Teodor Jeske-Choiński's incomplete and not always scrupulous calculations, one can speak of thousands of Jewish families who, before the beginning of the twentieth century, had accepted Christianity in Poland, be it Catholicism or Protestantism. New historical conditions had developed that were eminently favorable to that process.

First of all, changes occurred in the Jews' legal position. Official equality of rights came first in the area of the Prussian partition, where the number of Jews was negligible. Equality even caused their exodus, chiefly into Prussia. Later on, legal equality came to Galicia, where Jews formed a significant percentage of the population. In the area under

Russian partition (with the exception of Congress Poland, where the Jews were emancipated in the 1860s), however, it was only the Russian authorities' departure during the First World War that abrogated the legal limitations to which Jews in the Russian Empire were subjected.

Equality before the law obviously did not mean that the caste system had been eliminated. A caste does not have to be a legal institution. It is an institution of custom, the result of definite attitudes and social traditions. But official equality had a positive influence on the frequency and ease of leaving the caste. Legal difficulties fell away, and new impetuses and motivations arose.

Second and more important, however, were other changes occurring both in the life of Poland as a whole and in that of Polish Jews. The country's economic structure had slowly begun to be transformed. The first large industrial enterprises appeared, the first railroads were constructed, and more modern banking methods came into use. No doubt this was a far cry from the tempo and dimensions of capitalism's development in Western Europe, but it did revolutionize Polish life.

The Polish Jews necessarily played an important role in these changes; they were the only social element in Poland prepared for such tasks. They did not produce Rothschilds, Montefiores, or Lazares, but they did produce Kronenbergs, Blochs, Wawelbergs, Natansons,[5] Rotwands, Bersons, and many others. Jan Bogumił Bloch built the first railroad line in the Congress Kingdom of Poland; others were pioneers in the fields of banking and industry. Their part in economic life fitted the traditional image of the Jew. For centuries the Jew had been a businessman who dealt with trade and with organizing production of every sort and at every stage. He had a "head for business," experience, a tradition, and he knew how to establish commercial relations with the world at large.

Moreover, there existed a group of rich Jews who had amassed a supply of capital. One can have doubts about the size of those Jewish fortunes; probably none of them equaled the great fortunes of the magnates. But those possessing them were not afraid of taking risks, and knew how to invest their money, make it bring a profit, and increase it. They were aided in this by the experience of many generations.

We know quite a lot about those first Jewish captains of Polish economic development. We know their beginnings and their fates. We even have biographical details concerning people like Bloch and Leopold Kronenberg. They came from wealthy backgrounds and, it should be stressed, backgrounds with traditions of education. Sometimes—as was the case with the Eiger family—there were famous rabbis among their ancestors. Also, a tradition of secular, non-Jewish education prevailed in all those families by the beginning of the nineteenth century. Bloch was a man of great learning, knew several foreign languages, and of course spoke perfect Polish. He had traveled the world a great deal in his youth and had studied in Germany. The same may be said of the first Kronenberg. By background, the Wawelbergs, the Rotwands, the Leos, the Natansons, the Wolfs, the Fajanses were not only wealthy but also educated. That education was not always very high, and it was often quite one-sided; but it was probably no worse than that of the majority of Polish landowners of the time.

These people began to play an important role in the life of the country. They created great fortunes and engaged in wide-ranging economic activity. And not only economic activity. During the January Uprising of 1863 Kronenberg was one of the leaders of the White party.[6] Henryk Wohl and the two Neuding brothers occupied high positions in the ranks of the insurgents. The famous book *The War to Come*, which had a great influence on world political thought at the time, was Bloch's work, or, more precisely, arose under his auspices. Hipolit Wawelberg and Stanisław Rotwand founded a well-known technical school. Natanson became a book publisher. One could cite many similar examples.

One can understand that it was unbearable for such people to remain in the caste; none of them could accept playing the traditional roles of *parch* or *żydek*. And, as a matter of fact, all, or nearly all, had begun their careers with a decisive step—they had left the caste through baptism. Both Bloch and Kronenberg became Christians as young men. Over the course of time they would spare no efforts to distance themselves from the caste as much as possible. They would acquire titles of nobility and establish family ties with the Polish aristocracy through marriage. Large dowries served to lure the young aristocrats, although there were also instances of genuine affection.

Not all the new Jewish tycoons followed the example set by Kronenberg and Bloch. Some remained formally true to the faith of their forefathers. There were even those who placed great emphasis on their religious affiliation with Judaism. This, however, rarely had anything in common with the old orthodoxy. In matters of culture, custom, and ideology, the Jewish bourgeoisie attempted to leave the caste.

The socioeconomic changes that Polish Jews encountered caused further breaches in the caste's traditional ethos. Secular trends began infiltrating the Jewish ghettos. The Jews of Western Europe had been subjected to secularization somewhat earlier, a process in which Moses Mendelssohn became a leading figure. Word of him and his writings began to reach the small towns in Poland and Lithuania. The end of the eighteenth century saw the beginning of a movement among East European Jewry that has gone down in Jewish history under the name Haskalah.

The secularization of the Jews was the aim of that movement. It did not reject the old traditions and was not an antireligious movement.

Instead, it strove to "enlighten" the Jews, to modernize them culturally. While not acting against the caste system as such, the adherents of Haskalah believed that by changing their customs and reforming their ethos Jews would gradually be able to free themselves from the narrow confines of caste, would cease to be a despised group, and would develop a sense of their own dignity and importance.

Haskalah had an influence on the Jews in Poland as well. It developed tendencies toward secularization, tendencies that also sprang from other sources. In time Haskalah would become an important influence in awakening aspirations for national emancipation among Jews. However, in the early phases, through its secularism, it provided an incentive for individuals to leave the caste through baptism and assimilation.

Secularization created an atmosphere in which changing religion ceased to be a matter of such profound inner conflict as it had formerly been. A time of religious indifference began. It did not affect the Jewish masses, who remained faithful to the rules of the order. But it did affect the periphery of the caste, the people who, through wealth, education, and constant contact with the outside world, were losing their connection to the caste and gradually becoming alienated from it. There were more and more such people all the time. Undoubtedly, in relation to the Jewish masses, that periphery was not substantial in number, but it increased steadily, forming a category of marginal people. Those people sought to leave the caste. If changing their religion could achieve that, they saw it as no cause for great moral perturbation. And there is no doubt that opportunistic consideration had begun to prevail. Religion was becoming a social convention; the acceptance of another convention could make possible a fundamental change in one's social standing. It is significant that many Jews at that time converted to Protestantism, which was considered closer to Judaic deism and, at the same time, less rigorous than Catholicism, more rationalized. Calvinism enjoyed particular success among Polish Jews.

It does not follow that no Jews converted out of genuine conviction. Of course, there were such cases, but it was not they who created the social image of the new neophytism. To an increasingly greater degree, this neophytism was conditioned by nonreligious motives.

Such motives were social, cultural, even political. Baptism, which became very common after 1863, was now often an expression of the desire to identify fully with Polishness. In reality, it was the final seal to the process of assimilation. At times it was connected with "mixed" marriage, an increasingly frequent occurrence toward the end of the nineteenth century. This was also related to a new social phenomenon in Polish life: the formation of the urban intelligentsia, whose origins reach back to the first decades of the nineteenth century. From the end of that century, the intelligentsia in Poland, quantitatively and qualitatively, became an important factor in public life. And among the intelligentsia, an ever-increasing role was played by people of Jewish origin. The tradition of the book was of great significance here. Social advancement through education was particularly meaningful for Jews, more so than for other elements in Polish society. In keeping with the tradition, it seemed the best route for liberating oneself from the caste. We see analogous tendencies in other caste systems in various civilizations throughout the world. Social advancement through education is characteristic of the blacks in America, colonial peoples, and European national groups in the process of emancipation, like the Ukrainians, Lithuanians, Latvians, Belorussians, and so. In the case of the Jews this process was greatly intensified by the peculiarities of the Jewish ethos, which placed such value on books and knowledge.

Julian Klaczko may be considered the first outstanding Polish writer of Jewish origin.[7] He began his career writing poetry in Hebrew and ended as a prominent publicist, historian, and politician. In Klaczko's case, baptism was the final confirmation of his Polishness. It should be added that Klaczko treated his new religion with great seriousness.

Before Klaczko, those who had left the caste often found themselves among the Polish intelligentsia, which was then in its early stages. After him, their influx was increasingly greater. People even spoke about the "Jewification" of the Polish intelligentsia.

VIII

This is how the question of conversion by Polish Jews appears from a social and cultural standpoint. In other European countries a similar pattern prevailed. By changing his religion, a Jew would leave the caste, enter the world outside, and attempt to identify with it as fully and as quickly as possible.

That identification consisted in developing a loyalty to that new world and in rejecting any remnants of loyalty to the old. This meant adopting the mores of the new world, its rules, its ethos, its entire culture. And it meant a final break with the past. If permitted by law, the converts would change their names to ones that did not sound Jewish. New genealogies were contrived, attempts were made at acquiring titles of nobility, and marriages were made with non-Jews. The denial of one's Jewish origin was frequent.

When Jeske-Choiński and, later, Korwin published their books "unmasking" the Jewish origin of a great number of Polish families, those concerned diligently bought up copies of the book and destroyed them. As a result, Jeske-Choiński's *Polish Converts* is an antiquarian rarity today.

The question of conversion, in turn, brings us to a considerably broader problem: the assimilation of the Jews. It was both a program and a historical process: the advocates of assimilation saw it as a means of solving the Jewish question in Poland; but it was also a social phenomenon. There is no doubt that thousands of Polish Jews took the route of assimilation, some changing their religion, some remaining true to Judaism, even if only formally. And although assimilation was condemned by Jewish nationalists and dismissed or rejected by anti-Semites, it remained of great significance in Polish life and of great significance for Polish culture. Without the sociohistorical fact of assimilation, Polish science, Polish art, all creative Polish culture would have been seriously impoverished. But assimilation was also of significance for Jewish culture. Most likely, without assimilation Jewish national and emancipationist tendencies could not have developed fully. Today's Israel owes more than a little to the Polish assimilationists.

Within the Caste or Outside It?

I

From the mid nineteenth century on, the abandoning of caste by changing religion became increasingly common among Jews in Poland. It was not only factors of personal religious experience that were decisive here. In an ever-larger number of cases the motive for changing religion had very little to do with religious experience. National-political, social, and general cultural motives began to come more and more into play. In reality, conversion became the conclusion of and the seal on individual instances of a process considerably more general, and it was conditioned by that process. This process is what in Poland and in many other countries was called the assimilation of the Jews.

When speaking of assimilation in general, we mean the process by which a group or its individual members adopt the culture of another group. This can be the culture of a national group or any other group with specific cultural values of its own. In certain epochs the wealthy city bourgeoisie took over the values of feudal knightly culture and assimilated to it. In today's world, workers—and not only in Western Europe and North America—are clearly assimilating to so-called middle-class or burgher culture, adopting values that until now had been considered specific to the middle class. In Poland, assimilating Jews took on the qualities not only of Polish culture but also, and to a remarkable degree, of gentry culture. The features of Polish gentry culture have been prominently preserved in the milieus of the assimilated Jewish intelligentsia and plutocracy up to the present time.

Assimilation occurs, to one degree or another, wherever and whenever there are points of contact between groups with different cultures. When such contacts take place, exchanges of cultural qualities ensue. Those exchanges can include all realms and all types of values. Dress and diet, instruments of work and war, social customs and pastimes, linguistic borrowings and philosophical concepts, religious beliefs and aesthetic views—there is no end to the list of the forms and directions taken when various qualities are mutually adopted, all of which fall under the general concept of assimilation. The processes of assimilation are particularly comprehensive and far-reaching in contemporary civilizations that, on the one hand, create a uniformity of living conditions and, on the other, possess extremely powerful means for influencing masses of people.

If, however, in all those cases objective instances of assimilation do occur, we do not always realize it, and even if we are aware of adopting the values of other groups, we do not define this as assimilation. At most, we speak of a partial, incomplete, fragmentary assimilation, something which is different from total assimilation. But what we now have in mind is full and complete adoption by one group of another group's culture, especially of a national culture. When speaking of assimilation, we most frequently mean national assimilation.

In the nineteenth century the growth of national aspirations and the formation of nationalistic philosophies narrowed the concept of assimilation to the domain of national language. At the same time, the term *assimilation* itself took on a marked emotional coloration. It offended some, attracted others. Poles spoke favorably of assimilation when it referred to the Polonization of Ukrainians or even, at certain periods, of Jews. On the other hand, for Ukrainians and Jews, people from their milieus who assimilated to Polishness were renegades. The Poles thought the same of Poles who became Russified or Germanized. Orzeszkowa was passionate in condemning Joseph Conrad's "renegation." Obviously, the specific political conditions in which Poles, Ukrainians, and Jews lived had a decisive influence on the formation of those emotional attitudes.

However, irrespective of the emotional attitudes of the groups involved, the processes of national assimilation occur everywhere. In national societies founded by emigration—the United States, Canada, Brazil, Argentina, Australia—the existence of a "melting pot" means an incessant process of assimilation of various ethnic elements that adopt the qualities of the dominant culture and at times add their own values to it. In America ethnic groups from the world over assimilate either to an Anglo-Saxon culture that has been transformed on the spot or to a Hispanic or Portuguese culture that has undergone no less a transformation, while at the same time themselves contributing to that transformation. This process may require more or less time, but it occurs constantly and successfully, especially because it has the support of the entire machinery of the state, of the society, and of the groups assimilating to it. National societies owing their emergence to emigration were able to maintain their existence and develop in no other way than by assimilating newcomers.

In all these countries the processes of assimilation are furthered if the society is friendly to the groups assimilating into it and creates conditions that facilitate the absorption of new elements. In these instances the demands placed on the assimilating groups are modest, at least for the first generation. Citizenship—very easy to receive in those countries—some mastery of the language, the adoption of certain customs held to be basic, loyalty to the government, all this is entirely sufficient in American or Canadian society for assimilation to be recognized as a fact.

The demands are infinitely more severe in Europe's old nation states. In France or in England many years are needed before a foreigner is recognized as fully assimilated, and much bias, mistrust, and suspicion have to be overcome. Naturalization alone is not sufficient. In England it was only the unprecedented influx of foreigners during the last war that weakened a number of biases and somewhat liberalized the society's relation to those assimilating to it.

It is not difficult to observe that this attitude changes depending on time and various other factors, among which the society's assessment of those who are assimilating to it is of particular significance. In the United States the attitude toward the Dutch or Scandinavians was always incomparably more friendly than that toward Italians or Poles, and the society was considerably more liberal in the degree of assimilation it required of Dutch and Scandinavians than of many other immigrant groups. If that is the case in the United States, it must be infinitely more acute in the countries of old Europe. The French, who are extremely exclusive, will sooner accept an Italian than a German, a Pole than a Russian, as part of their national society.

Noble Poland was characterized by a very great receptivity to the assimilation of foreigners, especially if they were Catholics and noblemen. There was a strikingly large number of Scottish, German, and Italian newcomers, not to mention Tartars and Armenians, among the Polish nobility. They found easy acceptance, a friendly attitude, and equal treatment. That friendly attitude toward assimilating foreigners survived noble Poland and may even have lasted until the present time. A certain number of Russians remained in Poland after 1915, a group that increased with time owing to the influx of émigrés after the revolution. Those Russians, whose younger generation adapted easily to Polish life, received friendly treatment, were considered Poles, and met with none of the resistance encountered by foreigners attempting to assimilate in France or England.

The case of what might be called internal assimilation, assimilation of the "lower" orders—peasants, burghers, and Jews—to the culture of the nobility presents a somewhat different appearance. If Polish noble society's exclusivity, especially in earlier periods, was not overly great in regard to Jews who had changed religion and received noble status, it was very great in regard to those peasants and burghers who had accepted the "lords'" way of life, which in the nineteenth century occurred with increasing frequency. Noble society was averse to the newly rich parvenus who imitated the nobility. And not only to them. Until the nineteenth century intellectuals of common origin met with unfriendly treatment, mockery, and mistrust. Żeromski's Tomasz Judym and Andrzej Radek are literary characters who symbolize the attitude of the nobility toward intruders.

In the nineteenth century the attitude of the nobility toward Jews who were assimilating began to assume a similar character. To an increasing degree, such people began to be treated as intruders. Here, however, the case was more complicated than that of the peasants or the burghers. On the one hand, especially after 1863, the mass assimilation of Jews to Polishness was viewed as the sole solution to the Jewish question in Poland; on the other hand, a distance was kept from those new Poles of the Jewish faith. As we shall discuss again, that distance increased as the assimilation of Jews to non-Jews gathered momentum. *Mutatis mutandis*, something similar can be observed in the American South, and to a degree also in the North, in relation to black people. The absolute cultural assimilation of blacks to the rest of the American population has not only failed to reduce discrimination but has rather increased it.

These are very general statements on the process of cultural assimilation. I strongly emphasize that assimilation always depends both on the group assimilating and on the group assimilated to. The rate of assimilation and how common and complete it becomes depend much on the receptivity of the milieu that is the goal of assimilation.

II

However, assimilation can be understood not solely as the process of one group's adapting itself to the culture of another. It can also be understood as a *program* for the purposeful attainment of that adaptation and as the *method* for realizing that program. Both aspects are two-sided.

First, assimilation can be the program and the method of the group that is being assimilated to. The dominant group in the national culture (this can, of course, relate to groups of other sorts as well, e.g., classes), operating on territory inhabited by groups of various other national cultures, puts forward a program of assimilation for the latter groups and attempts to put that program into practice. Often, though not always, this takes the form of forced assimilation imposed by legal and governmental machinery. The methods of Russification used by the czarist governments and those of Germanization in Prussia can serve as classic examples of forced assimilation accompanied by the subjugation and persecution of cultures held to be alien. In these instances forcible means were used with particular brutality and ruthlessness. In certain periods they did not shrink even from such drastic measures as the extermination of the subjugated people. The people, and the culture they represented, were eliminated. Nazism was the last attempt to apply such methods of assimilation on an enormous scale.

Forcible means can, however, be considerably milder, for example, denying the other cultural groups schools of their own and imposing on them a school system unified by language. Brazil's policy toward foreign-language immigrant groups at a certain period can serve as an example. In Poland before the outbreak of World War II, the policy toward the schools for national minorities had similar goals (which were not, by the way, carried out with great consistency). In the Soviet Union, after periods of physical extermination (e.g., that of the Ukrainian intelligentsia), the fight against the "nationalism" of non-Russian groups took the form of a policy of Russification "from within" while preserving the cultural autonomy of the Soviet peoples on the surface. This is careful Russification, one that avoids brutality and seemingly does not violate the freedom of the local cultures; nevertheless, it achieves a program of assimilation.

In the United States, on the other hand, methods of forced assimilation are not applied, even though Americanization is recognized as one of the chief aims of national policy. And Americanization is nothing other than the assimilation of various immigrant groups to American culture, an assimilation that begins with their adoption of American English. Americanization is achieved with excellent results and without using compulsory means; it proceeds through evolution, through the spontaneous absorption of differing cultural elements.

In Poland, after the Four-Year Sejm, the assimilation of Jews to Polish culture was preached constantly and, almost until the period before the Second World War, was considered the best solution to the Jewish question. Of course, forced assimilation was possible only in those periods when a Polish state existed. In the nineteenth century the assimilationist program was not a state policy but rather a postulate enjoying great approval in certain circles of Polish society, especially among the intelligentsia. Those circles thought that no efforts should be spared to attain the Polonization of Jews as quickly and fully as possible, within, of course, the possibilities of a society that was not a state.

But second, assimilation can also be understood as a postulate and a program adopted by the group that is assimilating. This occurs when the group ceases to treat its own traditional culture as superior and begins to acknowledge its inferiority to the culture of another group. In the United States Americanization progresses primarily because American life is accepted as something considerably better than the old traditional cultures. This is particularly characteristic of the children of immigrants who view their fathers' traditional culture as inferior, unattractive, or embarrassing. Breaking from that culture, endeavoring to become an American in the full sense of the word (to cease being a hyphenated American), is very common. In this case one may speak of a program of assimilation consciously adopted by the descendants of immigrants from any country. The success of such a program is greatly favored by the absence of any compulsion except the influence of public opinion.

Innumerable parallel examples can be cited of the adoption of assimilationist programs by various groups and their individual members who feel their own cultural traditions to be inferior. This does not mean that, objectively speaking, those traditions are of little value. On the contrary, they may spring from splendid sources. An Italian or a German who becomes Americanized descends from cultures that are certainly not inferior to American or even English culture. However, in their own mind, influenced by American conditions, they consider their forefathers' culture less attractive than the culture of America. In most cases, those forefathers had been common people in the old country, and their connections to the great cultural traditions of Italy or Germany were loose and fragmentary.

The process of assimilation through which those people passed and still pass was assimilation not only to a national culture that was considered superior but also to the culture of a social class that, regardless of its national traditions, was valued as something especially attractive and better. In similar fashion, those who had left the world of the peasants or the petite bourgeoisie in Poland as they advanced socially as individuals assimilated to the culture of the nobility. That culture was especially attractive and provided areas of opportunity significantly greater than those offered by the culture of the common people. At the same time, partaking in the culture of the nobility allowed a person to demonstrate his worth in accordance with the objective position that wealth or acquired education allowed those *homines novi* to occupy.

Among Western European Jews at the end of the eighteenth century and among Eastern European Jews after the mid nineteenth century, the assimilationist ideology began to play a prominent role, and it became the driving force behind profound changes. Up until the beginning of the twentieth century, that ideology would continue to attract the younger generations of Polish Jews who were seeking a way out of the ghetto's traditional confines. In the twentieth century the objective role played by the assimilation of Polish Jews was often disregarded or even denied. The Polish side questioned the sincerity of the assimilationists and considered the entire movement a phenomenon with little significance for Polish life and with only weak influence on the Jewish masses. Many people—like Jeske-Choiński, for example, not to mention the racists who came later—saw assimilation as the pernicious infiltration of Polish culture by elements that carried alien and hostile values. The Jewish side, especially with the increase in trends toward national emancipation, saw assimilation as defection and the assimilationists as defectors from the Jewish cause. Assimilation was harmful to Jewish life, it impoverished it, and the assimilationists were traitors to their own people. No one perceived that assimilation was a fundamental precondition for awakening the Jews' national aspirations. Without the assimilations the later leaders of the Jewish national renaissance would probably have never appeared. Analogous accusations and analogous misunderstandings can be found in all other cases of contemporary national emancipation movements both in Europe and in the colonial countries. Everywhere a period of assimilation preceded those movements and served to pave the way for them, and everywhere it was condemned by the developing nationalist ideologies.

III

Assimilation, both as program and as process, would have been impossible without the socioeconomic and cultural changes that took place in the European arena after the mid eighteenth century and that spread to Poland in the nineteenth century. These changes, known as the creation of the capitalist economy, revolutionized all areas of life, putting an end to the traditional villein economy, creating new forms of urban life, destroying old social stratifications, and replacing old cultural values with entirely new ones. The changes, which were comprehensive and deep, did not run a smooth and harmonious course. They were accompanied by powerful political upheavals—wars and revolutions. In some countries they moved faster, in others slower. They usually moved in a zigzag course, allowing obsolete elements to coexist with new ones. Few periods in human history have been so dramatic, so full of conflict and contradiction, as that which began more than two centuries ago and has still not ended.

These changes also affected Polish Jews. The great agrarian economy had entered a period of prolonged crisis from which it would never recover. The magnates' fortunes dwindled, or they were forced to change their farming methods. The age of villein service was now past. These changes were accompanied by an end to the Jews' traditional functions in the economy of the gentry landowners. There was no longer any place for the Jew as saloon keeper, innkeeper, leaseholder, or general factotum. Here and there, some Jews maintained their old positions, but as relics of the past that, in the period between the wars, began to be consigned to oblivion. During this time, one could still encounter the Jewish innkeeper, but only in certain areas of Poland, and his functions had increasingly less in common with those he had once performed. He had become a primitive hotelier and restaurant manager as opposed to an actual innkeeper.

The large developing cities began to attract masses of Jews from the countryside and the small towns. Toward the end of the eighteenth century, there began an exodus of Jews from the area under Prussian partition into the industrializing cities of the Reich. This exodus was so large that, by the beginning of the twentieth century, Jews constituted only a small percentage of the population of the Poznań region and Pomerania. It was only in highly industrialized Silesia that the percentage was somewhat higher. The once-popular conception that the Polish population had, by a deliberate and planned campaign, "de-Jewified" the area of Prussian partition was an obvious misunderstanding. The Prussian partition owed its "de-Jewification" to the colossal development of industry and trade throughout the Reich. Moreover, a certain number of Jews had moved from the Prussian partition to the Congress Kingdom, which was also industrializing.

But even the Austro-Hungarian Empire, whose economic development was considerably weaker than that of the Reich, became an attractive area for many Galician Jews. They were drawn in particular to Vienna, whose Second District became not just a Jewish but a Galician-Jewish quarter.

Of course, the larger urban centers in Poland itself—Warsaw, Łódź, Lvov, Kraków, Częstochowa, Sosnowiec—absorbed large numbers of Jews who were leaving the countryside and the small towns. The latter, though, remained extremely important centers of Jewish life. In large measure they maintained their old economic functions of supplying simple commodities to backward agricultural regions. To an increasing extent, such small towns had to take into account the needs of peasant villages, which could not have had a positive influence on the type and structure of their trade. The primitive, dirty Jewish market stall was an offshoot of the primitive, dirty peasant village, which in turn was an offshoot of the primitive, dirty small town and the general economic level of the country. All these sorry affairs were, of course, interdependent. Not everyone was aware of this, and many people thought that the replacement of the Jewish tradesman by a Polish one would raise the level of the villages and the small towns, invigorate trade, and regenerate the entire country. Attempts at putting those convictions into practice produced results that did nothing to contribute to an economic renaissance of the country. Thus, such exceptional thinkers as Wawrzyniec Surowiecki, who already in the first half of the nineteenth century had come to an excellent understanding of the crux of the problem, are all the more worthy of admiration. But there were not many Surowieckis in Poland.

A large portion of Polish Jewry underwent urbanization to an ever-increasing degree. And urbanization involved the Jews in fundamental social, economic, and culture-creating processes that were compatible neither with a ghetto-bound life nor with the caste-structure model. These conditions necessarily led to conflicts among the masses of Jews between the ideals of the past, traditions, the old ethos, and the new reality with its objective demands and allurements. As always, the conflict was chiefly between the generations. For young Jews in particular, the clash between the old ideals and the new reality was irreconcilable. The new reality was chosen, and that in short order led to the adoption of the patterns of the goys' world, that is, to assimilation.

We have already spoken about social conditioning in cases of Jewish conversion. Obviously, those same factors were also at work here. But conversion as a rule led to a complete break with the caste and, in practice, to erasing traces of caste and of Jewish origin. Assimilation was something considerably broader than conversion, although in individual cases it led to conversion. It included various degrees of adaptation to non-Jews and various levels of personal identification with Polishness. It did not always necessarily indicate a break with the past, at least not a complete one.

We must stress again that absolute isolation exists only in theory. Even under the caste-ghetto system there was some contact and mutual influence. This was already true in the sixteenth century, the era of Ezofowicz, and it took place to a greater degree in the nineteenth century, when all of Poland, including Polish Jews, began to be drawn into the orbit of the new socioeconomic processes. One result was a more lively economic connection between the area of the Russian partition and Prussia. This was accompanied by an influx of German, especially Silesian, Jews into the Congress Kingdom, chiefly to Warsaw, Łódź, Częstochowa, and Sosnowiec. Those Jews were well-to-do and educated people who, to a significant degree, had already managed to separate themselves from the traditional caste organization that existed in the Reich. The German Jews who had found their spiritual leader in Mendelssohn had already begun assimilating to German culture at the end of the eighteenth century. The German-Jewish newcomers to the Congress Kingdom were extremely Germanized and tried to maintain the separateness of their cultural identity from the mass of local Jews.

Those German Jews played an important role in Poland. Most important, they began to attract the elements of Polish Jewry that were seeking a way out of the caste. If those elements were, for a certain time, under the spell of German culture, this proved only temporary, and the Jews from Germany themselves began to be affected by the Polonizing influences of the larger environment. By the end of the nineteenth century the overwhelming majority of those formerly German Jews had become Polonized, and quite a few had even assumed Polish-sounding names along with a change of religion.

It is difficult to determine the size of that immigration of German Jews into the Congress Kingdom. Relative to the number of Polish Jews it was not large, but their impact was significant. They served as a link connecting Polish Jews with another world. That the Jews from Germany and the Polish Jews seeking to advance in society were, in terms of wealth and education, close to each other, facilitated their relations. Mixed marriages created new connections among families. All of this favored the progress of assimilation.

The groundwork had been laid by the Haskalah movement, which had developed among Eastern European Jewry, not without influence from Germany. As discussed above, Haskalah sought to break with the traditional forms, to rebuild life through nontraditional education in keeping with the new demands. The leaders of Haskalah believed that the Jews' lot would be improved by the spread of "European" education and by the introduction of new customs and forms of economic activity. At the same time, they rejected the concept of a radical break with the past. The Jew was to remain a Jew but one adapted to the new reality. For all its moderation, Haskalah had an enormous influence both on furthering individual assimilation and, with time, on awakening the desire for national emancipation among the Jewish masses.

The Haskalah movement contributed to the emergence in Warsaw of the School of Rabbis, the first large-scale center for creating a Polish-Jewish intelligentsia. Under the influence of Haskalah, young Jews assumed the dress, customs, and language of the goys and, sometimes at the cost of enormous effort, acquired education. The way had been made much easier for the children and grandchildren of those people to find places for themselves among the Jewish-Polish intelligentsia or bourgeoisie.

IV

How can we determine the number of Polish Jews who assimilated in the course of more than a century? In practice it is impossible. Even those situations in which the assimilationists acted as a political group, for example in the elections to parliament or to the agencies of self-government or those within the Jewish community, do not tell us a great deal. The results of the elections were a chance matter, and the electorate could have been guided by a variety of motives. The circulation of such publications as *Jutrzenka* (Dawn), *Izraelita* (The Israelite), or *Nowa Gazeta* (The New Gazette) cannot serve as an accurate indicator either. The data in population censuses regarding those who declared themselves Poles of the Jewish faith are also quite doubtful. The first such census in independent Poland indicated that there were half a million people who gave their native language as Polish and their religion as Jewish. Today we know well how dubious the value of this census of 1921 was.

However, the most important point is that the concept of "assimilation" is not and cannot be limited to a single meaning. In the world of cultural values there are so many variations, nuances, and distinctions that one must not apply rigid formulas. To what degree is one Pole more "Polish" than another, one Frenchman more "French"? If we apply certain criteria here, they are ideal criteria—models with which we want the Pole or Frenchman to comply and according to which we wish to classify him. But the ideal Pole, American, Frenchman, German, or Jew is only an ideal whose counterpart cannot be found among living people. Let us say that a Pole, Jew, American, Russian, German, or Italian should act in one specific way and no other, that that is what national ideals and traditions and the honor of the fatherland demand. That would obviously be mere journalism. What should be is extremely far from what actually is.

When studying Polish anti-Semitic literature (and this also applies to similar literature in other countries) it is easy to conclude that the authors placed extremely severe demands on assimilating or assimilated

Jews, much more severe than those they placed on Poles. To be acknowledged by those authors as an indisputable Pole, an assimilated Jew had to display all the virtues of Polishness: an excellent mastery of the language, a total adoption of all Polish customs (the good and the bad), total unselfishness, self-sacrificing devotion to the cause of Poland, courage, a complete renunciation of his Jewish past, contempt for business, utter integrity—in short, he had to be an ideal denial of the image of the Jew that prevailed among people hostile to Jews. Moreover, and especially later on, the anti-Semitic writers denied, somehow a priori, that an assimilated Jew could in fact ever attain all those qualities. There was no mention of those writers displaying all those qualities themselves. Such severe criteria no doubt had their influence on the exaltation of things Polish that could be found among assimilated Jews.

An actual, living Pole is, in practice, completely different from an ideal Pole. And, in practice, assimilated Jews were a heterogeneous lot, exhibiting various degrees of adaptation to Polishness. Until the end of his life Wilhelm Feldman spoke with an accent that in Poland was considered gratingly Jewish. Markedly Jewish traits were maliciously ascribed to Julian Klaczko and Szymon Askenazy. And one would be hard-pressed to say just how accurate that might have been. Especially since it is no simple matter to define what "markedly Jewish" traits are. Józef Piłsudski constantly stressed his Lithuanian characteristics, as did Mickiewicz. In milieus that are not ethnically homogeneous and in which intercultural influence is constant, no one is culturally monolithic. It would be a tragedy if anyone were, for it would indicate that the various sources from which the current of cultural life flows had dried up.

Given this situation, an attempt at producing a statistical formulation of the dimensions of assimilation among Polish Jews would be a thankless task. There were various degrees and shadings of assimilation, and there were contradictory attitudes within the same person. Later, when the national emancipationist processes thrust to the fore a group of leading Jews, that group included people who, in their way of life, thought, speech, and feeling, could be considered entirely assimilated. And in fact they were. Some of them—Jakub Apenszlak, for example,[1]—began learning Yiddish only as mature men and never mastered it. Their cultural connection to things Polish—language, history, literature, traditions—was powerful and comprehensive. There was more of the Polish nobleman than of the traditional Jew about Apenszlak. And in that he was no exception. On the other hand, quite a few of those who unreservedly identified with Polish life and had left Jewish affairs behind, and quite a few of the ideologues of assimilation, spoke Polish with a so-called accent and in many other respects betrayed their recent departure from Jewishness. The degree of assimilation was not measurable in any of these instances. Like everything human, it was full of contradictions and inconsistencies.

The situation is no different wherever similar processes of intercultural influence occur and various groups adapt to each other. The assimilation of the natives to English, French, or Spanish culture in the colonial countries is accompanied by similar changes, which are universal in the great melting pot that the United States has been for over a century. And it is only against the background of the processes going on in these other countries that one can get a better understanding of the absurdity of the remarks and reproaches directed against assimilating Jews in Poland.

Thus, if we leave aside all these considerations of quantity and quality, we will be able to limit ourselves to stating certain basic facts. It was a fact that Jews adapted to non-Jews, and that this process expressed itself outwardly in changes in dress and behavior, and inwardly in the form of increasing mastery of the Polish language and the adoption of Polish customs and values. This did not necessarily mean a total identification with Polishness and, especially in the later years, could go hand in hand with a growing national Jewish consciousness. Bilingual Jews were a common phenomenon in the period between the wars. Schools in which the language of instruction was either exclusively or primarily Polish left deep traces on the younger generation of Polish Jews. There is also no doubt that there existed a type of Polish Jew different from the Russian, German, or Lithuanian type of Jew. The best indication of how advanced those differences were is found in the relations among immigrant groups in the United States. There the Polish, Russian, German, Hungarian, Austrian, and Lithuanian Jews created separate groups that as a rule kept their distance from one another, while maintaining an individual character that resulted from their connection to the culture of their former countries. In America a Polish Jew has more in common with things Polish than with a Jew from another country. And the same holds true for German, Russian, or Hungarian Jews. Assimilationist currents occurred everywhere, and everywhere the Jews took over the cultural values of their native lands. It is only against the background of the United States that one can properly evaluate the strength and versatility of old Europe's assimilationist tendencies.

V

The life of a Polish Jew was delineated by his participation in the caste organization. For centuries the Jew had reconciled himself to that fact and accepted the resulting social role. Individuals revolting against the caste had only one route of escape: to change religion and merge totally with the Christian world. As we know, in noble Poland, such individuals were not rarities; and the phenomenon of conversion, though involving a relatively small number of Jews, was not without importance. In the nineteenth and twentieth centuries, cases of conversion became very frequent. Gradually, however, this became less and less of a serviceable means for leaving the caste. At the same time, new factors thrust conversion's social significance into the background.

From the end of the nineteenth century, the contradiction between an individual's objective role and his forced participation in the caste began to be felt with increasing keenness. Most important, the number of individuals whose objective role in society was not in keeping with the caste was steadily growing. A quick change in the objective role of individual Polish Jews was a fundamental aspect of assimilation. The very meaning of assimilation consisted in an individual's adoption of cultural values, economic functions, and ways of behaving that departed radically from the model delimiting the caste and obligatory within it. An assimilating Jew changed his social countenance, changed the world of his values, and underwent a professional and economic transformation. Nevertheless, if he did not succeed through passing, that is, in changing his religion and in leaving the caste entirely behind, he would still be seen by the surrounding world as a man of the caste and still be termed a *parch* or, at best, a *żydek*. In certain periods these definitions were not applied too precisely, and the sense of conflict between the objective role and membership in the caste would lessen. For example, during the January Uprising a friendly attitude toward the Jews and a belief in their rapid assimilation prevailed in Polish society. Later, however, periods of heightened antagonism toward Jews were coupled with a tendency to retain the caste nature of Polish Jewry. Such was the case, for example, in the Congress Kingdom around 1912 and throughout Poland between the two wars. Under those conditions, the sense of disparity between the objective role and the socially conditioned compulsion to participate in the caste was especially painful for assimilated Jews. Marian Hemar, a Polish poet of Jewish descent, ably expressed the feelings of his milieu in a well-known verse: "That I'm hobbling with grace seems true/alas, I remember: I'm a Jew." Black intellectuals in the United States and colored intellectuals in the colonial countries would be able to understand perfectly the meaning of the Polish poet's verse.

This created tension, even in cases in which passing had been successful. Although all traces of the past had been erased, there was the constant danger of discovery, which would entail a radical change in the way others related to an individual of "bad" origin. In America that tension is well known to individuals who, like the hero of Sinclair Lewis's novel, seem to have passed perfectly. It was no different in Poland. Hundreds of Polish families from the higher social spheres experienced painful moments when Jeske-Choiński published his *Polish Converts* in 1904. In the years preceding World War II, the "unmasking" of a political opponent's Jewish origin was a favorite polemical tactic on the right and the left (albeit for different reasons). Zuzanna Ginczanka, a Polish poet of Jewish descent murdered by Nazis, wrote: "The hunters are dashing off into remote history where the trail is overgrown and the scent is weak; in the thickets of the past, persistent as ants, they're searching for a grandmother, a Jewish grandmother. . . ."

Toward the end of the nineteenth century, complete passing became increasingly difficult. Even changing religion and surname was of less and less help. At times, passing was easier for women in "mixed" marriages who had taken their husband's surname. Unfortunately, "Semitic" facial features, the maiden name, and the long memory of friends presented serious obstacles. Several anti-Semitic political figures in the period between the two wars were distressed when publicly reminded of their mothers' origin.

If to pass totally was increasingly less possible, however, the effort to free oneself of the conflict between the objective role and the fact of caste was assuming new forms. One such form was to demonstrate to oneself and to others that all the rules of the caste had been rejected, that one was free of its qualities and of those features traditionally ascribed to Jews. This would lead a person to behave as if he had never been part of the caste, an attitude that at times assumed grotesque forms. We observe the same attitudes and behavior everywhere individuals from the lower social or economic strata attempt to assimilate to groups that are considered higher. Examples include Molière's *bourgeois gentilhomme* and Aleksander Fredro's Mister Geldhab.

The effort to convince oneself and others that one has nothing in common with the caste led to that exaltation of things Polish that was frequently encountered among assimilated Jews. (The exaltation of things German was common among German Jews, and things Magyar, among Hungarian Jews.) This involved an exaggerated care in using perfect language, a pedantic observation of customs considered specifically Polish, a cult of Polish literature and art, and sometimes outright fanatical nationalism and chauvinism. It was maliciously said that an assimilated Jew tried to be more Polish than a Pole. Others added that this excess of Polishness attested instead to incomplete assimilation. And in that there might have been a grain of truth. Even the most sincere enthusiasm for things Polish bespoke a need, not always conscious, to prove that the test had been passed and that one had ceased to be a member of the caste.

One of the forms of such proof was participation in Polish independence movements and the courage the Jews displayed there. The percentage of intellectuals of Jewish origin in the Polish Legions was considerable. A great number displayed particular courage in battle and leadership ability, and many were awarded the Virtuti Militari cross. One of them, a close friend of mine, when describing the action for which he had been awarded the Virtuti Militari, added, "You see, I had to be brave. If I had acted like a coward, they would have said—the Jew's a coward!" There was something deeply poignant about those words spoken by a courageous officer, important scholar, and later senator of the republic. While in uniform as a Polish officer, he never forgot the shadow of the caste trailing behind him.

The shadow of the caste trailed behind thousands of people whose objective role was a complete denial of the traditional model. It trailed behind eminent government figures like Szymon Askenazy, Hipolit Gliwic,[2] and Sokol; famous scholars and scientists; doctors; lawyers; officers; great artists; poets; and writers. The shadow of the caste fell over the creative work of Julian Tuwim, Józef Wittlin, Słonimski, and so many others; and their creations reflect that shadow. Hemar's little verse is infinitely more serious than a trifling joke in rhyme. It expresses the deep conflict that not only existed among Poles of Jewish origin but had also penetrated all of recent Polish culture.

In those who sensed that conflict there grew a feeling of uncertainty in relation to others, of mistrust toward them. Am I accepted, what am I to do to be accepted, can I trust my friends? And are they really my friends? I am constantly suspected of not being a Pole. And I must suspect others of having that attitude toward me. This created a vicious circle of suspicion and mistrust.

But it is precisely such attitudes that typify how people from a caste relate to the outside world. In the old days this was expressed as uncertainty about whether one would be treated as a *parch* or a *żydek*. Later, during the period of assimilation, it was uncertainty about whether one would be treated as a Pole or a Jew. The latter situation was probably even more difficult and more painful than the former. It required constant testing with no assurance that one's attempt, albeit objectively better, would be viewed by others as sufficient. And the survival of such attitudes was the best proof of the durability of the caste, its trailing behind those who had long ago attempted to leave it far behind, and who had thought they had done so.

VI

It must be remembered that the Jews, while forming a caste, were not a national group in the modern sense of the word until the end of the nineteenth century. True enough, one spoke of the Jewish "nation," but the same was said of the Gypsy "nation," and even of the "nation" of the nobles. But the significance, so essential for the concept of contemporary nationhood, had not yet been attached to that term. Of course, the Jews were a specific cultural group. They had their own language, religion, customs, traditions; the memory of their great past as a nation was a fundamental component of Jewish tradition. But the memory of a national existence had become a part of the religious system, had taken the form of a religious cult, and had nothing in common with the modern ideal of a national community. That ideal began to be formed among the Jewish masses only in the second half of the nineteenth century, paralleling its development among a great number of other cultural groups in Europe and the rest of the world. In fact, only Zionism and the various currents of Yiddishism gave the Jewish masses a new conception of national emancipation and a new ideal that in time was to lead to the creation of the state of Israel.

This was of fundamental significance for the problem of assimilation by Polish Jews. At that time, assimilation did not mean abandoning one national group for another, nor did it mean being a renegade or an apostate. Later, the ideologues of Jewish nationalism would fling that accusation at the assimilationists. In their eyes assimilating Jews were betrayers of the Jewish cause. Those charges were based on a mistaken assessment of historical processes, on an anticipation of events that were yet to occur. An assimilating Jew did not move from one nationality to another, although he did move from one cultural system to another. What he was abandoning was not a nation. It became one only later. He was attempting to abandon a caste, with all its attributes of cultural separateness and the stigma of humiliation. There could be no question in this case of calling anyone a "turncoat" as the word was applied to Russifying Poles or Polonizing Russians.

An assimilating Polish Jew attempted to leave the caste and enter the nation. But that nation was not homogeneous. In reality, it represented a symbiosis of various cultures, each of which expressed the values of a definite social and economic milieu. Roughly put, one could speak of a gentry culture and a folk culture, or even folk cultures. Of all those cultures, only the gentry culture defined Polishness. This was the culture of the group that determined the direction of Polish history; created the literature, art, and science; and decided on the goals and methods of education. In relation to gentry culture, the other cultures making up the whole of Poland's life were marginal. It was obvious that an assimilating Jew would assimilate to the culture of the gentry. Assimilation was not only the adoption of a new national culture but also, and perhaps primarily, the adoption of the culture of a specific social class. A few factors played a fundamental role here.

It must be stated clearly once again that, throughout the course of their history, the Polish Jews as a caste were most strongly bound to the nobility. The overwhelming majority of the leading Polish anti-Semites came from the bourgeoisie or minor nobility. In contrast, aristocratic circles produced a number of individuals well disposed to the Jews and their historic role in Poland. The line of Polish "philo-Semites" ran from Ksawery Korczak-Branicki[3] to Piotr Dunin-Borkowski. Of course, one may speak only of a certain tendency here. Wincenty Krasiński was ill disposed toward the Jews, while their defenders included Orzeszkowa, the distinguished Polish linguist Baudouin de Courtenay, and the geographer, writer, and journalist Wacław Nałkowski.

The gentry and the aristocracy formed the class in Poland with which the Jews, especially the wealthy, had the most frequent and most permanent contacts. Those contacts, however much conditioned by the fact of caste, were often close and many-sided, and they opened a route for certain of the nobles' cultural values to penetrate Jewish milieus.

In the period when assimilation became common, the nobility's way of life, by the nature of things, held great appeal for the new plutocracy of Jewish origin. This was the upper-class way of life; to adopt it meant to identify both with what was socially "better" and with things Polish. Acquiring land and adopting the landowners' way of life became commonplace. Those new landowners and the airs they assumed met with mockery, but that mockery did not halt the overall tendency. The young generation of the Jewish plutocracy found it very easy to adopt the ways of the young aristocrats, including their inclination to squander the fortunes made by their fathers and grandfathers. Marriages between wealthy Jews and impoverished landowning families were in themselves an important factor in the adoption of aristocratic manners. The fathers-in-law had to demonstrate that they were equal to their titled sons-in-law. The Bersons owned a stable of racehorses, others played at hunting; they all led sumptuous lives, built palaces, scrambled for titles of nobility, and so forth.

It is striking that among Jews—in contrast to Protestants—fortunes usually are short-lived. That was pointed out by Roman Dmowski, but, as always, he gave it the most fantastic interpretation. The impermanence of inherited Jewish wealth is, to a great extent, connected with the traditional Jewish ethos, the belief that wealth is only a means and not a sign of charisma. Also, in many cases wealthy Jews considered their life's goal achieved if their descendants distinguished themselves in science or literature. And it is also not unlikely that the Jewish ethos was a factor favoring the adoption of certain of the magnates' qualities, including the tendency to squander one's money. To the Protestant Puritans such an attitude deserved condemnation. Riches must be increased, for thereby one serves the glory of God, and the very fact of increase attests to God's grace. The permanence of certain, though not all, Jewish family fortunes in America and Western Europe may indicate that Jewish assimilation there moved in the direction of adopting middle-class rather than aristocratic values. However, the German and Hungarian Jews displayed a process of assimilation rather closer to that of the Polish Jews.

The history of Jewish fortunes in Poland and certain other countries may be reduced to the following, somewhat simplified outline: the grandfather made the money; the father, if he did not waste the family fortune, did not increase it and often reduced it by becoming a patron of the arts, a collector, a sports backer, a man of leisure; the grandson, representing the third generation, was already a litterateur, an artist, a scientist or scholar, sometimes an officer, sometimes a socialist or communist activist, and, as a rule, no longer had money. Wars and revolutions, of course, were also important corrective factors in making fortunes dwindle. But even without such upheaval, those fortunes did not display any permanence and betrayed a tendency to pass from the economic foresight of the grandfathers to the purely intellectual activities of the grandsons. The life stories of various Polish *hommes de lettres*, scholars, and political figures could tell a great deal about the ups and downs of Jewish family fortunes.

It was of particular significance that this road ended in the intellectual professions because the most important form of Jewish assimilation to gentry culture was their entering the specific milieu of the intelligentsia. The complaints about the "Jewification" of the Polish intelligentsia had grounds. There is no doubt that both quantitatively and qualitatively the role of the Jewish element in the Polish intelligentsia was very important. Something similar held true in other countries as well. Everywhere it is in the so-called intelligentsia that Jewish assimilation finds an important outlet.

VII

We have stressed that in the Jewish ethos wisdom was a fundamental value. The God-fearing Jew's ideal was to raise his son to be a learned rabbi. This tradition continued when the Jews entered a phase of secularization. To have a son who was a doctor (or sometimes a lawyer, but in any case educated) became the dream of even the poorest Jews. This was a basis for social distinction and honor that wealth could never provide.

The attempt to leave the caste by obtaining an education is a common phenomenon and typical not only of Jews. Whether it be the case of the Ukrainians, the Belorussians, the Lithuanians, the Slovaks, the colonial peoples, or the blacks in the United States, the formation of an indigenous intelligentsia is always the first step in the struggle against caste and marks the beginning of all the great emancipation movements. In its first phase, that new intelligentsia as a rule assimilates to another culture that is considered higher. The first Ukrainian or Belorussian intelligentsia assimilated to Russian culture or, in certain cases, to Polish culture, the Latvians to German or Russian culture, the Slovaks to Hungarian culture, the Indians to English culture, the Dahomeans to French culture, and so forth. Obviously, the black intelligentsia in the United States assimilates to the culture of educated classes of Americans, which means no change of nationality. A black American fighting to leave the caste or to abolish it operates within the value system of the general, national American culture and is at all times an American. It is precisely in the existence of the caste that he sees a limitation on his Americanness, and he fights against caste in the name of American ideals.

If those same tendencies operated in the Jewish world, however, they were intensified by the traditional ethos that gave pride of place to wisdom and knowledge. And hence the Polish Jews assimilated to the greatest extent by entering the intelligentsia.

Here I must devote a few words to the general question of the Polish intelligentsia, a subject that has been often and amply discussed. Great credit for this is owed to Józef Chałasiński, who in his *Przeszłość i przyszłość inteligencji polskiej* (Genealogy of the Polish Intelligentsia [Warsaw, 1958]) provided valuable points of departure for my own research. (For a fuller treatment of my position see "The Case of an Eastern European Intelligentsia" in the *Journal of Central European Affairs*, 1951.)

Unlike that in Western Europe and Russia, the Polish educated class was not connected by social origin to the machinery of state and officialdom. In old Poland that machinery was so rudimentary as to be beyond consideration. The Polish bureaucracy began to be created during the period of the Duchy of Warsaw and the Congress Kingdom of Poland, but those entities lasted for too short a time to produce a class of professional civil servants of the type found in other European countries. It was only in Galicia that a sizable Polish civil service with a tradition of its own was able to arise. The task of both of Galicia's universities was to create a base for recruiting officials for the country's administrative apparatus.

Galicia aside, the Polish intelligentsia owes its development to the disintegration of the noble landowning class. And even in Galicia itself, until the end of the nineteenth century the majority of educated people and of the bureaucratic apparatus were either of noble origin or from the Jewish milieus assimilating to the culture of the Polish nobility.

When speaking of the social genealogy of the Polish intelligentsia, we must accept that the great majority came from the noble landowning class and the minority from the Jewish caste. Of course, especially after the end of the nineteenth century, people from other social groups as well entered the ranks of the intelligentsia; but the mass influx of Tomaszes, Judyms, and Andrzej Radeks[4] was to take place only in the twentieth century, mainly in the period between the two world wars.

The essential point, however, was that the culture represented by the Polish intelligentsia was, in form and content, the culture of the nobility. And regardless of the social origin of its individual members, the Polish intelligentsia as a whole bore the cultural traditions of the nobility and expressed ideals and values whose roots were in the world of the landowning nobility.

We cannot enter here into a detailed analysis of the intrinsic "nobleness" of the Polish intelligentsia. Such analyses have already been done. We shall touch only on a few points of particular importance for our discussion.

In Poland before 1918, the chances to make good use of the qualifications that come through education were meager. Apart from that in Galicia, no Polish bureaucratic apparatus existed to absorb even a fraction of the educated. Nor did industry, commerce, or banking provide any such opportunities on a great scale. Even the economically advanced section of Poland under Prussian partition offered no greater prospects for educated people. From the area under Russian partition, technicians and engineers emigrated in large numbers to Russia itself, where it was easier to find employment than in their own country. In brief, as opposed to the highly developed countries of Western Europe and the United States, the acquisition of an education did not mean the acquisition of a corresponding level of economic employment—hence, the striking disparity between the degree of education and economic function among many Polish intellectuals. Important historians and writers served as minor railroad officials, worked in banks, or gave private lessons. More than one talented writer struggled through life on modest earnings as journalists. Various memoirs and biographies have made us aware of the poverty suffered by people destined to occupy permanent places in the history of Polish culture.

The situation improved when Poland regained its independence. A large bureaucracy was created, higher education developed, and the country began to be industrialized here and there. But, at the same time, progress in democratizing social life considerably expanded the base from which educated people could be recruited. In Poland critics began to speak of an overproduction of intelligentsia. Obviously, in comparison with the economically developed countries, Poland had a shortage of properly qualified, educated people rather than a surplus. The "overproduction" of the intelligentsia was a measure of the country's backwardness, its low level of industrialization, and its poverty.

A characteristic phenomenon in Poland for many decades was a separation between acquired education and its practical application. This concerned primarily education in the humanities and exact sciences, but even included medicine, law, and engineering. A young educated person could not be reasonably certain that he would be able to put the knowledge he had acquired to any practical use.

Nevertheless, a high value was placed on education. The phenomenon of knowledge acquired in school being a value per se, regardless of its practical application, is not something peculiar to Poland. We encounter it in all countries and social systems that are economically and culturally underdeveloped and in which emancipation movements find it necessary to create their own leading elite. Parallel tendencies are observable in all the Latin American republics; in the colonial countries attaining independence; among Ukrainians, Belorussians, Lithuanians, Latvians, and others in the period of awakening national aspiration and of attempts to build nation states of their own; among American blacks who reject the caste system; and among European Jews. In all such situations education becomes a form of social distinction and is a value in and of itself, separate from its practical application. Complaints about the overproduction of the intelligentsia arise in all those cases. Those complaints sound odd in many Latin American countries, though undoubtedly they have their justification.

The high value placed on education per se in Latin American countries is unquestionably bound up with the traditions of the *Hispanidad*, the philosophy that the *hidalgo*, not a man of productive economic labor, is, by the nature of things, called to a higher mission for the nation and state, and that formal education gives him the right to fulfill such a mission. A degree is always a sign of social distinction; a *licenciado*, through the very fact of possessing a degree, enters the higher class and actually becomes a *hidalgo*.

The attitudes, philosophies, and traditions that we encounter in countries within the range of the *Hispanidad* are strikingly similar to those of the Polish intelligentsia. Despite the utter separation of those two civilizations, we find similar traditions of aristocratic culture, strengthened both by the entire course of their historical development and by their socioeconomic backwardness. In both civilizations, noble descent went hand in hand with contempt for economic functions performed for profit. In both civilizations, education—primarily in the humanities and law—was a mark of social distinction, a form of ennoblement. And in neither civilization did there emerge a middle class with a social philosophy of its own which would have been able to introduce its values into the world of the nobility, as was the case in England, for example.

Theoretically speaking, in Poland such values could have arisen from the assimilating Jewish middle class. But in the Jewish world itself knowledge and economics had been separated for centuries; it was precisely in the Jewish world that education was a value per se and provided the most important basis for social distinction. Moreover, in Poland that world was under the strong spell of the culture of the nobility.

Unquestionably, there was no lack of practical men of action among Polish Jews, people more representative of Western European middle-class virtue than that of the Polish nobility. It is to people like Bloch, Kronenberg, Epstein,[5] Natanson, Rotwand, Wawelberg, and others that the Congress Kingdom of Poland owed in great measure its early economic achievements. But those people quickly adopted the qualities, way of life, and philosophy of the nobility. And by marrying into the aristocracy, they further lost their own distinct social character. They were not able to leave their mark on the Polish nobility in the way that the wealthy British middle class did on the English aristocracy. In England members of the middle class also entered the ranks of the nobility but did not adopt the model of the country squire; on the contrary, it was they who were able to reshape the squire.

The assimilating Polish Jews, by becoming part of the intelligentsia and, to an important extent, by helping to form it, adopted not merely Polishness but nobleness. They assimilated to the culture of the nobility with all its features, good and bad. Like the Polish intelligentsia as a whole, its Jewish members were the heirs to the Poland of the nobility.

VIII

The processes of assimilation are common and constant wherever groups representing different cultural values come into contact with each other. Every intergroup exchange of cultural values is a form of assimilation. In that sense, Jewish assimilation to things Polish was an old phenomenon, regardless of the facts of caste and ghetto. Of course, the caste and the ghetto, by impeding intergroup contact and by conditioning it a peculiar way, narrowed the channels of that exchange, thereby hampering and limiting it. They did not, however, eliminate it entirely. Exchanges of some sort went on constantly and were accompanied by a certain assimilation which, in individual cases, was quite far advanced. That the Jews constituted a lower and despised caste and that their traditional culture could only be of scant help to them in the world outside the caste caused them to assimilate to non-Jews but not the reverse. Certain Jewish values did penetrate the non-Jewish world but never on the scale that non-Jewish values penetrated the Jewish world.

The processes of assimilation increased greatly in the nineteenth and twentieth centuries. This was the result of basic, objective changes taking place in Europe that had reached as far as Poland. There was a significant increase in the number of Jews who not only adapted objectively to the outside world but who also, owing to their education and organizational abilities, began to play an ever-increasing role in it. The social and cultural positions these people occupied and the objective role they played in Polish life were in striking variance with the traditions of the caste to which the outside world still continued to regard them as belonging. At the same time, the processes of assimilation, though considerably less intensive and comprehensive, also reached the world of the ghettos, of those masses who had accepted their place in the caste unconditionally. Here those processes were expressed primarily in the increasing secularization of Jewish life. Of course, in this case one cannot speak of any conscious or programmatic assimilation to Polishness, or even of any Polonization. The Jewish masses did not cease to be caste Jews, but they had increasingly begun to adopt new cultural values from Polish life. This was the prelude to the development of broader national emancipation tendencies among those masses. Bernard Singer's memoirs, *Moje Nalewki* (My Nalewki Street), are, in that respect, a treasure trove of information.

In prewar Poland the most difficult and fundamental problems arose in connection with the assimilation of upper-class Jews, assimilation that *was* programmatic and sought to merge fully into Polishness. Socially speaking, this meant leaving the caste entirely and freeing oneself from its stigma. In many instances, the goal—as it used to be in former times—was to erase all traces of the past connected with the caste. That was the purpose of changing one's religion and name. However, in a great number of cases no effort was made to erase the traces of the past, nor were name and religion changed; the goal was to occupy in Polish society a position that would be free of any hint of caste, in other words, that a Pole of Jewish extraction should cease to be the traditional *parch* or *żydek*.

That goal was achieved in certain periods, in 1863, for example. Later it was achieved with increasing rarity. Undoubtedly, there were Polish circles, especially among the liberal and radical intelligentsia, that accepted the Jewish *Poloni novi* unconditionally and rejected the old definitions. They did not, however, create a pattern for Polish society as a whole. In the period between the two wars, the tendency to treat all Jews as members of the caste intensified in Poland, regardless of the objective characteristics of those Jews, the degree of their identification with Polishness, and the role they played in Polish life. In the light of prevailing judgments, people like Askenazy, Handelsman, or Tuwim were still *parchs* or, at best, *żydeks*.

That left a profound and tragic mark on the psyche of assimilated Jews, on their attitudes and their relation to the world. Hemar's seemingly jocular poem, quoted earlier, expressed this perfectly. One could write a long psychological study on the various neuroses, traumas, and mental and spiritual disorders that developed against that background.

Another factor here was the lack of faith in the possibility of eradicating traces of caste, a distrust of the outside world, hypersensitivity, a looking for anti-Semitism even where it did not exist. Once again, these are symptoms well known in the experience of American civilization or in colonial countries. In this matter, Poland was nothing new. These highly pathological phenomena are, unfortunately, extremely human and occur in various ages and civilizations. It is to America's great credit that the abnormality of these phenomena is understood and properly evaluated, and constant efforts are made to eliminate them.

In the years preceding the Second World War, Poland saw an increase in the number of assimilated Jews who were profoundly pessimistic about the possibility of identifying fully with Polishness. Strictly speaking, that was a pessimism about the larger environment's accepting them as free of any shadow of caste. Such pessimism developed among people who had thought of themselves as Poles for generations—former members of the Legions, individuals who had dedicated their lives to the cause of Poland. As a result of this pessimism assimilation declined as a political program, and there was an effort to draw closer to the Jewish masses. Favoring this tendency were the new aspirations that had begun to arise among those masses at that time. The thrust of those aspirations was toward liberating the entire Jewish community from the caste system while retaining and developing its distinctive national and cultural character. In this case, what was at issue was not the flight of individuals or larger groups from the caste, but the elimination of the caste as such, its transformation into a national community. This tendency found its fullest expression in Zionism.

Assimilated Jews began to turn to those mass movements in increasing numbers and, in certain instances, became their leaders. This quest to return to Jewishness was neither easy nor always successful. In many cases a new assimilation became necessary, this time from Polish to Jewish culture. That this new assimilation is no easy thing is best attested to by Israel, with its profound problems in transforming Jews from every national culture into a single national cultural community. Israel can also serve as the best evidence of the depth and thoroughness of assimilatory processes among Jews from every country of the world.

Against the Caste

I

The rise of mass emancipationist movements among the Jews was a particular instance of the large social movements that became one of the most important factors in forming contemporary civilization as it now stands. In all these cases and with all the variety of local situations, a similar mechanism of change was at work; similar motivations, means, and goals were found. As a rule, in places where emancipationist aspirations were national in character, they joined with aspirations for social and economic emancipation. In places where emancipationist aspirations arose within a caste system (the more frequent case), the liberation of the entire collectivity from caste, the overthrow of the system as such, constituted the basic driving force behind the changes taking place. And it was this that caused the greatest resistance from the outside world, which saw its reason for being and the basis of its prestige in the preservation of the caste system. The relation of Russians and Poles to Ukrainians or Belorussians, whites to blacks in America, and Europeans to colonial peoples are all fundamentally consistent with what, in relation to Jews, was defined as anti-Semitism.

Undoubtedly, each case mentioned above had its own specific local qualities. The Jews were not a territorial society but an extraterritorial group, everywhere a minority. In that respect, they were like American blacks, and, like them, the Jews formed a clear-cut caste, closed and despised. But there were major differences as well. American blacks generally do not aspire to national separateness. In struggling to free themselves from the caste, they desire to identify fully and completely with American national society, of which they are, culturally and historically, an integral part. The Jews, however, formed a specific cultural group, one extremely rich in tradition, with developed institutions and a sense of mission. Among other ethnic groups seeking emancipation it is only in India and the Arab countries that one can find cultural traditions comparable to those of the Jews.

Thus, a peculiar characteristic of the Jews was that, on the one hand, they were everywhere a minority group (obviously, we are not speaking here of those areas where the inhabitants of the Jewish ghetto constituted a majority of the local population), treated as "newcomers," with contempt and antipathy. On the other hand, they possessed unusually strong and rich cultural traditions and were a group with a sense of its own historical continuity. If the first circumstance had a distinctly restraining effect on the development of Jewish national emancipationist tendencies, the second favored them greatly, creating a natural point of departure. In that respect, the Jews were an exception among various groups in diaspora. Even such groups as the Armenians or the Parsis did not have such strong traditions and such a highly developed sense of historical continuity. In this, the Jewish diaspora can be compared only with that of the Chinese. The latter, however, were constantly connected to their former homeland and considered themselves an extension of it.

As in all similar instances, the origins of Jewish emancipationist aspirations were understood and evaluated in a special way. The "falling away" of a caste group from its traditional role evokes anxiety and bewilderment within the larger environment. Polish opinion either deplored Jewish "separatism" and nationalism or saw it as proof of Jewish "arrogance" and attributed it to the intrigues of forces hostile to Poland. Its beginning was found in the influx of Litwaks[1] and their hostility to Poland or in plots by the Germans and by the Czarist government. Roman Dmowski blamed the American and especially the English Jews, ascribing to them a particular hatred of Poland. In similar fashion, an American Southerner is convinced that he would have no trouble with "his" blacks if it were not for the machinations of Yankees from the North. In Poland it was deeply and widely held that the Ukrainian question was an Austrian intrigue and that without Vienna's malicious influence, the Ukrainians would have remained good-natured Ruthenians. In Russia, on the other hand, the rise of the Ukrainian question was eagerly attributed to Polish machinations. Even today one can encounter the view that Arab nationalism is the product of British intrigues gone awry. And many other nationalistic tendencies in colonial territories are unhesitatingly ascribed to communist plots.

In reality, it is great historical processes, socially and culturally conditioned and embracing great masses of people, that have come to the fore in all these cases. Undoubtedly, diverse elements have attempted to exploit these processes. During World War I, the German occupation authorities took a favorable view of signs of Jewish nationalism in Poland. At present, the Soviets are very fond of nationalist movements in various "young" countries located outside the Soviet Union's territory. Lawrence of Arabia played an important role in awakening Arab nationalism. The Russian Jews had a large share in the history of Jewish nationalism in Poland. But Lawrence of Arabia did not create Arab nationalism; nor did the Litwaks create that of the Polish Jews, not to mention other even more absurd attributions. The nationalism of the "new" nations was an extremely complex phenomenon, one subject to multiple conditions and evolving from a great number of sources.

In all these cases of burgeoning national emancipationist tendencies a certain common factor of great significance was the attractiveness of the cultural model of the dominant group. And although, especially in later phases, the "young" group's programmatic attitude toward that model was usually negative and even hostile, it was still under its spell and, to a certain extent, attempted to appropriate it. The model of English culture had enormous significance in the development of Indian and African nationalism. The English and French cultural models had similar significance for nationalism in the Arab countries. The Polish and Russian cultural models left deep traces on Ukrainian, Belorussian, and Lithuanian nationalism. And it also seems certain that the Polish cultural model—next to the German and, to some degree, the Russian—had a definite influence on the formation of Jewish nationalism in Poland. There is much to be said for the idea that the nationalisms of "young" ethnic groups are offshoots of the cultures of dominant groups. From the Polish point of view, it would be extremely interesting to explore the degree to which Jewish nationalism in Poland was a product of Polish culture, just as in the Anglo-Saxon countries it is now said increasingly and with pride that, in their nationalistic aspirations, the colonial peoples are the children and inheritors of English and American culture and its entire historical development.

Let us now move on to a more detailed examination of these problems, which we have treated above in very general terms.

II

For the awakening of wide-ranging emancipationist aspirations, an ideology that would appeal to the masses and become a driving force for them is a necessity. In the case of nationalism, this must be a nationalist ideology that encompasses a given group as a uniform historical entity and sets before its eyes definite goals as well as the means of attaining them. (I should point out that the word *nationalism* is used throughout not in the sense accepted in Polish but in the sense accepted in English: a nation's aspirations in general, without any implications about politics or parties.)

The Polish peasant movement owes its ideology to intellectuals of peasant origin who came out of the villages, took on the noble, intelligentsia culture, and then furnished the Polish villages with a cadre of leaders. The ideologists of the national *risorgimento* of the Ukrainians, Belorussians, Lithuanians, Latvians, and others were people who, in the initial phase of their spiritual development, had lived in the atmosphere of Russian or Polish culture. It was only as adults that some of them learned the tongue of the nation (or rather, the people) they wished to serve. The indigenous intelligentsia in the colonial countries had been through English or French schools. Cambridge and Oxford on the one hand and the Sorbonne on the other were the nursery for those statesmen, thinkers, writers, and politicians who now guide the fate of the nations of Asia and Africa. A similar role, and on an increasingly greater scale, is now played by Harvard and Yale, the University of Chicago and Columbia, Princeton and the University of California. The great English, French, and American universities have occupied a place of great importance in the history of contemporary national emancipation movements.

The same may of course be said of American blacks whose aspirations are not directed toward national and cultural separateness. Their emancipation movements, directed against the caste system, have been headed by people who had completely adapted to the culture of white society. Although those people had no possibility of abandoning the caste, they did achieve complete cultural assimilation in relation to America's intellectual and spiritual elite.

All this indicates that, without the assimilationist period, there would have been no Zionism or Yiddishism among the Jews, none of those aspirations whose goal was to transform the caste into a national society. This must be stated clearly and emphatically. Assimilation was not a betrayal of Jewish national ideals—no such ideals existed when assimilation developed—but an inescapable historical phase that paved the way for those ideals to arise. Obviously, every instance of assimilation means a certain loss, often a considerable one, for the group that the assimilating individual leaves. In Poland, a great many intellectuals of peasant origin left the village behind them and attempted to erase all traces of their peasant origin. But there remained the Bujaks and the Cierniaks—to cite but two names—and to them the Polish peasant owes a great deal.[2] The Ukraine has given Russia and Poland a great number of its sons. But there remained the Antonoviches and the Drahomanovs to whom the Ukrainians owe the ideological foundations of their concept of nationhood. The colonial peoples bore similar losses, losses that were compensated by those who returned to their peoples and became their leaders. A substantial number of assimilated Jews succeeded in passing, left Jewry entirely behind, and were even able to erase all traces of their past. But Theodor Herzl was also an assimilated Jew, and from the circles of the highly assimilated came many of Zionism's leaders and ideologists. In Poland, besides those who left Jewry behind, there were also those who went through assimilation and returned to Jewry, like Stanisław Mendelson, Jan Kirszrot, Jakub Apenszlak, the Zionist leader and deputy to the Polish Sejm Apolinary Hartglas, and many others. Jewish emancipation would have been unthinkable without the ideological leadership of those people.

The losses caused by assimilation quickly diminish as the emancipation movement's intensity and scope increase. This comes under the influence of a series of circumstances that shall be discussed later on. In our time, when emancipationist movements have led to the emergence of numerous new states, those losses are relatively small. Losses are, of course, unavoidable, since the constant exchange of cultural values among various groups is itself unavoidable. Wherever various cultural groups come into contact, the processes of assimilation must occur. And it would be a genuine disaster for mankind were they to cease. National cultures would become impoverished, eventually sterile.

III

It is unlikely today that the "lower" classes, the despised peasant castes, or the indigenous societies in the colonies would be able to produce ideological and political leaders who had not been through some assimilationist training in the dominant culture acknowledged as "higher." Traditional experiences of those groups do not correspond to the demands made by contemporary industrial civilization. The Koran or the Talmud, the Hindu holy books or the writings of the Chinese sages, and the oral traditions of African peoples are all incapable of answering the questions posed by contemporary civilization to every national society in today's world. The answers must be sought in that industrial civilization itself, its history and development. An ideological leadership that has assimilated the concepts and values of Euramerican life is indispensable to achieving emancipation. Such a leadership must be made up of people who, to some degree, have assimilated to the culture of the others. And it is only such people who can reach back to the traditions of their own group in order to transform those traditions and adapt them to the demands of the current world. Then the Koran and the Talmud, the Chinese and Hindu holy books, and even African folk beliefs will assume new meaning and be included among the possessions of humanity. They too will pass through some process of assimilation. The peasant leaders of the Polish Peasant party—Szymon Bojko, Wincenty Witos—were not intellectuals in the generally accepted sense. Their formal education was incomplete and rather modest; they were actually self-taught men. Nevertheless, they were no longer representatives and products of the traditional culture of the Polish countryside. To some degree, even a considerable one, they had entered the realm of noble, intellectual culture, adopting many of its basic elements. Otherwise they would not have become the ideologists and leaders of the emancipation movement in the Polish countryside. Naturally, a great deal of their old peasant attitudes, their peasant way of thinking, and their peasant traditions stayed with them. But in the most fundamental respects, they had assimilated to the nonpeasant culture. The same may be said of many of today's African leaders. They may have little formal education, and their adoption of various elements of European culture is often superficial, but a certain assimilation does take place, as it must. Without it—shallow as it is—those people would still remain on the traditional level of tribal civilization.

The ideologists for groups striving for national emancipation could take the basic concepts and values essential for a national society only and exclusively from the cultures to which they were assimilating. It was only within those cultures that such concepts and values existed. Later on we shall discuss the significance of all this in the case of Polish Jews. The rise and formulation of Herzl's ideas would have been unthinkable were he not the product of Austro-German culture and had he not lived by that culture's values. There is no doubt that the anti-Semitism at the end of the nineteenth century in Austria, Germany, and Russia (and France with the Dreyfus case) had a decisive influence on Herzl's actions and on the direction of his philosophy, just as it did on the entire development of Jewish emancipation movements. However, what Herzl and his followers contributed to those movements originated in non-Jewish culture, its values and development. Jewish nationalism was the child of the nationalism of other European nations, just as are all the various nationalisms in the world today. And that could occur only thanks to the assimilationist processes that precede the awakening of wide-ranging aspirations for emancipation in all "folk" groups.

Other factors, also bound up with assimilation, were at work here.

The audacity to compare one's own social condition with that of others who occupy higher places in the hierarchy is a prerequisite both for an individual aspiring to advance and for masses seeking emancipation. Those others can be individuals or large groups. When such audacity arises, the acceptance of one's own inferiority as natural and unchanging begins to come to an end. The next step, and not a short one, is a belief in one's right to a higher position and the certitude that such a position is attainable. Here, in the most simplified form, is the psychological mechanism of the process that, in individual cases, leads to personal advancement and, in the case of the masses, to emancipation.

An enormous role in that process is played by the example of those persons who have achieved individual advancement and occupy some position in the world outside the caste or, if the caste system is not explicit, outside the lower class. To the world from which those people emerged they are living proof that upward mobility is possible, that the road to advancement is not closed. At the same time—and this is even more important—those people become a means for overcoming the sense of inferiority in their former world. That world cannot be so bad if it produces people who enjoy recognition and respect among those held to be "better and higher." The emancipationist aims of American blacks are stimulated enormously by the admiration and respect accorded George Washington Carver, Canada Lee, Marian Anderson, Ralph Bunche, and a whole galaxy of others. The objective value of their achievements is less important than that they gained white people's admiration and respect. However, was that gain theirs alone? No, because all black people partake of it to some extent. In his or her own way, each of those outstanding individuals demonstrates the great range of black people's possibilities. Hence the genuine adoration of everyone who succeeds outside the caste—the famous boxer, runner, nightclub or film star. They all contribute to increasing their "race's" prestige and thereby serve the cause of its emancipation.

None of those famous blacks has abandoned the caste, because this was impossible—its mark is always visible. But by remaining in the caste, identifying with its aspirations, and, at the same time, by occupying such a high position outside it, they serve the cause of eliminating the caste system and emancipating the masses of black America. However, things are more complicated in the case of individuals who, having advanced far outside the caste, abandon it and attempt to maintain a distance between it and themselves. In reality, advancement itself was tantamount to leaving the caste or was the obvious consequence of having left it. Very often that was the case with Jews.

We know the role Moses Mendelssohn played in the lives of European Jews. Orthodox Jews were severely critical of his philosophy and his entire way of life. But at the same time, word of the position that he held in the life of Berlin and all of Prussia reached the Jewish ghettos and won their admiration. Here was a Jew whose friends and admirers were the most eminent goys.

The influence of such prominent Jews or ex-Jews on the Jewish masses increased greatly in the nineteenth century. The myth of the Rothschilds became part of Jewish folklore. That they were people of fantastic wealth was not all that mattered. It was mainly the role they played in the world of that time; that they were lords and barons, and that kings and their ministers respected their advice. Moreover, the Rothschilds had not ceased to be Jews but had remained true to the faith of their forefathers. Thus, a Jew could attain such a summit, occupy such a position. There is no doubt that the Rothschilds, as well as the other lesser Jewish potentates of the time, contributed greatly to the waning of the sense of inferiority felt by the Jewish caste in relation to the outside world.

Other legends arose beside that of the Rothschilds and even began to surpass it. There was the legend of Disraeli, who had undoubtedly deserted the faith of his forefathers but was a Jew by origin and never denied it. And that Jew became the trusted adviser of a powerful queen, a premier, a lord, a person on whom the eyes of the whole world were turned. With each decade more and more Jews achieved glory, which also fell on those from whom they had sprung; especially if they were people who, like Louis Brandeis, Henry Morgenthau, and so many others, did not cease to be Jews and laid great emphasis on their connection with Jewry. After all, those people who had won the admiration of millions of goys *were not ashamed* of their Jewish origins. And the goys themselves did not hold it against them either. The meaning of this amazement and admiration and their influence on aspirations within the caste must be clearly understood.

As secularization progressed among the Jewish masses, legend also began to include those who had changed their religion and broken completely with Jewry. The family trees of world celebrities were eagerly scrutinized for Jewish traces. If anti-Semites traced such genealogies for purposes of discrimination, the young Jewish nationalists found here a source of national pride. Famous people only partially of Jewish origin, or even of dubious origin, were recalled. And there was nothing unusual about this. After all, American blacks have included Pushkin and Dumas in their pantheon of greats. In the formative stage of all cases of nationalism, such mythology is common. It serves to rouse the group's faith in its own powers and to open a prospect for changing the present situation.

The Jews were exceptionally privileged in this regard. No other ethnic or caste group could display such a number of illustrious individuals emerging from its milieu and achieving renown throughout the world. Since the end of the nineteenth century there has been an abundance of illustrious Jewish names in all areas of Euramerican civilization. There have been tycoons and statesmen, famous revolutionaries and great lawyers (most frequently, very conservative men), scientists, writers, and artists. Even though the caste could view their way of life and their breaking with the old customs critically or negatively, the caste was also proud of their achievements and fame and, in some way, partook of it.

If the legends of the illustrious served as a stimulus for new valuations, the achievements made outside the caste by people much less famous played no less a role in daily life. Taking any small-town Jewish ghetto in Poland at the end of the nineteenth century and the beginning of the twentieth, we see that it was increasingly common for the son of the local shopkeeper or tradesman to become a doctor, a lawyer, or even, in Galicia, a civil servant or a gymnasium teacher. He no doubt had ceased to be a "good" Jew, ate "treif" food, behaved like a goy, and associated with goys. But at the same time, for the Jews he was one of "their own," everyone knew his father and his grandfather and everyone knew him. Often—sometimes out of conviction, sometimes for family reasons or out of opportunism—he would keep close ties with the ghetto, pray in the synagogue there, and be a part of the congregational administration. The ghetto would say with pride that the most eminent local goys were his patients, or that he was legal counsel to important squires, even to the count himself. The ghetto could be proud of its son.

In this manner there arose local legends about Jews who had proved outside the caste that they were as good as the goys. And sometimes even better, because, for some reason, the goys were not drawn to the "learned" occupations that corresponded to the traditions of the Jewish ethos.

It must be emphasized again that those learned people had left the caste and its traditional model. Many of them were entirely lost to the Jewish world. But without them the national rebirth of the Jews would not have ensued, and without them the processes of emancipation could not have developed. Assimilation was an inevitable phase.

IV

Assimilation was also an inevitable phase in the sense that Jewish national rebirth would not have occurred if the Jewish masses had not adopted the basic values of the world outside the caste. For the caste to cease to be a caste and be transformed into a national group, it had to renounce the basic values, attitudes, and ways of life that made it a caste. And that meant a certain form of assimilation. For the Jews to become a nation in some sense, they had to depart from Jewry in some way. In Poland that meant adopting certain attributes of the Poles and their culture. One of Israel's most difficult problems today is to fuse into a single entity all the national cultures that Polish, Russian, German, Hungarian, Lithuanian, Rumanian, and Czechoslovakian Jews bring with them. The road to Israel led through all the cultures of the countries of the diaspora. It would be extremely interesting to explore how much of Polish culture and Polish tradition has gone into the newly arising culture of Israel. Who knows, Israel's swagger and its soldiers' romantic heroism may well contain some legacy of Polish noble traditions. And it is also possible that the traditions of the English gentleman carried by the English Jews, some of whom have occupied leading positions in the young country's diplomatic corps and armed forces, act as a restraining factor.

We have frequently emphasized that the assimilation of the Polish Jews was toward the culture of the Polish nobility. The instrument of assimilation was social advancement achieved primarily through the acquisition of education. That meant becoming part of the intelligentsia, the group that in Polish civilization was the product of the transformation of the nobility and the propagator of its ideals. A wealthy and educated Jew tried to assimilate to the world of the landowner. A Jew who had education but not wealth sought a place for himself among the intelligentsia. In each case assimilation was to the culture of the leading class.

The Jews who headed the mass Jewish national emancipation movements and formulated their ideologies were of the intelligentsia. In

Poland, they had their roots in Polish culture, more precisely, in the culture of the Polish nobility. Stanisław Mendelson and Jan Kirszrot, Jakub Apenszlak and Bernard Singer, Sholem Asch and Joseph Opatoshu, Apolinary Hartglas and Yitskhok Grunbaum, though differing greatly one from the other, each bore the impress of Polish noble culture. Of course, writers like Asch and Opatoshu were completely rooted in Jewish life and are Jewish writers not only by virtue of language. But at the same time, it requires no great effort to detect echoes of Polish romanticism, Żeromski, and Młoda Polska in their work.[3] When translated into Polish, their work is clear and familiar to the Polish reader. And how much of the old-fashioned Polish tale can be felt in the stories of a Shalom Aleichem or Isaac Leib Peretz. And Chaim Bialik's great poetry preserves something of Polish romanticism.

I am inclined to assume that Polish political romanticism had a profound influence on Zionism and related emancipationist trends among Polish Jews. And not only among Polish Jews. Vladimir Jabotynsky was not a Polish Jew by origin. And much of Józef Piłsudski's philosophy went into the concept of Jewish revisionism. David Ben-Gurion was reputedly an ardent reader of Piłsudski's letters. Even if that is only a legend, it is a telling one. To the sober-minded concepts of Herzl and the Western Zionists, the East European Jews—and primarily the Polish ones—added elements of romanticism and political mysticism, the ideals of service and sacrifice, dedication to the cause, the ideal of the Deed, all of which lent Polish political romanticism its specific coloration.

The role of Polish Jews in the creation of today's Israel is not a small one, so Polish culture has also played some role. Unquestionably, this was the culture of the nobility as absorbed by those who were inspired by Zionism. Israel seems the fulfillment of the motto: "Measure your strength by your goals, not your goals by your strength." Among Polish Jews who set about building a new nation there were many who found a source of faith and a rock of hope in Adam Mickiewicz. And not only in Mickiewicz, the creator of the Jewish Legion.[4]

V

The essence of Jewish emancipationist aspirations lay in transforming the caste into a national group. This holds true for many of the parallel aspirations that characterize our civilization. What is always at issue here is the rejection of a caste system and the transformation of the caste group into a national society with a definite cultural countenance and explicit political goals. Two elements interact. On the one hand, there is the struggle against the caste, the rejection of the ways of life and the customs that define the caste and its place in the world, and the achieving of true equality with the order outside the caste; on the other hand, there is the effort to endow a community free of caste limitations with explicit national features. Both factors supplement each other and provide the background for ideologies that attempt to find rational form for collective aspirations, to give them justification and an explicit goal.

There is no question that the directions taken by the Jewish emancipation movement were consistent with a negative attitude toward the caste. They were also consistent with the positive goal of transforming the caste into a national community. The differences—and they were fundamental—emerged when it came to a more exact definition of the nature of that national community and of the paths that were to lead to it. Here one comes to basic divergences in ideology that were to have far-reaching practical consequences.

In this respect, the Jewish national emancipation movement was something of an exception. Admittedly, serious ideological divergences were found in other national emancipation movements. Nowhere, however, were they as fundamental as they were among the Jews. Zionism and anti-Zionism, Hebraism and Yiddishism divided Jews into camps that advanced radically differing formulations of values so essential to any nation as location, language, and relations with other nations.

It is true that the question of language, for example, is becoming a serious problem for many of the young nations of Asia and Africa. Those are multilingual societies in which the national unifying force must, of necessity, be based on other values. Exceptional situations aside, none of those local languages has the tradition and the prestige necessary to be established as the national language. The language of the assimilated local intelligentsia, usually English or French, assumes that role. However, this cannot be compared with the problem faced by the Jews.

Yiddish was the language of the great majority of East European Jews. It was a reminder of the epoch in which Jews had assimilated to the German language. Since that time, the language had undergone a series of important evolutions while being influenced by the languages of the countries of the diaspora. Yiddish was the product of the diaspora. More important, however, it was the tongue of the caste, and it was one of the basic elements indicating the very existence of the caste and an individual's membership in it. If Yiddish was a person's daily language, that meant he was a member of the caste. This shaped the attitude of the non-Jewish environment toward Yiddish. It was not a language but a "jargon." A Jew who spoke it was said to "jabber in Jewish." That contemptuous attitude toward Yiddish was also widely shared in the milieus of assimilated Jews. Here, to admit to a knowledge of Yiddish was considered highly improper and might even be grounds for social disparagement.

And yet that "jargon" was not only the tongue of millions of people in the caste but also, from the middle of the nineteenth century, an increasingly literary language. Its grammar was elaborated; literary works were written in it. In the twentieth century, Yiddish literature, initially a "folk" literature, produced a series of eminent writers who were translated into other languages. There was a flourishing Yiddish press, and important scholarly works were written in Yiddish.

Nevertheless, in the eyes of the non-Jewish environment and of a significant part of the Jewish intelligentsia, Yiddish was still a "jargon," a ridiculous vernacular that met with universal derision. For many ideologists of Jewish emancipation, Yiddish was the language of the caste; it embodied the humiliations of the Jews and was unworthy of a national community with such great cultural traditions. National rebirth should return to the great linguistic traditions, to Hebrew.

There is nothing unusual about a national group in the process of emancipation that had lost its original language in the course of history and sought to return to it. It is sufficient to point to the case of the Irish, whose efforts to revive their ancient Gaelic culture have a great deal in common with Hebraism. However, the Hebrew tradition among the Jews was incomparably stronger than the Gaelic had been among the Irish. Hebrew was the language of scripture, of the liturgy in the synagogue, and was taught in school. A religious Jew was obliged to possess some knowledge of Hebrew. No doubt it was a rigid language, the language of scripture, and ill adapted to the demands of modern life. But it was a language with a great cultural tradition and was the Jews' "own." Also, it did not bear the explicit stigma of caste.

Thus, the question of language assumed especially great significance in the Jewish emancipation movement. But even more momentous than the problem of language was that of the external conditions under which emancipation could occur, and the question of its ultimate goals. Could emancipation occur in the diaspora? If not, what should be done to lead the Jews out of diaspora? Is it possible to create a Jewish national homeland? How is that to be achieved?

The many different answers to each of these questions caused deep ideological differentiations in the Jewish emancipation movement. A solution came through an unexpected course of events that swept millions of Jews from the stage of Eastern Europe and brought a new Jewish state into being in Palestine. Let us attempt to become somewhat more closely familiar with the two principal ideological currents in the Jewish emancipation movement in Poland.

VI

The first of those currents was Zionism. Ideologically, Zionism was the child of European romantic nationalism. It is not difficult to hear echoes of post-Hegelian nationalism, especially in its German formulation, in the writings of Herzl and other Zionist theorists. There were Polish echoes as well. Zionism held that a nation is a historical continuity with a unity of spirit and has specific historical tasks to fulfill. That unity is threatened, however, and those tasks cannot be fulfilled if a nation is deprived of its basis for development, that is, its own land. As long as the Jews remain in diaspora, they cannot be a nation and cannot fulfill their mission. The only solution to the Jewish problem is the renunciation of diaspora and the creation of a Jewish homeland.

There is no question that the Jews had succeeded in preserving their historical continuity and traditions even in the diaspora. It was not solely religion that was of decisive importance here. No less important was the very fact of their isolation, the fact of living in ghettos. Jews avoided the others; the others avoided Jews and held them in contempt. Wherever anti-Semitism is weak or nonexistent, the Jews are quick to lose their singularity as a people. In this sense, the diaspora, the ghetto, and anti-Semitism performed great services of conservation for the Jews.

But they were still evils. In the diaspora the Jews were everywhere and at all times a foreign body and had to be experienced as such by the larger environment. Zionism lay great emphasis on the Jews being alien to the nations among whom they lived. In that respect it agreed with anti-Semitism. It is telling that anti-Semitic writers frequently cited statements by Zionists in which they found arguments to support their own views. The Zionists, of course, spoke of the alienness of the Jews in the same spirit in which the romantic nationalisms of all young nations attempt to demonstrate their difference from the nations to which they have hitherto been subject. Ukrainian historians, as opposed to Russian historians, attempt to demonstrate that, from the dawn of history, the Ukraine and Russia were ethnically and culturally completely different.

In addition, the diaspora and the ghetto had depraved the Jews. They had imposed an abnormal economic structure on them, constricted their mental horizons, and morally distorted them. And, primarily, the diaspora and the ghetto had degraded them as individuals and as a collective body. Although the Zionist writers did not employ the concept of caste, they were aware that Jewish life in the diaspora was castelike in nature. In any case, that life attested to the marked degeneration of a great people. Here too the anti-Semitic writers made willing use of Zionist statements on the negative aspects of the Jews. In many cases they also agreed with the Zionists in their ultimate conclusions.

Anti-Semitism, of course, had to be considered an evil by Zionism. It was difficult to relate favorably to those who thought of the Jews as deadly enemies. The Jews were constantly feeling on their own hides the practical consequences of anti-Semitic philosophy. But, at the same time, the Zionists both rationalized the fact of anti-Semitism and perceived some useful elements in it. Like all other romantic nationalistic doctrines, Zionism, either explicitly or implicitly, accepted a division of the world into the "kindred" and the "alien," seeing their mutual antagonism as a historical necessity and a great historical driving force. Anti-Semitism impelled Jews toward national integration and compelled them to seek out and defend a homeland of their own. Among the masses of Jews, anti-Semitism led to the creation of a myth of the enemy—which, by the way, in the case at hand had a strong objective basis. All nationalistic philosophies viewed the myth of the enemy as a factor that cemented their national collective. Thus the "enemy" was useful and necessary. In this regard, Zionist ideas did not differ from those of the Polish League, the National Democratic party, or German nationalism, or from the Soviet myth of the "capitalist enemy."

Naturally, even with all their negative attitudes about the diaspora, the Zionists could not deny it as a fact of life. Moreover, they had to accept that, even given the most optimal achievement of their program of creating a homeland of their own, a certain part of the Jewish people would have to continue to live in the countries of the diaspora. Some theorists of Zionism (e.g., Ahad Ha-Am) even assumed that the future homeland would only have room for the elite of the nation so as to become a center radiating out to Jews throughout the world. Thus, Zionism could not abandon the program calling for Jews to struggle for equal rights in the countries of the diaspora where they still constituted a caste. This was necessary also from the vantage point of the ultimate goal—Zionism could not be the work of the unfree. In order to reach the point of being able to build a homeland of their own, the Jews had to go through a schooling in citizenship in the countries of the diaspora.

Although treating the struggle for emancipation in the diaspora as a necessity, Zionism had grave misgivings about that part of its program.

Complete emancipation within the framework of the diaspora could lead to a loss of national character, the disappearance of Jewish distinctness. Hence, East European Zionism looked with distrust on American Zionists. In the United States, the Jews had quickly ceased to be a caste and had achieved full and equal rights. They continued to think of themselves as Jews, of course, but significantly more in religious than in national terms. In regard to nationality, they viewed themselves primarily as one element in America's ethnically pluralistic national society. American Zionism was always philanthropic and patronal in nature. It helped other Jews settle in Palestine—and today lends Israel large-scale aid—but American Jews feel perfectly at home in the diaspora. In fact, they have ceased to think of America as a land of their diaspora, just as have all the other multiethnic elements of the American national society. The East European Zionists were aware of this and feared the consequences of genuine equal rights.

Viewed in the light of the world situation in 1939, the Zionist program appeared fantastic, utopian. Palestine, a Turkish province until the First World War, was a British mandate. The famous Balfour Declaration was so general that it could be interpreted in a variety of ways, and was so interpreted by the mandate authorities. The country was populated by Arabs. It was a small scrap of land, mostly desert. Economically and culturally, it was very backward. How could millions of people accustomed to completely different living conditions be settled there? Palestine was something entirely different from the American frontier, and the Jews did not much resemble the first pioneers. How was a migration of those dimensions to be accomplished on the technical level? Even millions of dollars from American Jews would not suffice. Besides, how does one prepare people for a migration of that sort and for a life under new conditions? The list of questions could be extended endlessly.

That this utopia became a reality is one of the most astounding events in human history. It happened as one of the consequences of the terrible disaster of war and the unparalleled extermination of European Jewry. However, even if Israel owes its origin to those circumstances, they do not explain everything. Israel would never have become Israel had it not been for the powerful aspirations for emancipation that had seized the Jewish masses of old Europe before the war. And here the role played by Zionism was enormous.

Zionism was able to give the Jewish masses a vision. It knew how to reach the mystical, messianic substance of Jewish cultural tradition and lend it new forms. This was different from Herzl's cool rationalism and was undoubtedly the contribution of East European Jewry. It seems highly probable that it also contained something of Polish romanticism. Young Jews were carried away by Zionism. It gave them faith, hope, and purpose for their life. It was an effective antidote to despair and hopelessness. If the objective situation in prewar Poland led to hopelessness, Zionism provided hope and activated people. Today's Israel is unquestionably the product of that colossal dynamic which developed in the Jewish masses of the diaspora in the twentieth century and to which Zionism lent direction and color.

Influenced by Zionism, young Jews began to study Hebrew as a living language. Here too utopia became a reality. The language of scripture was not a living language; yet it became one, creating a new literature and adapting itself to the demands of contemporary civilization. Young Jews began to study farming—also something utopian under Polish conditions. They set to work on physical and military training. The cowardly Jewish soldier, a universal laughingstock and the subject of innumerable jokes, had vanished. He was replaced by an excellent soldier led by superb combat officers. Today, Israel's army is considered the best in the Near East.

VII

Zionism, however, was only one of the ideological currents that expressed the emancipationist aspirations of East European Jewry, including those of Polish Jews. Another current existed that in many instances sharply opposed it. That current included various political groups in which the socialists, concentrated in the Bund, occupied the most important position. Their aim, too, was to transform the caste into a modern national community with its own cultural identity. Their ideological premises, however, differed from those of Zionism, and their goal was also defined differently.

Whereas prewar Zionism could justifiably be considered an extremely utopian concept, the current that opposed it was based on reality and sought a solution within those limits, setting itself extremely realistic goals. The course of historical events tipped the balance in favor of Zionism. The extermination of East European Jewry also meant the destruction of the second current of Jewish emancipation.

The Bund and related groups saw the fact of the diaspora as the only possible framework in which the Jewish collectivity could develop. But was it true to call it a diaspora? After all, at issue were countries in which the Jews had been living for centuries and with which they had the strongest historical, economic, and social ties. This was a diaspora as long as Jews were a despised caste, closed in ghettos, and denied a part in the greater life of the society. But it was not only the Jews who were in that situation. It could also be said of all underprivileged and exploited social groups that they lived in diaspora. Their native lands were foreign to them; the prevailing social systems debarred all the underprivileged from taking any real part in the life of the society.

In order that Poland could cease to be a land of diaspora for the Jews, a fundamental reconstruction of the entire social system would have to occur, eliminating the caste and providing full emancipation. And that precisely should be the goal of the renascent Jewish society, the direction in which it should strive.

The Bund saw the emancipation of the Jews as one element in the overall transformation of life in countries where—as in Poland, Russia, and Rumania—Jews were a very numerous group. Jewish aspirations could not develop separately from those of other underprivileged classes also seeking emancipation. It was only in connection with them that Jews would be able to maintain their own national identity and develop their culture.

Such a concept entailed definite practical conclusions. The Bund was decidedly a socialist, though not a communist, party. It arose on former Russian territory as one of the branches of Russian socialism and kept up close relations with the Mensheviks. Some of the eminent Mensheviks, like Abramovitch, for example, were also active members of the Bund. The Bolshevik Revolution put an end to the Bund's activity in Russia. It then drew its support from Poland and the Baltic countries. In Poland the Bund maintained close relations with the Polish Socialist party.

If the emancipation of Polish Jews could occur only together with the transformation of all Polish life, Jews should take the most active possible role in the struggle for that transformation. The Bund constantly stressed its positive attitude toward Polish statehood and its desire to participate fully in the life of that state. That it was not able to achieve this was a result of conditions existing in Poland.

While taking an active part in the life of Polish society, Jews would not cease to be Jews. In a Polish state, they would want to be a separate national group with its own language and cultural identity. Of course, that would be impossible as long as the concept of nation state prevailed in Poland. That concept was utopian and should be combated. The Jews were seeking a broad cultural autonomy that would create a framework for them to develop freely as a people within the Polish state.

Here the question of language was of fundamental importance. According to the Bund, only Yiddish could be the Jewish national language. It was the language of the masses, millions strong, a living language. Hebrew was a dead language, a sacred language. Yiddish was not the only language to have begun as a "jargon." So did many others, including English. Yiddish was demonstrating impressive development and producing a rich literature.

Unquestionably, the great Jewish cultural traditions were preserved in the form of the Hebrew language. But the new Jewish culture was becoming a secular one, departing ever further from its sacral history. It was not the distant biblical past but the centuries-long experience of diaspora that was of essential importance for the spiritual identity of the modern Jew, and only that experience could be his guide in emancipation. In other words, the basis for Yiddishism was the cultural continuity created in the diaspora.

To the Bund Zionism was a utopian and harmful concept. It was not possible to build a Jewish homeland on land the Jews had left long ago and which was now occupied by others. In preaching emigration, Zionism was in fact renouncing the Jews' historical continuity in the countries of the diaspora and relinquishing the struggle for their emancipation in those countries. The Zionists were so fixed on the myth of their own state that for its sake they were prepared to sacrifice the liberation of those millions of Jews who, no matter what, would have to remain outside the homeland in Palestine.

This position of the Bund and the criticism of Zionism it entailed were marked by great soberness of mind. There was nothing "utopian" about Jewish anti-Zionism. It was firmly grounded in reality. The Bund's program of cultural autonomy was far from radical. Its essential content could be reduced to some rather elementary requirements that today, when seen in the perspective of time, do not seem exaggerated. The program of cultural autonomy for national minority groups was popular with socialists in many countries and found adherents even among individuals otherwise very conservatively inclined. However, under conditions existing in prewar Poland, it seemed highly revolutionary and caused indignation. It was said in all seriousness that the Bund wanted to turn Poland into a Judeo-Polonia.

It must be stated clearly that it was not only in Poland that the chances were slim for carrying out a program of cultural autonomy. Even in Czechoslovakia or Latvia, where serious attempts were made to put it into practice, results were meager. All of Europe had been inundated by a broad wave of nationalist fanaticism. Both national "majorities" and "minorities" suffered from the disease. Czechoslovakia, which had been so genuine about taking the path of cultural autonomy for its minorities, fell victim to a revolt by one of them, the Sudeten Germans. In the Soviet Union, after a period of national self-determination and broadly conceived cultural freedom, came a brutal policy of destroying "nationalisms," the first victims of which were the Jews. In Spain the systematic persecution of cultural separateness in Catalonia and the Basque region persists to this day.

It is characteristic that, in prewar Poland, the anti-Semitic camp was more hostile to the Bund than to Zionism. The anticommunist Bund, representing a restrained form of socialism, was irrevocably numbered among the "seditious" parties. A particular hostility to Poland was ascribed to the Yiddishists. From the anti-Semitic point of view the reasons for this were self-evident. Zionism furnished arguments for the anti-Semites' positions and, were it successful, could help "purge" Poland of Jews. The anti-Zionists, on the other hand, proclaimed that the Jews should remain in Poland, considered them a component of Polish life, and claimed a part for them in the machinery of the Polish state. In other words, it was much stronger than Zionism in rejecting the traditional role of the caste Jew. That had to be perceived as the height of "arrogance."

Nevertheless, the anti-Zionists, and especially the Bund, had particularly strong ties with Poland and its culture. The Bund had not begun on Polish territory. But after the Bolshevik Revolution, when Poland had become its most important arena, the Bund underwent rapid Polonization. Its leaders had strong bonds with Poland and spoke and wrote excellent Polish. After all, the Bund's theorists included Liebmann Hersch, to whom nothing Polish was alien.

VIII

Jewish emancipation trends in Poland cannot be understood outside the context of Poland and Polish culture as a whole. This does not mean in the least that Polish Jews were undergoing Polonization. Assimilation as a program was a thing of the past. The goal of the Polish Jews was to define themselves as a separate national community. But in seeking to transform the caste into a collectivity of that sort, they took on new values that resulted from the fact of living in Poland and that originated in Polish culture in one way or another. Obviously, the great majority of those values were universal in nature and had come to Poland from elsewhere. But they had in some way been assimilated by Polish culture, and it was chiefly through that agency that they reached Polish Jews.

These things were not understood in prewar Poland, and it is doubtful whether they are understood today. The maturity of the British, who see the development of the separate cultures in the commonwealth as the greatest triumph of Anglo-Saxon civilization, was foreign to the Poles. British imperial nationalism was free of the traditions of narrow-minded romantic nationalism, free of the traditions of Fichte, Hegel, and the German nationalist school. A broad view was taken of Britishness, which was seen as a far-flung reach of cultural influence with room enough for a gamut of local cultures.

If similar ideas existed in embryonic form in Poland during the Jagiellonian period (1386–1572), they vanished entirely in the course of time. The long period of statelessness ultimately put an end to them. After the fall of the Polish state, all that could remain was a mystical concept of nation as a closed society of compatriots, different in every respect from other national collectivities. That formulation could allow only for the assimilation of "aliens" to Polishness, an assimilation that had to be total, leading to complete conformity of the alien with the accepted definition of being a Pole. And that was an extremely rigorous definition. In many instances it placed non-Catholics outside the sphere of Polish life. Similarly rigorous definitions are easily detectable among

Jews in the process of emancipation. Comparable historical conditioning and motivations were at work in both cases.

Poland entered its new period of statehood with a philosophy that found its expression in the concept of nation state. That concept was put into practice at a time of general crisis of which Poland was only one particular instance. One aspect of that crisis was an enormous intensification of mass emancipation movements, social and national. Traditional Polish political, social, and philosophical concepts—themselves undermined from every side—were particularly ill suited to this situation.

The Crisis

I

There is much to be said for the idea that future historians will view the period between the two world wars as one of the most critical in human history. One era was coming to an end; the elements of another were beginning to emerge. This was expressed by crises in politics, economics, culture, and morality. Like every major turning point in history, the period between the wars was rent by vast internal contradictions; it was a stage for violent fall and violent rise, for mass insanity, and for the shattering of entire value systems based on age-old traditions, whose place was taken by irrational, alogical substitutes that attempted somehow to fill the void. Ideologies arose which, confronted with objective historical reality, were anachronisms from the very start. However, those ideologies corresponded to the attitudes of people who felt lost, deprived of the compass that had served them for centuries, and who were feverishly seeking something to provide answers and a rational basis for existence.

It was a period in which the exaltation of nationalism reached its peak. Even in countries that were socially and culturally stable, prophets of national mission appeared. Fortunately for those countries, the influence of such prophets was limited. In unstable countries where the disintegration of traditional values was far advanced, the mystique of nationalism found a perfect seedbed. This mystique expressed itself in outbursts of mass hysteria, in the emergence of savior leaders who had seized power through revolution and were creating new political systems. Those systems were conceived to last for millennia and to assure power and happiness to the weak and unhappy human masses. In fact, all those nationalistic ideologies, when confronted with objective reality, proved to be anachronisms, attempts to turn back or halt history. When read before the war, *Mein Kampf* could have been thought by many to be the ravings of a crude madman. But for millions of people the book came as a revelation. When read today, what is striking about *Mein Kampf* is that the author had no understanding of his epoch and that the world he constituted for himself was a historical fiction. He had a tremendous feeling for human weaknesses, but he did not understand the times in which he and his contemporaries had been fated to live. And in that he was not alone.

This period of general crisis determined the historical framework in which the new Polish state was created and took form, and it also had a fundamental influence on the fate of Polish Jews.

To the mass of the Polish Jews the birth of the Polish state was unexpected and not quite comprehensible; they were doubtful and mistrustful of it. In that sense, the Jews in 1918 were "native foreigners." But not only the Jews. In 1918 it could be said that the great majority of all citizens of the Polish state, including the indigenous Polish population, were "native foreigners." Among the masses there was no feeling that the new state was a state of their own; they did not identify with it and regarded it with no small dose of distrust and skepticism.

The new state was the outcome of the exceptional historical situation caused by the defeat of the three partitioning powers. A small group of radical intellectuals understood the situation and attempted to draw conclusions based on that understanding. That group found some modest backing among those elements of the workers who had been schooled by Polska Paria Socjalistyczna (PPS), the Socialist party of Poland, and among the radicalized peasants, especially those in *Zaranie* (Daybreak). There were a good many assimilated Jews among those radical intellectuals. Bronisław Mansperl was one of the first Legion officers to fall on the field of battle. Wilhelm Feldman, Stanisław Posner, Feliks Perl, Herman Liebermann, Herman Diamand, to take but a few, all played important roles both in the campaign for independence and in creating the foundation for the new state. There were also people like Szymon Askenazy among those initial architects of the Polish state. All told, it was not a large group because the team that gathered around Józef Piłsudski was not a large one.

Although by and large the general public remained aloof, the Polish-Soviet war of 1920 did arouse a certain enthusiasm in people. There was the feeling that the country was being threatened, and the public grew aware of the need to repel the enemy. And, regardless of our assessment of that war, it must be acknowledged that it was of major educational significance for the mass of Poles. It remains true, however, that in general those masses were not strongly involved in the process of creating the new state and that their emotional commitment to it was weak. Indeed, the Jews were not the only "native foreigners."

It must be remembered, though, that the tradition of Polish statehood was uncommonly frail, in many respects nonexistent. The peasants, with few exceptions, had for centuries been outside the orbit of the nobles' republican state. The same held true for the middle class and the Jews. In the peasants' memory, the times of the Polish state were times of villenage. In the Jews' memory, those were the periods when the caste system had been rigorous, ruthless. The traditions of statehood were preserved, in part, among the nobles and were brought to life by the heirs of the nobility—the intelligentsia, especially its radical wing. But although a large portion of the landowning nobility viewed the traditions of Polish statehood as something venerable and moving, they did not treat them as something to be taken seriously.

All the same, after 1918 the Polish state was a fact. And regardless of how it functioned, its very existence became a factor of great educational influence. It was a reality, and it created the framework within which millions of human beings lived, acted, and developed. It is to the Piłsudskyites' credit that they appreciated the significance of training people for citizenship. Their program for such training was conducted poorly and inconsistently. But the premises of that program were correct: to make the masses into citizens to some extent, to join them with the state in some way.

If we compare the Poland of 1918 with the Poland of 1939, we must admit that, despite everything that occurred in Poland after Brześć,[1] the citizenship process has advanced greatly and that, especially among the indigenous Polish population, the number of "native foreigners" had undergone a significant reduction.

But was that the case only among the indigenous population? There is also much to be said for the great advance in the process of connecting the Jewish masses to the Polish state, in spite of all the factors that impeded that process.

II

As we mentioned earlier, the Jewish masses were unenthusiastic about and mistrustful of the new Polish state. Apart from the general factors causing similar attitudes among the Polish population, there were special factors operating in the case of the Jews. The economic struggle against the Jews that had played such a political role in the Congress Kingdom after 1912 was still fresh in memory. To some degree, the slogans of that struggle had been echoed in Galicia as well. The Jews of the eastern frontiers of Poland were very much under the sway of Russian culture and had little in common with Poland. The events in Lvov during the battles between Poles and Ukrainians had produced a shocking impression. Of course, many assimilated Jews had been fighting on the Polish side, but the Jews of Lvov as a whole decided to be neutral in the conflict, which, given the conditions of the time, seemed to them the only sensible approach. Neutrals, however, must sometimes pay heavily for their neutrality. The Jews of Lvov laid themselves open to both the Poles and the Ukrainians and were the victims of major anti-Semitic riots. The events in Lvov cast a shadow on the further development of Polish-Jewish relations. On the Polish side there was the heightened conviction that the young Polish state could not trust the Jews, and on the Jewish there was a greater fear of the future and mistrust of the new state.

In any case, the events in Lvov are only one illustration of the state of mind existing on both sides at that time. The indisputable fact that people of Jewish origin played an important role among the then Bolshevik leaders had a special resonance in Poland. Official propaganda exploited that fact, and the right-wing press made use of it to an enormous extent. It was then that the myth of the "commie Jew" began to be created, a myth that had its counterparts in other countries as well.

Poles returning from Russia would relate their experiences with the Bolshevik commissars, who most frequently were Jews. This was extremely influential in the persistent identification of Bolshevism and the

Jews. Naturally, few people considered that the Jewish commissars constituted a negligible minority among the masses of Jews. Although known to a handful of serious sociologists, it did not penetrate the consciousness of the community at large that groups that are marginal and discriminated against have always furnished revolutions with their leaders. In the end, there was no lack of Poles among the leading Bolsheviks, to name but Dzierżyński and Marchlewski, and there were also many Armenians, Georgians, Latvians, and so on.

Nevertheless, the image of the Jewish Bolshevik had a tremendous influence on the attitude toward Jews at the moment of the creation of the Polish state. It was a source of the extreme distrust of Jews as an unreliable social element. The tradition of the caste system was also of great significance here. It was easier to accept communists of any other origin rather than Jewish communists, who were so radically departing from their historic role. Things reached the point where soldiers of Jewish origin were interned in a special camp in Jablonna. Those internees included many people who had volunteered for the Polish army and who felt themselves wholeheartedly Polish.

Naturally, distrust gave birth to distrust. The Poles' mistrust of the Jews was matched by the Jews' mistrust of the Poles and Poland. This entailed serious consequences whose reach exceeded Poland itself. American and West European Jews, disturbed by the fate of their coreligionists in Poland, did not regard the young state with any enthusiasm. And that was not without influence on the so-called minority treaties. Meanwhile, in Poland itself relations grew more tense. From Jewish political circles issued the initiative to seek a rapprochement with the other national minorities in Poland. And since those groups also did not feel secure in Poland, the idea of a political bloc composed of all the national minorities could easily appeal to them.

The concept of a nation state, which in practice became the basic philosophy of the young Polish state, had an unmistakable influence on the mood of those minorities. We will not enter into an analysis of the concept of nation state, its philosophical assumptions, its social conditioning, and its political consequences. Instead we will limit ourselves to the most general of observations.

The idea of a nation state was the work of Polish right-wing groups, primarily Roman Dmowski and his school. It was opposed to the concept of "federation" preached by the ideologists of Józef Piłsudski's camp and by the Polish left. In the struggle between those two concepts, the former had every chance of success.

Let us set aside the impediments that, independent of Poland, lay on the road to carrying out the idea of federation. The very concept was difficult and visionary, imposing great renunciation on the Poles and compelling them to make enormous efforts. It did not and could not appeal to the imagination of the masses. It was the concept of a small team of intellectuals.

The concept of nation state could appeal both to the masses and to those intellectual circles that were opposed to radical slogans. For a hundred and thirty years or so, to a Pole the state had meant the state of the partitioner. The program then had been to survive as a national society by resisting the denationalizing policy of the partitioning state. For the Polish nation the ability to survive had become primary; the fundamental values that defined its identity had to be preserved, protected, and venerated. Hence, the very word *nation* possessed a special emotional implication, was a symbol of something profoundly mystical with emotional power for everyone. At the same time, the nation was seen as a collectivity that was as uniform and compact as possible, a community of the "kindred," like, and familiar. In sum, this was a concept both markedly conservative and explicitly exclusive, rigorously defining every member of the national community. And above all, this was a concept with a strong emotional coloration.

It was with these ideas in mind that the Polish right-wing intelligentsia reacted to the emergence of Polish statehood. The new state's ideology would be a continuation of the previously existing national ideology. The Polish state was to be the state of the Poles, each of whom had to correspond to the traditional definition of a Pole. In other words, the Polish state was to be an in-group community and was to serve to maintain that in-group's ways.

That concept was well suited to the mood of the more educated elements of Polish society. In a more simplified form it was also able to reach the broadest masses, whose sense of Polishness, hitherto weak, now began to develop quickly. To those masses, Polishness was synonymous with the rejection of everything not Polish and with an unfriendly attitude toward minorities.

But in a state where every third citizen was not considered a Pole and did not consider himself one, the concept of a nation state was utopian. The more rational ideologues in Piłsudski's camp and on the Polish left were well aware of that. They had to relinquish the idea of federalism but could not reconcile themselves to that of a nation state, whose consequences they saw as a danger to Poland's future.

This concept was not only utopian. It quickly became anachronistic as well. Because the existence of a Polish state had a deep educational influence on Poles, it also had a similar influence on the so-called national minorities. In practice, it became an agent favoring the development of emancipationist striving among those minorities. This had not been foreseen by believers in the national concept and, when confronted with the new realities, they were unable to comprehend them. Worse still, they attempted to oppose those realities by bringing pressure to bear. A utopian concept was followed by utopian methods of operation.

Poland of the period between the wars can hardly be called a democracy. Attempts at establishing democracy were timorous and clumsy. Nothing else could have been expected from a country whose social and economic development had been so retarded. But still, certain institutions, containing democratic elements and with an educational influence, did function, albeit poorly. And that influence was felt by both Poles and non-Poles. The Polish parliamentary institutions and the Polish political parties of that era are open to great criticism. But some parliamentary institutions did exist, some elections did take place, and some political parties were active. The press, though severely hampered by censorship, did offer some possibility of free expression. There were agencies of local self-government that, though badly encumbered by a self-willed administration, could display initiative, could, within certain limits, take constructive action. There was a certain scope for organizational life—for cooperatives, and for educational, union, agricultural, sport, and other organizations.

The twenty-year period between the wars set the scene for an ever-increasing expression of emancipationist strivings among the so-called national minorities. This related primarily to Ukrainians and Jews and, to a somewhat lesser degree, to Belorussians and Lithuanians. The ethnic Germans constituted a group apart. The Ukrainian was ceasing to be a "Ruthenian": a hayseed, sometimes unruly but always picturesque, and speaking a language that was melodious but of the peasants. The Ukrainians were producing their own intelligentsia, creating their own literature, constructing ideologies of their own, and operating within organizations of their own. They had clear national political aspirations. They were Ukrainians and did not wish to be Ruthenians. The Jews wanted to free themselves from the limits of the caste; they were secularizing their life and had a national political leadership, a literature, a press, ideologies. They no longer wished to be *parchs* or *żydeks*.

There is no question that participation in the life of the Polish state was conducive to forming those aspirations. Minority groups developed their activity within the framework of the Polish state and its institutions. Although that activity was being limited and frequent attempts were made to halt it, it was stronger than all the obstacles. And, after all, those obstacles also had certain limitations. Despite some juggling with ballots, the minorities had their representatives in parliament. Each minority had political parties, associations, cooperatives, a press. On a meager scale, there was even instruction in minority languages, Ukrainian, Belorussian, Hebrew, or Yiddish. Members of national minority groups complained of being treated as second-class citizens; and undoubtedly they had grounds for such complaints. Nevertheless, they did receive from the state something constructive that furthered their own national development.

Though it sounds paradoxical, the national minorities—for all the Polish state's ill will toward them and theirs toward it—were drawn into the state's sphere of action and connected to it. That applied to the Jews in particular. Though the Jews might not be happy in Poland and might encounter proof of the state's ill will toward them at any step of the way, they began to lose their initially intense feeling that the state was alien; and they began to accept it as an important element in their own reality. Even many years after the Second World War, Polish Jews encountered in émigré situations offered ample proof of how far the process of assimilation to the Polish state had advanced among them. To a certain extent, the same may be said even of the Polish Ukrainians and Belorussians.

That process would have been infinitely stronger had it not been for the prevailing doctrine of a nation state. That doctrine, utopian and anachronistic, was unable to halt the processes of national emancipation among the national minorities. It alienated those minorities from Poland and created difficult and insoluble political situations. But it was not able to wipe out the educational effects that, by the nature of things, stemmed from the very existence of the Polish state and from the participation of minority groups in its functions. And thus, alongside the constantly increasing national emancipationist strivings among minorities, processes of assimilation to the state were making the Polish state a part of the experiences and feelings of non-Polish groups.

III

In 1929 Piotr Dunin-Borkowski published a lengthy study of the Jewish question in Poland in the Warsaw monthly *Droga* (The Road). At the same time Tadeusz Hołówko wrote a series of articles for *Gazeta Polska* (The Polish Gazette) on the national minorities in Poland, giving considerable attention to the Jewish minority. Proceeding from different assumptions, both writers came to very similar conclusions: of all the national minorities in Poland the Jews were the only one that was pro-state, acceptant of Polish statehood as the framework for their life and actions, and free of irredentism. The Jewish program was very modest: that the provisions of the constitution be genuinely put into practice and that the Jews be treated no differently from the rest of Poland's citizens. The views of Dunin-Borkowski and Hołówko were shared by a small team of experts on the minority problem in Poland concentrated at Instytut Badań Spraw Narodowościowych (The Institute of Minority Affairs). That team was small, however, and entirely isolated in its views.

With the perspective time affords, we can now better assess the validity of Dunin-Borkowski's and Hołówko's conclusions. If the Jews were initially mistrustful of the newly created Polish state, they accepted it relatively quickly and made it a part of their reality. A group, a considerable portion of whose members are professionally engaged in the exchange of economic goods, is always interested in a strong, well-organized state that would be able to ensure the free movement of goods and services and create a legal system that would make economic activity possible. The Jews wanted a lawful state that would not discriminate against them and that would secure peace in economic relations.

It is not difficult to demonstrate that the Jews always and everywhere supported a strong central authority, strove for stable political relations within the state, and were victimized by all decentralizing forces. In countries that did not discriminate against them, like the United States, England, France, and Italy, the Jews produced a series of eminent statesmen who were most frequently of a conservative stripe. In the kaiser's Germany and the Austro-Hungarian Empire, the Jews were ideologists of unity of the state. The German Jews even became zealous Germanizers in areas ethnically non-German, and the Hungarian Jews became equally zealous Magyarizers. Even in czarist Russia, for all its brutal policy of discrimination, the Russian Jews were advocates of the idea of Great Russia. We shall have occasion later to speak of the Polonizing functions of the Polish Jews.

It can of course be said that, in their tendencies toward state centralism, Jews were guided by their own interests. That was undoubtedly the case. But it is difficult to demand that Jews not be guided by self-interest. Had they not been, they would have made an exception. In order to exist, every human collectivity must be guided by self-interest.

During the time of the Polish state, Zionism had a particularly great influence among the Jewish masses. Zionism was not in the slightest an irredentist idea. It had no intention of taking away a part of Polish territory; its idea was that the Jews would emigrate from Poland. Zionism also envisioned that such emigration should take place in an organized fashion, under conditions of legal order, with aid from the state people would be leaving. The Zionists sought to reach an understanding with the state and were prepared to rely on it.

Of decisive significance here was that the Zionists were perfectly well aware that the mass emigration of Jews from Poland was a long-term matter and that the bulk of the Jewish population would continue to live in Poland for a long time. No one was able at the time to foresee the course future events would take. In their daily activities as a political party operating in Poland, the Zionists had to accept that millions of Jews lived in Poland and took part in Polish statehood. Practically speaking, the Zionists did not differ from other Jewish political parties, putting forth as their basic political postulate that the Jews be assured genuine equality as citizens. That was a moderate program, one that both affirmed the fact of Polish statehood and sought ways to cooperate with it.

To attribute antistate or "seditious" tendencies to the Zionists or to the other Jewish political parties was patent nonsense. Irredentist tendencies existed among the Ukrainians, the Belorussians, the ethnic Germans, and the Lithuanians. It is an absolute certainty that they were alien to the Jews.

There was, however, the matter of communist influence on Polish Jews. No doubt such influence existed. A significant number of people of Jewish origin were in the leadership of the Communist party. Communist ideology had adherents among the young Jewish intelligentsia. Those things intruded on the attention of society at large and served as material for the myth of the "commie Jew." Besides, they went hand in hand with the myth about the specific revolutionary qualities of Jews in general. In certain instances, that attribution was even approving.

Jews were seen as mental "yeast," an agent of the healthy ferment that brings progress. However, considerably more often, the revolutionary or corruptive qualities of the Jews were used as an accusation by their enemies. The conjecture of the destructive role of the Jews always occupied a leading place in anti-Semitic ideologies.

That conjecture used arguments that sounded convincing. Jews had furnished humanity with many famous revolutionaries, iconoclasts, critics of the existing order, and satirists who ridiculed that order. Jews played a prominent role in the Bolshevik Revolution, providing it with outstanding leaders. There were many Jews in the Polish Communist party, especially on its leadership team. Those facts appealed to the imagination of people already hostile toward the Jews. Those people accepted the facts emotionally, without caring about a rational interpretation of them.

Like every marginal group that is discriminated against and, at the same time, strives for emancipation, the Jews were predestined to furnish humanity with revolutionaries and critics of the established order. Communist influence on the masses of blacks in the United States is negligible, yet one is struck by the high percentage of black intellectuals in the leadership of the American Communist party. This phenomenon is well understood in America and has justly been connected with the caste position of black citizens. A black intellectual's chances in American life are very limited. A Jewish intellectual's chances in prewar Polish life were most likely even more limited. Radical slogans find fertile ground in milieus of this sort. In addition, the role Poles have played in various nineteenth- and twentieth-century revolutions is worth noticing. They too were marginal people—émigrés, products of the breakup of the noble class, down-and-out people of every sort, derelicts. And some of Poland's greatest writers were to be found among them.

Communist influence was relatively small even in the milieu of the déclassé Jewish intelligentsia in Poland. Zionist influence was much greater. Among the Jewish masses, communism met with a very weak response.

Thus, putting aside the proposition about the "seditiousness" of Jews, we must acknowledge as correct the arguments of those who stated that the Polish Jews as a whole were an element grounded in Polish statehood and were nonrevolutionary and nonirredentist. Their political demands were marked by moderation and were entirely within the framework of Polish law. Their sole concern was that those laws actually be put into practice.

IV

The years between the two world wars were a period of one of the great crises in modern times. In all of mankind's history, perhaps only the years of the fall of the Roman Empire are comparable. But the fall of Rome was a process that occurred at a substantially slower rate and in a social and economic system infinitely less complicated than ours. Their technology, too, was, comparatively speaking, at an infant stage. The great crisis of our times occurred with dizzying speed, in a very complex society, in an economy immeasurably more differentiated, and with technology at a fantastic level of development.

The crisis was political, social, economic: a crisis in all cultural and moral values. In 1918 old Europe collapsed—the work of the Vienna Congress and the centuries preceding it. On the rubble of the old empire arose new, inexperienced states, their borders uncertain, their economies weak, and their social antagonisms acute. With the exception of the few years immediately after the war, the world was in the grip of a frenetic economic crisis. It struck such economic giants as the United States and England and mercilessly battered the weak new states. That crisis did not come out of nowhere but was the result of economic development since the beginning of the Industrial Revolution. A complete rebuilding of the entire economic and social system was needed to combat the crisis. That, however, required time, vision on the part of leaders, and maturity among the masses.

All fixed cultural values broke down. Violent departures from the old ideals and values took place in literature, art, and science. The belief in Progress, Brotherhood, and Humanity had come to an end. Extremist revolutionary concepts found expression—radicalism of social class or of nationalism—and those concepts stood in brutal opposition to the old ideals. The age of political adventures and adventurist philosophies had begun. New myths were born and savior-dictators arose: the Hitlers, the Stalins, the Mussolinis.

The crisis affected Poland severely, and it affected Polish Jews as well. This was the context in which Jewish life in Poland was to form itself, and in which the emancipation of the Jewish masses was to progress.

In fact, throughout the period between the two wars, Poland lived in conditions of an economic crisis encompassing all areas of the national economy. At certain points—for example, the period after the coup d'état of Marshall Józef Piłsudski, immediately after 1926—the crisis lessened, only to reemerge with greater severity. There was constant unemployment in industry, and the agricultural situation was disastrous. The most optimistic figures spoke of three million "superfluous" people in the countryside. In reality, the figure was substantially larger. And those who were not "superfluous" lived a vegetative life. Business and exchange did not, of course, present any better appearance. Business, as primitive as the rest of the Polish economy, was pitiful and grappling with the greatest difficulties. The same held true of the trades. The situation of the mass of Jews would have been very bad even without the prevailing discrimination against them. Moreover, an end had been put to emigration overseas, which, since before the time of independence, had acted as a regulator on Poland's demographic and socioeconomic relations. The introduction of a quota and visa system in the United States, the limits set on immigration by Canada and the Latin American countries, the reduction of emigration to Palestine to a minimum, all had a powerful impact on Polish life as a whole.

However, the desperate economic situation determined only the framework for the basic historical processes taking place at that time. When the war broke out in 1914, Poland was the Poland of the nobility. Its entire social system, formed through the centuries, rested on the supremacy of the noble class. It is true that after the middle of the nineteenth century the nobility's position and role were in decline. But the product of that decline, the urban intelligentsia, continued the nobles' traditions and took over their historical role.

After 1918, however, distinct transformations began to occur. There is no question that the traditions of the aristocratic past continued to be strong, just as they are in Poland today. Fundamentally, Polish culture has not ceased to be aristocratic. Ideologies, inarguably noble in origin, permeated all elements of Polish society, from right to left. They were strong in Piłsudski's camp, were easily detected among socialists and peasant parties, and permeated even to the Jews. But at the same time, the social foundation of those ideologies and traditions was undergoing decline and decay.

The countryside of the noble manors gradually became a thing of the past. From the end of the eighteenth century, Poland, along with nearly all the rest of Europe, was the scene of an agrarian crisis that destroyed numerous large farming estates ill adapted to contemporary circumstances. The crisis intensified in the twentieth century. Even without agrarian reform, the Polish gentry economy was bound to decline. The agrarian reform of the early 1920s—a halfway measure introduced as a compromise—was only one of the factors that furthered this overall trend. The landowning gentry as a historical class was losing its basis; it grew impoverished, left the land, and became objectively déclassé.

The bad economic situation hampered the social changes occurring among peasants in the countryside but was unable to halt them. Those changes were comprehensive and far-reaching. The traditional social pattern of the Polish village, based on relations of neighbors and family and built around the squire's manor, the presbytery of the priest, and the Jewish inn, was quickly vanishing. New social relations and new forms of organization took its place. The old leaders of the peasant community were losing their authority, and new types of leaders emerged—the teacher, the instructor of an agricultural group, the co-op worker, the activist in the peasant youths' political organizations Wici or Siew. The number of peasants' sons entering the ranks of the Polish intelligentsia was steadily increasing. New ideals and new ideologies came into being. Mental horizons expanded; new needs and new interests were stimulated. The peasant was becoming a political force that had to be reckoned with. Unquestionably, all this was still very far from full political, social, or cultural maturity. In comparison with the Western countries, the Polish village was still backward and primitive. However, in comparison with what it had been some years before, it displayed striking progress. There was every indication that the Polish peasant village was now within the orbit of the great processes of social emancipation.

As we know, emancipationist processes also encompassed other elements of Polish society. They occurred among the national minorities, in whom national and social aspirations were united. In the world of the Polish Jews, those aspirations sought to replace the traditional caste system with a modern national cultural community. In fact, the goal of the Polish peasants was also the elimination of those forms of caste existence that had for centuries defined the place and role of the peasant village.

It was a misfortune that all these processes went on under highly unfavorable conditions, which encumbered both the nature of those aspirations and the forms they took. The country's disastrous economic situation, the faulty vocational structure, the lack of jobs, inept organization, and the absence of clear guiding principles, all had a tragic impact on the changes that were taking place.

A sense of uncertainty, of unrelenting menace prevailed. This was not peculiar to Poland alone. At that time an atmosphere of catastrophism lay over a great part of the world. After 1929 it was no longer alien to America, and it seized Germany on an immense scale. Danger seemed to threaten from every side, and it was difficult to understand clearly where it came from and what its causes were. It brought with it a state of constant panic, alarm, fear for the future and provided sustenance for visionariness, for a mystique of revolution, for anticipations of a new era.

That was nothing especially new in human history. The past provides sufficient examples of analogous situations. Periods of great political, social, and economic crisis always gave birth to apocalyptic moods among the masses and collective hysteria. And as a rule, those were epochs in which magical thought and feeling dominated.

In his collective actions, man rarely makes use of rational thought, even though he always tries to rationalize his emotions. This is true even in periods of balance and stability. In times of great panic, rational elements disappear from human thought to be replaced by magical elements, although man subjects them to rationalization or pseudorationalization.

In magical thinking all of reality is divided into spheres where two opposed forces operate—Good and Evil, White and Black, the Pure and the Impure. Most frequently, this is tantamount to a division into the Familiar and the Alien. The Good, the White, the Pure are that which is ours, which favors us, and which we can trust. The Evil, the Black, the Impure are alien, hostile to us, and we must protect ourselves against them. Our misfortunes are the result of the machinations of Evil. If we are to free ourselves from adversity, we must oppose and combat the Evil. Above all, however, we must separate ourselves from it. For Evil is impure and every contact with it defiles the Good which is within us and which we serve. In other words, Good and Evil must be absolutely separate from each other.

That idea is as old as mankind. It is found in various religious systems, to mention only Judaism's dietary rules and certain rules of Hinduism, of other Eastern religions, or of the religion of ancient Rome. Manichaeanism is a more sublimated form of this idea. But it is not difficult to detect its presence in various modern political systems and philosophies either, for example the pseudo-Marxism accepted in the communist world or the various racist doctrines, Nazism chief among them. In pseudo-Marxism, Good and Evil assume the form of class, leading to a division of all reality into the socialist and the capitalist spheres. Racism divided everything along racial lines, the Good concentrated in the Aryan race, Evil in the race of the Jews. Both in pseudo-Marxism and in racism, the ancient magical idea has undergone rationalization and makes use of pseudoscientific arguments. When, however, a communist true believer fights for class purity in socialism and when a racist true believer purges the defilement stemming from the influence of alien races, they are both employing the age-old magical concept that divided reality into Good and Evil.

None of us is ever completely free from magical elements in our thinking, feeling, and acting. Magic is man's inseparable companion on the road of history. However, in times of great panic magic dislodges the strictly rational elements and achieves its greatest triumph, because it gives a clear answer to the questions posed by a man who is terrified and menaced. In extremely simple and concrete terms it shows him who is guilty of causing his misfortune and reveals the means to free himself from adversity. Those answers lead to disastrous consequences, but the panic-stricken man discovers that too late.

V

It is noteworthy that in Poland, and outside it as well, antagonism toward the Jews increased as the objective differences between Jews and non-Jews diminished. Jewish life was undergoing increasing secularization: there was a decrease in the influence of the Talmud, which Staszic's contemporaries had seen as the chief source of the Jews' harmfulness. Knowledge of the Polish language was growing; the old forms of dress were disappearing (it is worth noting in passing that the costume of the Galician Jews was a survival of the dress of the sixteenth-century Polish burgher); Jewish customs were being modernized; Jews were taking a growing interest in Poland's national concerns and obviously desired to take part in public life. Both culturally and in terms of civic awareness, Jews in the period between the wars were infinitely closer to Poles than Jews of the nineteenth century were, not to mention those of earlier times. The professions, such as innkeeper and usurer, traditionally thought to be specifically Jewish were also on the wane. Though the conditions were not propitious, a certain professional transformation was taking place among the Jewish population in Poland. Jewish workers began to appear, chiefly in the clothing and textile industry, and the cadres of the Jewish intelligentsia were on the increase. The Jews were also beginning to distinguish themselves by their physical skill. One Jewish type—the coward, the weakling afraid of dogs and water—was replaced by the athlete from the Zionist sport organization Maccabee. The accusations leveled at the Jews in the nineteenth century were clearly losing their basis. Antagonism, however, did not decrease; on the contrary, it grew. The old accusations were now multiplied by the new.

It is not unusual for antagonism toward a certain group to grow, even though that group loses the objective features that had been considered the source or cause of the hostility toward them. Similarly, it is not uncommon that the hostility of one group toward another increases as they come to resemble each other. In the American South, hostility toward blacks increases as the blacks socially and culturally more and more resemble the rest of the population. Moreover, in some circles, antagonism is greatest toward those blacks whose assimilation to white society is the most advanced. The situation is no different in the Union of South Africa, where the primary victims of apartheid are those blacks who have assimilated the most to whites. An entire series of similar examples from other countries, epochs, and civilizations could be cited here.

This does not mean, however, that all assimilation must increase antagonism. For assimilation to be accompanied by increased antagonism, a basic condition must be fulfilled: the group assimilating to us ceases to act the way we believe it *should*. Fundamentally, all assimilation means a change in the behavior of those who are assimilating. But this is not always in accord with certain social valuations, strengthened by firm tradition, that for centuries delimited relations between the two groups. Assimilation that occurs in defiance of those valuations, that rejects them, and that is a "leaping out of the role" as traditionally understood shocks and galls us, offends our feelings, and challenges our basic philosophy.

That, as a rule, causes an increase in antagonism toward the group that was assigned a very low place in the hierarchy of our world before assimilation and that now, through the very fact of assimilating to us, attempts to overthrow that hierarchy. This is evident in the American South and also in the case of the "untouchables" in India. However, in both those countries the increase in antagonism toward those acting "out of their role" is restrained by the state and by a considerable portion of public opinion that looks with favor on the changes taking place. In the United States, even in the South, a significant portion of white society is fighting discrimination against blacks. In prewar Poland, the state's influence on restraining antagonism was weak and inconsistent. Public opinion, a few exceptions aside, approved the growth of antagonism and itself contributed to it.

But in the Poland between the wars, all elements of society were acting "out of their role" and had ceased to behave in accordance with the pattern hitherto binding. This primarily applied to the peasants, who had begun a radical rejection of their traditional image as *chams*. To no less an extent, it applied to the Jews, who had also begun a radical rejection of their traditional images as *parch* and *żydek*. In the case of the Jews, however, these changes were especially irritating and disturbing.

Contrary to the opinion commonly held outside America, the greatest enemies of integration in the southern states are not the well-to-do elements but the poorest ones, the "white trash," small tenant cotton farmers, small farmers, workmen, and, in part, industrial workers. In other words, elements that are definable as proletarian. Equal rights for blacks pains them as the prospect of their losing the one "superior" position they have in a segregated society by virtue of having white skin. In those social strata the traditional caste system is valued extremely highly. It provides white people, even the poorest among them, with a definite higher place, a permanent social position. For them, integration means social disaster, the overthrow of the entire recognized order which gave the "white trash" a place under the sun. It is those strata that most oppose the program of integration imposed by the federal government, and that complain most loudly about the arrogance of blacks, their insolence, garishness, pushiness, and so forth. Those accusations are astonishingly reminiscent of those leveled at the Jews in Poland.

The similarity is not accidental. In both cases, similar motivations and patterns of social conditioning are at work. In prewar Poland, the entire traditional order was in the process of collapsing. In different circumstances and for other reasons, it also broke down in the American South. In Poland, however, that collapse was particularly great and dramatic. Hitherto wealthy strata were under threat of becoming or already were déclassé. The country's poverty was vast, its economic possibilities limited. And at the same time, on every side individual and collective aspirers to advancement appeared. By the nature of things, all conflicts grew more acute, the general tension increased, and the sense of menace grew stronger. In that state of affairs, the Jews' departure from their traditional social role, their rejection of their traditional image, intruded on the attention of the society at large, creating indignation and antagonism. The Jews' emancipationist strivings were undermining the traditional social hierarchy and overthrowing the existing order, which was already in a state of increasingly pronounced decay. Thus, the assimilation of Jews to non-Jews added to the general sense of menace and alarm that was prevalent anyway in the life of that period. Never before in Poland had so much been spoken about Jewish arrogance as during those times.

The Jews were not the only large social group in Poland that was developing emancipationist tendencies. However, in no other group was the disparity between those tendencies and the traditional image so grating as it was in the case of the Jews, because in no other group was the contrast between past conditions and current aspirations so great. In Germany, where Jews had rejected the traditional image and made the transition much earlier and under infinitely better conditions, the first signs of Nazi-like anti-Semitism already appeared by the second half of the nineteenth century. It would seem that, in the catastrophic years of the period between the two wars, the Jews in Germany, Poland, and a few other European countries were, as if in some fatally mounting series of events, doomed to play the tragic role they in fact were to play.

VI

Magic in people's attitudes during periods of great panic always leads to the personification and the concretization of Evil. This then produces a specific magical sociology that rejects the impersonal nature of great social processes. Someone must be guilty of our misfortune. Someone must be responsible. The myth of the enemy emerges, the enemy who is guilty and responsible. Sometimes specific individuals —politicians, thinkers—are the enemy; more often it is groups to whom, for one reason or another, we ascribe ill intentions.

In the United States after World War II, the "communist" became the popular personification of the enemy responsible for everything evil. A woman farmer I know who is otherwise a reasonable person assured me that a certain government ruling on sanitation that had caused cranberry farmers great losses had to be the work of a communist conspiracy. I do not think she is any stupider than those who thought the economic crisis in Poland had been deliberately unleashed by the Jews.

There is no doubt that the Jews in Poland and several other countries were particularly well suited for the role of the enemy, the source of our misfortune. In this case personification was an easy matter and had been prepared by the entire course of events.

A study of Polish anti-Semitic literature between the wars permits a better understanding of the mechanism of mythicizing the enemy as it operated in regard to the Jews. That was not an original literature but primarily a reworking of similar German or French sources that attempted, not always with success, to adapt those models to Polish conditions. It does, however, have important documentary value.

That literature achieved codification in Henryk Rolicki's *Zmierzch Izraela* (The Twilight of Israel). Published in 1933, it went through several editions and enjoyed great popularity. Today, of course, it is entirely forgotten, but in the thirties it was representative of Polish anti-Semitic ideology.

The book is historicophilosophical in nature. The author attempts to interpret all human history from the point of view of the role Jews played in it. According to Rolicki, from the beginning the Jews sought both to "separate themselves" from non-Jews and to subjugate them. To that end, they conducted a policy that corrupted the non-Jewish world and caused it to decay in order to make it spoils for the Jews. But as a rule that policy had turned against them, and they themselves fell victim to the calamities they had prepared to destroy others. So it has been throughout history and so it is today. The Jews have prepared new calamities—primarily communism—and again they themselves will fall victim to it. But they will not regain their might anymore; humanity is beginning to understand what Jews really are, and the twilight of Israel is inevitable.

In great detail, Rolicki demonstrates that the Jews were the mainspring in the fall of great powers and in the rise of heresies and revolutionary ideas of every sort. It was the Jews who caused the fall of the Roman Empire and the invasions by the Germans, Arabs, and Tartars. Neo-Platonism, Manichaeanism, Gnosticism, and Aryanism were their work. Their machinations produced the Albigensians, Hussitism, Humanism (the author thinks humanism an evil), and the Reformation. Obviously, Free Masonry and the French Revolution were the fruits of Jewish intrigues. The Jews' ultimate products are capitalism and Bolshevism. He does not hesitate to reduce the entire Polish Reformation to Jewish intrigues.[2] In short, it could be said that the Jews were the driving force of history, that anything of importance that occurred in history originated from the Jews.

Rolicki's book created controversy. Some people simply mocked it while others, mainly Jewish publicists, replied heatedly to it. However, to criticize a book of this sort was both easy and altogether hopeless. It was easy to demonstrate that, scientifically speaking, the book was sheer nonsense, that it was rife with striking historical errors and full of internal contradictions, and that the author either did not know the facts, altered them, or lent them fantastical interpretation. Rolicki's book contained comical mistakes. For example, one figure appearing in its pages was a mysterious Duns Scot Erigena, clearly a fusion of two philosophers from different areas, with one of the names undergoing distortion. There were also incredible linguistic interpretations and confusions of concept and fact.

But if rational criticism of the book was an easy matter, it was also hopeless. Rolicki's book was the product of belief, not of knowledge and rational thought. The people who were taken in by it were not guided by the criteria used in scientific research. In Rolicki's book they found what they already believed or wished to believe. Moreover, they found a confirmation and justification for their own fears and hopes. Rolicki told them clearly why things were bad, while at the same time providing them with hope for the future. Those guilty of their misfortunes would themselves fall victim to their own perversity. The twilight of Israel is approaching and, when it comes, happiness will prevail on earth.

Rolicki revealed the full power of Evil to his readers. The omnipotence of the Jews was truly terrible. This was, of course, not entirely in accord with the traditional image of the despised caste of *parchs* which was still alive in the minds of those who read *The Twilight of Israel*. But that contradiction was more apparent than real. It was precisely because the Jews, while being the despised caste of *parchs*, were indeed able to achieve such omnipotence that made their machinations all the more sinister and Rolicki's effusions all the more revelatory. The reader also received immediate reassurance. The greatest powers in the world had been the victims of Jewish perfidiousness. Was there anything surprising about each of us also having been its victim? Evil is so powerful that it can penetrate everywhere and corrupt everything. But—and here came further reassurance—for all its power, Evil is doomed to defeat. It is strong but at the same time it is weak. It is terrible but at the same time it can and must be destroyed. We don't have to submit to its might; we can combat it. And that won't be difficult. The twilight of Israel is in sight; Israel's reign is coming to an end.

The paradox of Evil that is omnipotent but at the same time weak emerges in all anti-Semitic ideas, just as it always does in analogous magical ideas. Those who sent the witches to the stake experienced a sense of relief in knowing that Satan, for all his might, was powerless to save his own servants. The Jews too are a great force but at the same time they are weak and for that reason can be combated. Dmowski, though undoubtedly on a considerably higher level than Rolicki, repeatedly stressed that the Jews, for all their power, were weak and that victory in the struggle against them was absolutely guaranteed.

Such magical interpretations of history are extremely well suited to the minds of the masses in epochs of panic and social cataclysm. Rational arguments do not reach them, nor can they. The story behind *The Protocols of the Elders of Zion* was no secret. It had been irrefutably proved that it was the work of the Russian Okhrana, that it was a falsification, a plagiarism of a political pamphlet from the time of Napoleon III with only the dramatis personae changed. The original pamphlet did not even speak of Jews. All the same, millions of people strongly believed in the authenticity of the *Protocols*. Some editions were even furnished with a note to the effect that even if the book was a falsification, it was still an excellent rendering of the Jewish spirit and that the councils of the Elders could in any case have occurred, must have occurred, and did occur just as they were presented in the *Protocols*. *The Protocols of the Elders of Zion* was one of the few publications in Polish that the Germans issued during the last occupation. And even then it found diligent readers in Poland.

In his book *Anonimowe mocarstwo* (The Anonymous Power), Adolf Nowaczyński provides a detailed description of the power of Jewish bankers in the United States. The belief that Wall Street is a Jewish stronghold remains widespread outside the United States to this day. Since banking is at all times and in all places the work of the Jews, it is obvious that American banking too must be in Jewish hands. In Nazi Germany someone even located the place where the Elders of Zion met —in the basement of the Chase Manhattan Bank! Although well known in America, it was generally ignored elsewhere that the role of the Jews in American banking was secondary and that Protestants played the decisive role. What is more, it was never acceptable. It just couldn't be so. That wouldn't fit the mental pattern that prevailed in Europe. Hence, the power of Jewish capitalists in America was spoken of everywhere, and the appropriate conclusions were drawn. It seems highly doubtful, however, that Nowaczyński and others with similar views would have changed their opinions even had they become familiar with the facts. Of decisive importance here was the accepted pattern and the emotions on which it was based.

In the early thirties Karol Hubert Rostworowski launched a program to protect the purity of Polish literature. This was primarily a philippic against Tuwim. For Rostworowski, Tuwim was of course not a Polish poet but a Jewish one. Still worse, being a Jew, Tuwim had introduced destructive elements into Polish literature. Using examples from his poetry, Rostworowski diligently demonstrated the basic features of Tuwim's Jewishness: his sensualism, his lack of feeling for nature, and so forth. A Polish-Jewish journalist, S. J. Imber, spoke out against Rostworowski. In *Asy czystej rasy* (Aces of Pure Race), published in 1934, Imber demonstrates that the specifically Jewish traits Rostworowski attributes to Tuwim were present in identical form in the work of other poets of the time, and poets whose Polishness could not be doubted. Imber, who in his book also passionately attacked Rolicki, received a reply from Rostworowski that was surprisingly weak and evasive. Nevertheless, it was clear that Imber had not changed Rostworowski's conviction, nor could he have, for the author of *Judasz* was a man of faith. Since Tuwim was a Jew, it was obvious that his poetic works had to have Jewish traits, meaning everything that did not meet with Rostworowski's approval. It was not important whether those traits (e.g., a lack of feeling for nature) existed in Tuwim's poetry. What was important was that, in keeping with a definition accepted a priori, they had to exist. And all rational argument was shattered against the indestructible rock of that definition.

VII

Anti-Semitism is one of the symptoms of the antagonism of one group for another. Such antagonisms assume various forms, are supported by various rationalizations, and are caused by various external conditions. Human history abounds with them. Even anti-Semitism is not monolithic. First of all, not every negative attitude toward Jews has to be considered anti-Semitic, just as not every negative attitude of one person toward another is necessarily a sign of antagonism or conflict. A Polish noble inveighing against a Jew as a *parch* and a peasant as a *cham* was neither an anti-Semite nor an enemy of the peasants and was not necessarily unfriendly toward the one or the other. He was just classifying the Jew and the peasant socially, employing the generally accepted patterns. The historical periods in which the Jews were held in contempt were not necessarily periods of anti-Semitism. The latter emerged when the attitude toward Jews began to be marked by explicit hostility, when rationalizations for that hostility were created, and all this went hand in hand with certain actions. But even here it is difficult to speak of any monolithic anti-Semitism. The persecution of the Jews during the Middle Ages was something different from Nazism, although Jews were the victims in both cases. Polish anti-Semitism at the end of the nineteenth century was completely different from that of the 1930s. Polish anti-Semitism was different from German. Russian anti-Semitism had completely different conditioning, forms, and rationalizations than did Ukrainian anti-Semitism, for example, which in turn was different from both the Polish and the German varieties. If symptoms of anti-Semitism have emerged in the modern era in France, England, or the United States, they are absolutely different from those in Eastern and Central Europe.

In any case, all these types of anti-Semitism—as with other related forms of interpersonal antagonism—had certain things in common, besides that Jews were the target. It is highly likely that, had there not been a single Jew in Poland or Germany in the period between the two wars, antagonism would have emerged and been directed at some other group. The myth of the enemy that always arises in times of great historical catastrophe is by no means always personified by the Jew—and this is true not only in places where there are no Jews. In the United States the myth of the enemy was not anti-Semitic in nature even though several million Jews live in that country. This myth focused on the foreigner in general, the uppity black, the communist, the intellectual, and others. The Armenians played the role of Jews in nineteenth-century Turkey. In many African countries the white man is the enemy. But the starting point of all mass myths of the enemy is always the same: a disaster, a breakdown of the established social order, a disintegration of accepted value systems, a growing sense of isolation, uncertainty, menace. The individual feels lonely and thus uncertain, deprived of a sense of direction and meaning in life. The traditional bonds that joined individuals are being torn away. At a time of economic decline, the individual can find no application for his skills and strengths. He becomes déclassé, heading for the bottom, or else is shunted to marginal status.

These are perfect conditions for the creation of myths that unite mysticism and magic. The weak dream of being strong, and so they follow the one in whose strength they believe, whose might can assure them protection and return lost meaning to their lives. Charismatic ideologies are born and savior dictators arise. None of this can do without the myth of the enemy. To Fidel Castro, the myth of the American enemy is indispensable. It does not matter whether Americans have really done Cuba the wrongs Castro claims. What is important is that, given the specific local conditions, Americans are suited to the role that someone had to play in Cuba. No other group, including the Jews, who are one of the elements of the island's population, were suited for the role.

The anti-Semitism of the prewar period cannot be interpreted in rational terms. Of course, it made use of rationalizations, but its contents were purely magical. It was the product of panic, of historical calamity. Seen from that vantage point, it tells more about the state of the society it took hold in than about the Jews. It was one of the symptoms of a powerful social disease. Anti-Semitism at that time was far and away more of a German, Polish, Rumanian question than it was a Jewish question.

It does not follow that the Jews were themselves free of all disease. The general state of calamity could not pass them by untouched. Worse still, the very fact of being the objects of discrimination produced the worst possible social and psychological consequences. Living in a sick world, they could not be healthy. Among them, too, were mystical ideologies, magical attitudes, and the conditions for a charismatic leadership.

As a practical policy, anti-Semitism could not provide any solution whatsoever to the great problems of the time. The economic struggle against the Jews in Poland weakened the country's economy without benefiting anyone. No other element in society grew richer from the Jews' financial suffering. The country's abnormal professional structure, particularly striking in the case of the Jews, was a result, not a cause, of Poland's economic backwardness. Perhaps worst of all was that anti-Semitism as a plan of action, while failing to provide any real solutions, created the fiction that the problems facing Poland were being solved. In his comments on Stanisław Brzozowski (*Kultura*, July–August 1960), Czesław Miłosz quotes a passage from *Sam wśród ludzi* (Alone Among People) in which a Russian says that Poles are convinced that Russians are the sole source of all their misfortunes; if there were no "Muscovites" in Poland, paradise on earth would reign there. That sort of thinking is universal and as old as mankind. In prewar Poland millions believed that if the Jews left, all the country's problems would disappear at once. That fiction screened reality and released people from the obligation of looking at reality more clear-sightedly.

After 1945 only a handful of Jews remained in Poland. The vast majority of the former Jewish community had departed through the gas chambers and crematoria. Most of those who survived left Poland. But they took with them many things Polish. A thousand years of history could not be blotted out. They took with them the basic values of Polish culture, definite traditions and attachments. They did not cease to be Polish Jews. Only later will their descendants lose those ties with the past, as will the descendants of the great throng of postwar Polish refugees. But among the memories still alive in the souls of Polish Jews are also the years of that wave of anti-Semitism that swept Poland on the eve of the great calamity of war. Those are painful memories, which cast their shadow on Polish-Jewish relations. Not in Poland, of course, where only a few Jews remain, but on the wide spaces of the world where Jews and Poles encounter each other.

The Image of the Jew

I

Among the most interesting and most important problems in sociology and cultural anthropology is how the image of one group and each of its members is reflected in the minds of the members of another group. Research on this problem is of major significance for understanding intergroup and interpersonal relations. Our own group's experience forms the images of other groups and their members, and we make use of definitions based on those images whenever we enter into relations with people from those groups. Those images, and the definitions based on them, are never the fruit of sober reflection and do not provide an adequate representation of reality. And it could not be otherwise. Those images are the outcome of our daily experiences and have nothing in common with the thorough and meticulous search for truth that scientific inquiry needs. Those experiences boil down to chance encounters and casual judgments in which emotional factors prevail over reflection. The result is the stereotypes that make up the "wisdom of nations" and their knowledge of others. Those stereotypes pass from generation to generation and become part of a given group's collective tradition.

The objective cognitive value of those images is slight, most often nonexistent. Those images are abbreviations, fragments, distortions, and always have a powerful emotional coloration. But in the life of society those images have tremendous significance. They decide the way we behave toward others, motivate our judgments and actions, and are reflected in our politics, our economics, and our spiritual culture.

They are of particular importance in the relationships between national groups. The image of the Englishman in the French mind and the image of the Frenchman in the English mind, the image of the Pole in the Russian mind and the image of the Russian in the Polish mind, are all of enormous practical significance.

Modern scholarship has done relatively little in exploring this matter. Even American scholarship, which has earned such merit for its research into the mechanisms of intergroup relations, has made only modest achievements in research on the images of one nationality in the minds of others. However, the research done in America on the whites' image of blacks, and the blacks' image of whites, is a valuable point of departure for research on national groups. A great deal of interesting material has also been collected in America on the images of various ethnic groups among both immigrants and Americans.

The scarcity of such research is no doubt related to its difficulty, for this kind of research is exceptionally intricate. To be of real value, it cannot be satisfied with banal and haphazard observations but has to be as many-sided as possible. Most important, that research has to be fieldwork conducted on a large scale. The researchers have to get into direct contact with people in order to find out how they see others, especially when those others represent a specific national group. The research must include vast areas of folklore—proverbs, songs, stories, riddles, folk art, and so on. It must study the press and political platforms and slogans. How one national collective is reflected in the literature and art of another also requires diligent research. In short, at issue here is research with tremendous range which cannot be carried out by isolated individuals but requires entire teams.

Some fragmentary approaches have been made. The young German scholar Kurt Lück has studied the image of the German in the minds of Poles. His book *Der Mythos vom Deutschen in der polnischen Volksüberlieferung und Literatur* (Poznan, 1938) was the product of careful research and is of uncommon scholarly value. Unfortunately, Lück was killed during the Second World War.

I know of no work that has given serious study to the image of the Jew in the Polish mind. Needless to say, I omit cheap publicist works and propaganda, which at best are of dubious scholarly value. Some Polish researchers, for example Bystroń in his book on Polish proverbs, have touched on this question but have not devoted a great deal of attention to it.

In fact, the first attempt to approach the problem was a work on the image of the Jew in Polish proverbs written by a German Nazi during the occupation and published in *Die Burg*, an organ of the occupying authorities. The author, Jozef Sommerfeldt, was in charge of Jewish affairs at the Institut für Deutsche Ostarbeit in Kraków. His work, *Die Juden in den polnischen Sprichwörtern and sprichwörtlichen Redensarten*, was published in 1942, in the July edition of *Die Burg*. Both the person of the author and the place where his work was published necessarily give rise to doubts about its objectivity. This is unquestionably a slanted work, especially in its interpretive sections. The author was a Nazi racist and wrote in that spirit.

Nevertheless, Sommerfeldt's work cannot be denied its scholarly value. With German meticulousness, the author collected 477 Polish proverbs and sayings on the subject of Jews. While remaining entirely critical of the method he used to systematize the proverbs, it must be admitted that his material is rich and his work pioneering. The work is worth remembering, especially since *Die Burg* is now becoming a bibliophilic rarity.

All told, however, there is little on the subject. The difficulty is that as time passes, and as a generation matures in Poland which never had direct contact with Jews, the image of the Jew loses its freshness, its life, and becomes an increasingly vague memory more and more transformed into legend. It will become a static image, unmodified by the experiences of direct interpersonal contact.

A static image of that sort cannot tell us a great deal. Wherever experiences are immediate, the image of one social group as it exists in the minds of another is never static and uniform. It is always conditioned by society and history. The image of the Jew was one thing in the world of the landowning nobility and another in the world of the peasants. The liberal intelligentsia had one idea of the Jew and the lower middle class another. The image of the Polish Jew after 1863 was radically different from what it became in the years directly preceding the Second World War. Anti-Semitic propaganda, so intense in the prewar years, left a deep trace on the image of the Jew that was formed in various Polish milieus at the time.

Thus, if an image is alive and truly part of direct collective experience, it is a kaleidoscope, changing in time and space, full of contradictions, rarely consistent, always fragmentary, and highly fluid. One must go to many sources to fix that image. Popular novels and the press and publicist work of every type are also material that must be taken into account. In fact, this is material of considerably greater importance than folk creations like proverbs, adages, jokes, or songs.

To collect and solidly work up this material is an enormous task, especially since one must begin from the foundations. I am under no illusion whatsoever that the present book can provide the image of the Jew as it existed in the Polish mind. That achievement exceeds the capabilities of any one man, especially one who has been living far from Poland for a good many years. Others will have to carry out that task. My intentions here are infinitely more modest: to initiate such work, to raise certain issues, to deal with questions of method. It seems to me that this can be of help to those after me who will study this problem more thoroughly.

II

Let us begin with the image of the Jew in the Polish folk tradition. Astonishingly little has been done on the subject. In fact, Sommerfeldt's work was the first serious attempt at an approach to the image of the Jew in Polish proverbs. Among Polish authors, Franciszek Rawita-Gawroński (1845–1930) studied Jews as they appear in songs and folk traditions in the Ukraine. What he wrote on the subject is only a chapter of a larger work on Jews in Ukrainian history. Unfortunately, that work is of very little value. Ill inclined toward the Jews, Rawita-Gawroński attributed responsibility for the peasant uprisings in the seventeenth century to them and interpreted the Ukrainian folk poetry of that era from that vantage point. He collected a fair amount of material, but it all related to the Ukraine and not to Poland proper. Besides Rawita-Gawroński, only a few ethnographers, Bystroń, for example, touched on the image of the Jew in Polish folklore, treating it in a fragmentary and rather marginal fashion.

In all folk arts we find judgments on and images of people who belong to other ethnic and cultural groups. These are the fruits of historical experience, the results of our contacts with others from outside our group. The nature of those contacts is conditioned by a variety of circumstances. We encounter "others" as enemies, and sometimes as allies; we encounter them in business, in ways where we depend on them or they on us. There are an immense number of areas of encounter. Most frequently, those are purely outward encounters and casual or haphazard. The dominant chord in those relations is the clash between the way others behave and the model that we consider our own and therefore the only proper one. Hence, aliens and their ways grate on us and we usually find them ridiculous. We do not approve of how they act, how they look, what ends they pursue; and, most frequently, that disapproval is expressed in mockery. The ridiculousness of a foreigner, of a person of another religion, of anyone in general who is alien to us is the basic motif in the proverbs, sayings, and adages of the folklore of every nation in the world.

As a rule, we are struck and amused by the details of an alien's behavior that most depart from our own. This most frequently applies to things that are external but that in our experience are important since they make for the stuff of our daily life. The cuisine of foreigners is an object of disapproval throughout the world. In the Anglo-Saxon countries, Frenchmen are to this day called frogs or frog eaters, an expression of Anglo-Saxon disapproval for the French custom of eating frogs. In this case, one small detail of French cuisine so caught the attention of the Anglo-Saxons that it provided a nickname for all Frenchmen. However, in the popular mind that is an important detail, touching on something as familiar as dietary customs. In Poland, Italians were known as "macaronis." Jews as a rule were thought to smell of garlic, and some delicate noses could detect the smell of garlic on Jews who never ate it. In passing it is worth mentioning that assimilated Jews in Poland held garlic in great contempt. It was a reminder of the past. That excellent and most useful plant, which has been the delight of all southern peoples since antiquity, had a suspect aroma in Poland.

Folklore, in disapproving a certain detail in the customs or behavior of alien people, makes that detail a basic characteristic typical of the entire collectivity. The method of *pars pro toto* is commonly found when the image of one human group is formed in the minds of members of another. These again are stereotyped formulas that have enormous importance in human relations. A further step in the same direction is the ascribing of everything evil and ugly to the alien. Syphilis was known as the French disease (in Turkey it was the "Christian" disease, in Moscow the "Polish" disease), in Poland cockroaches are called "Prussians" (and in certain countries "Frenchmen"), an ink blotch is a "Jew," and so on.

A small number of exceptions aside, folklore is never friendly to outsiders. The attitude expressed is not always one of open hostility. More frequently it is one of mockery. Along with the sense of the laughable created in us by the outsider's behavior that does not accord with our norms, compensatory tendencies are at work. In mocking an outsider, we affirm our own sense of importance; we assert our superiority to the outsider. This is especially important in cases in which we objectively feel that we are being surpassed or menaced by an outsider. There is no question that the Poles' experiences with Germans have been extremely unfortunate. And hence the image of the German in Polish folklore—as is well demonstrated by Lück—is especially negative and abounds in diabolical traits. At the same time, however, the German is derided. The German is stupid and ends up falling into his own traps. It is my impression that in the image of the Russian as created by the Polish folk tradition ridiculous elements far outweigh all others. Primarily, the Polish people held the Russian in contempt and tried at every turn to affirm their own sense of superiority to the "Muscovite" barbarian. It would be extraordinarily interesting to study the image of the Russian in the popular Polish mind of today. However, under the present political conditions in Poland, this is a hopeless dream.

An examination of the hundreds of proverbs on Jewish subjects that Sommerfeldt collected demonstrates that the ridiculousness of the Jews was the dominant motif. The Jew is a figure of fun. "He sways like a Jew over the Talmud"; "As pretty as a Jew's beard"; "Each to his own: a pig to garbage, a Jew to onions "; "He's afraid of water like a Jew"; and so on. Jewish customs, dietary rules, occupations, religious rituals, and the like are derided. The comical *żydek* appears in these proverbs, a figure we encounter in other Polish folk arts, to mention but the Christmas puppet shows. The Jew's cowardice, his lack of veracity, his "impertinence" are further motifs in the proverbs.

However, a large group of proverbs exists in which disapproval of the Jew is not necessarily expressed in ridicule. In these proverbs, the Jew most frequently appears along with non-Jews, and the proverb condemns some character trait that is more general, a trait that belongs to Jew and non-Jew alike. "A Lithuanian's sincerity, a woman's constancy, and a Jew's kindheartedness are all good for nothing"; "A German, a Jew, and the devil—all children of one mother"; "A Polish bridge, a German's fast, a Gypsy's riches, a Jew's conscience, and a peasant's wit—none of them worth a damn"; "A girlfriend's word, a Jewish oath, both uncertain"; "The Jew and the noble contrive to ruin the peasant"; and so on.

An enormous number of the contacts between Polish peasants and Jews came as a result of the economic functions performed by the Jews. The peasant bought from a Jew and sold to a Jew. The Jew was a source of credit. There are a great many sayings that relate to those economic functions. The most well known of them is: "When things are bad, go see the Jew" (reportedly, in Poland people now say: "Though things are bad, there's no Jew to go to"). But there were other sayings as well: "Hard as a Jew doing business"; "Every Jew praises his goods"; "A Jew may be poor but he isn't stupid: if you sell cheap, he'll buy everything"; "As fair as a Jewish scale"; and so forth. The very fact that a Jew engaged in merchandising met with disapproval. In Poland a person who engaged in commercial business was not held in high esteem. This does not mean that the Polish peasant and, even more so, the nobleman, had no knack for business. A fair was an important event in the life of a village, and not just because it provided a chance for socializing and amusement. The peasant also participated in the market as a seller. The nobleman too might have a passion for commercial transactions. He might trade in grain, lumber, or horses. He did not shrink from risky speculation and did not always fare poorly in such dealings, as can be seen clearly in descriptions of the life of the nobility. But, for both the peasant and the nobleman, business was a sideline, secondary, an offshoot of their basic economic activity, which was farming. The nobleman "played at business," but he saw it only as one of the aspects of farming. Business per se, business as an autonomous economic activity, was considered "base" and contemptible. Over the course of time, this attitude was passed on from the nobility to the intelligentsia, and it became a part of the Polish peasant's ethos as well.

But the Jew was not a farmer. A series of Polish sayings provide a sharp reminder of that censurable fact. The Jew was solely and exclusively a merchant or trader. In Poland business had been given over to the Jews and had become an expression of their caste status. At the same time, this was an extremely primitive form of business, employing methods possible only within the framework of a backward economy. The Russian saying "You don't cheat, you don't sell" (*Nie obmaniesh, nie prodash*) characterizes those methods to a tee. (That saying, by the way, was a purely Russian product and had nothing to do with Jews.) The small Jewish merchant, of course, played by the only rules possible under the given conditions. He met with disapproval both because he was given to an economic activity that was held in contempt and because he played by rules that were considered improper. It was another matter that those rules were in general usage among non-Jews as well.

It would be no exaggeration to say that the Polish people ascribed to Jews characteristics no different from those that the peoples of underdeveloped countries ascribe to all professional merchants, regardless of religion or origin. "Swindler," "slippery," "bloodsucker"—epithets of this sort are in common use in colonial countries and are applied to the local merchants, who are rarely Jewish. The Chinese merchants in Indonesia and Malaya are the object of widespread aversion and innumerable accusations, often not without some basis. American tradition has preserved the memory of the dishonest merchants of the colonial and early capitalist periods. What was said about the merchants and saloon keepers in the Wild West exceeds in severity all the accusations leveled at the Jews in Poland. A minuscule number of Jews, if any, were among those American merchants and saloon keepers.

However, in all primitive economic systems the image of the merchant is not painted solely in dark colors. There are brighter shades as well. The image can be said to have a markedly ambivalent emotional coloration. Despite the antipathy for Chinese merchants in Indonesia and Malaya, their role in the society is important and often authoritative. The same may be said, to an even greater degree, about the merchant and the saloon keeper in the American tradition. And it fully applied to the image of the Jew in Poland. The Jew was "wise," his opinion had to be taken seriously. In fact, the innkeeper was one of the recognized authorities in the traditional Polish village. We have already spoken a good deal about the positive role that the Jew played in the world of the manor.

Even though Polish folklore treated the Jews with ridicule and aversion, it also expressed its respect for the Jew's intelligence and his positive qualities. It is the same inconsistency we observed when examining the role of the *parch* and the *żydek*. By virtue of his economic functions the Jew was held in low esteem; but at the same time, and to a great extent for the same reasons, the same Jew would be treated as an authority and viewed positively. Like everything human, the relationship here was markedly ambivalent, full of contradictions.

It is my impression that fundamental research toward establishing the image of the Jew in the Polish popular mind will necessarily come to indicate this ambivalent nature. That ambivalence was undoubtedly not something static. In certain periods, negative assessments of the Jew would come to the fore and cast the positive into shadow. In other periods, the reverse would be true. But even in the periods of the most intense anti-Semitism, a certain duality in the assessments existed. During the German occupation it was not exceptional for a peasant to aid his Jewish neighbors because of his favorable opinion of them and of the role they had formerly played. In the light of various memoirs from the time of the occupation, it is clear that such purely social motives emerged along with moral, religious, or simply human ones.

III

We can treat here the question of the image of the Jew in Polish folklore only in very general terms. Our concern is to raise the issue itself and to initiate a project requiring great collective effort. We must also treat in similar fashion the image of the Jew in the popular conceptions of journalists, publicists, and political parties. Leaving the area of the folk arts, we now shift our attention to that of literature per se. The latter, however, attempts to influence the minds of the community at large, to form the views of the masses, and at the same time, to one degree or another is itself based on the views and images that have been accepted by the masses.

The image of the Jew encountered in Polish journalism and popular political writings after the beginning of the nineteenth century was, of course, an offshoot of the beliefs and images prevailing in one or another Polish milieu in a given period. In that respect, newspapers, brochures, and political leaflets all constitute an extremely valuable source of information. That material must, however, be treated with extreme caution. This applies to statements with strictly practical goals which influence the opinion of broader social groups. Statements of that type programmatically avoid objectivity; when constructing an image, they are indifferent to whether it is adequate or not. They put forward only certain factors, those especially useful in influencing mass opinion. The choice of those factors is determined not only by the store of knowledge in the person making a given statement but also, and primarily, by his personal convictions, opinions, and the practical goals he has set for himself. This is closely connected, however, with the attitudes and aspirations of certain larger social milieus. Thus, seen from every point of view, statements in the press and in popular publicist works are important material for grasping the image of the Jew in the mind of Polish society at large.

There is an enormous amount of such material. After the beginning of the nineteenth century, the Jewish question was one of the most-discussed issues in Polish journalism. In certain periods, especially in the twentieth century, it even seemed to be the most important issue of all. In the years preceding World War II, for a segment of the Polish press the Jewish question had become the central issue obscuring other issues of the time.

When analyzing statements made in the Polish press since the beginning of the nineteenth century, we find confirmation for the thesis we discussed earlier: the existence of two opposite ways of viewing the Jew in Poland, two contradictory concepts of his role. We shall define those concepts as the pessimistic and the optimistic. Those were political and journalistic concepts, neither of which was based on a conscientious analysis of well-established facts. Each concept made use of sloganized stereotypes, and each had a powerful emotional coloration.

There is no doubt that it was the pessimistic concept that appeared most frequently in the Polish press. The opposing, optimistic concept prevailed at certain times, for example in 1863 and during the positivist period. But in the twentieth century the more optimistic views were supplanted in the Polish press by a pessimistic conception of the Jew, and ultimately that pessimism reached the point of flagrant anti-Semitism and racism. This concept had been initiated by Staszic and Wincenty Krasiński; adopted by publicists like Jeleński or Jeske-Choiński in the second half of the nineteenth century; and later developed by writers and political activists like Dmowski, Niemojewski, Nowaczyński, Rolicki, and the entire school of the so-called national camp.

Here the image of the Jew is painted in dark colors. The Jew is an antisocial and anti-Polish creature, an alien element in Poland, not bound to Poland and injurious to it. For a long time, Polish journalists had connected those Jewish qualities with Jewish religious life and its ethos. The Talmud and Jewish "religious superstitions" were the source of the evil. Could they be eliminated? The pessimistic concept did not believe they could. And for that reason, the Jews must be kept separate from Poles, and the sphere of harmful Jewish activity should be limited by law and custom. Over time, as secularization progressed in the world of the Jews, the negative assessment of the Jew was no longer based on his religious views. The Jew was organically evil, evil per se, by the very nature of things. Niemojewski did not think that the evil Jew was the product of the Talmud—it was the Talmud that was the product of the evil Jew. Dmowski, the nationalist, saw a fundamental opposition between Polish and Jewish national aspirations. Toward the end of his life, Dmowski was clearly inclined toward a racist philosophy. In any case, a Jew was organically alien and organically hostile or injurious. We have already spoken of the role played by magic in all such thinking.

It is noteworthy that, especially in the early period, there were certain pessimistic attitudes even among those who must be considered optimistic. These people also thought that the Jews were alien, in any case different, and attributed to them many traits that were harmful to Poland. Moreover, like Staszic, they believed that those traits originated in the Talmud and the Jewish ethos. For example, in 1830 an essay entitled *Tu chazy czyli Rozmowa o Żydach* (A Conversation About Jews) by Stanisław Hoge was published in Warsaw. Taking the form of a dialogue between a Polish Christian and a Jewish convert, it advances the idea that the harmfulness of the Jews to Poland—the author has no doubt that they are harmful—is a problem that will be solved by itself when the Jews either become Christians or reject the Talmud and reform their beliefs. Hoge thus believed in a positive solution to the problem, which he reduced to the otherness of the Jewish ethos. In his view, the harmfulness of the Jews is the result of the development of historical events. However, a change is possible, and were it to occur, the Jews could become useful citizens.

Czacki and Łukasiński were at one in painting the picture of the Jews in dark colors. But they did not see the Jews solely in a pessimistic light and, more importantly, were convinced that their negative aspects were not organic in nature but historical, and so they could be eliminated. Orzeszkowa preached the same message, as did all positivist political writers.

An exceptional position was taken by Wawrzyniec Surowiecki. While acknowledging that Jews possessed socially negative traits, he thought those traits the product of Poland's entire historical development. The Jews in Poland had become what all of Poland had become. Their moral decline was an offshoot of what had befallen all the other elements of Polish society. Moreover, it should be noted in the Jews' favor that they preserved certain values that were lost in other milieus. Polemicizing against the theory that made the Jews the cause of the decline of Polish cities, Surowiecki wrote in "On the Decline of Cities and Industry in Poland" (*Works*, Turowski ed., Kraków, 1861, p. 139): "Because of the position in which our cities and their industries have found themselves for more than a century and a half, they inevitably had to deteriorate and decline without any other additional cause; and thus, even without the Jews, they would not have escaped that fate." And he adds (p. 140): "With the exception of a few of the more important cities where from time to time the magnates squandered their income, Poland owes the survival of trade and the crafts almost solely to the Jews."

It should be affirmed that in Poland a stance like Surowiecki's was entirely isolated. Even serious historians attributed the decline of Polish cities to the Jews, and to anti-Semitic journalists this was axiomatic.

Surowiecki had the courage to demonstrate that what was considered a cause was, in reality, an effect of a considerably broader and more general process. But he was completely forgotten in Poland and has only now begun to be discovered.

Surowiecki's views could not have penetrated into popular journalism; they were too rational an attempt at a sober-minded analysis of Poland's historical processes. Publicism, on the other hand, uses slogans, and its motivations are of a highly emotional nature. This factor is what made the pessimistic view prevail. Compared with the alternative, the pessimism was far better able to create an image of the Jew that was monolithic, appealing to the imagination of the masses and corresponding to their emotional state. In that image the Jew was evil, harmful, alien, and hostile. The journalists who took that view mythicized the Jew and could thereby, especially in times of panic, count on evoking a response from the broad masses of society. The optimistic view—even if we leave Surowiecki's sober rationalism out of account—required reflection and a deeper knowledge and analysis of the facts. And thus the voices of political figures like Dunin-Borkowski, Hołówko, and Wasilewski, who in the period between the wars attempted to approach the image of the Jew and the entire Jewish question in a rational manner, met with no echo.

IV

There is one field in which research on the image of the Jew in Polish collective consciousness can be especially fertile and, relatively speaking, poses no great difficulties. That field is literature. Undoubtedly, the image of the Jew as it appears in Polish literature was not necessarily common to all elements of Polish society. Literature always had a limited range of influence in Poland. It reached only certain segments of society. On the other hand, it attempted to depict all segments of society, and to include even those that as a rule did not constitute its readers. For our purposes, its value as a source of knowledge is immense. How is the Jew presented in Polish literature, how is his image refracted in the light of Polish writers' assessments and descriptions?

This is an enormous subject, one to which an entire book could be devoted. Jeske-Choiński wrote such a book, but it is without value. A 1937 book by Irena Butkiewicz examines Eliza Orzeszkowa's novels and short stories about Jews but it is limited to that narrow theme. Everything remains to be done. In the work at hand, we shall once again limit ourselves to raising the problem and to advancing certain points that can be of importance to future research.

Let us begin with the most general of statements. First, the Jew appears relatively often in Polish literature, which simply could not overlook his presence in Poland. Second, the attitude toward him is, most frequently, friendly and at times even warm and affectionate. In this respect, Polish literature represents a clear departure both from Polish folk arts and from Polish political journalism.

It also departs from the literature of other countries in which Jews formed a significant part of the population. Let us take Russian literature as an example. Russian writers rarely noted the Jew, and their attitude toward him when he was noticed was cool, even unfriendly. Jews are overlooked entirely by Pushkin, who, it is true, spent his life in the part of the Russian Empire where Jews were a rarity at that time. But Gogol, whose works to such a great extent revolve around Ukrainian themes, writes little about Jews and, as a rule, in a very unfriendly fashion. Jews do not appear in Turgenev's works (with the exception of a short story entitled "The Yid," which is so flagrantly unrealistic that it hardly can serve as an example of "reflecting the image of the Jew"). Jews are incidental figures in Dostoyevski, for example in *The Brothers Karamazov*, and are treated with aversion and contempt. As a journalist, Dostoyevski was openly anti-Semitic. There are no Jews in Tolstoy's work, although as a journalist he was vocal and unswerving in his condemnation of anti-Semitism and the pogroms. A Jewish woman is the heroine of one of Chekhov's stories and not a pleasant character. A calculating and subtle seductress, she corrupts a naive officer in order to avoid repaying a debt and does the same with his supposedly more experienced cousin. However, in his play *Ivanov* Chekhov treats a Jewish woman character with definite sympathy. Jewish characters appear in the works of certain of the lesser pre- and postrevolutionary Russian writers, but they are merely incidental background figures. It is only some Russian writers of Jewish descent, like Yushkievich and Ilya Ehrenburg, who deal with Jewish themes. And of them, only Yushkievich can be considered to portray Jewish life in Russia.

The case in Poland was entirely different. It is enough to acquaint oneself with Jan Winczakiewicz's excellent anthology *Izrael w poezji polskiej* (Israel in Polish Poetry [Paris, 1958]) to be struck both by the profusion of writing by Polish poets on Jews and by their frequently warm attitude. Polish poetry at its greatest created the image of Jankiel, who must be considered one of the central figures in *Pan Tadeusz*. No interpretation can diminish his part in that masterpiece. Mickiewicz assigned a fundamental role to that character, which was undoubtedly an expression of his views on the place of the Jews in Poland. Here let us also note that in *Wesele* (The Wedding), Stanisław Wyspiański assigned Rachela the role of unleashing the mystery. It is she who introduces the element of poetic vision that leads to the liberation of that "which is a dream in everyone's soul."

Polish poetry viewed the Jew from various angles. In his beautiful poem about a street book vendor, Władysław Syrokomla perceived one of the most important culture-creating functions of Polish Jews—that of disseminating the great values of Polish culture. Polish poetry lamented the sorrows of the Jews in the songs of Jan Kasprowicz and Wiktor Gomulicki, and it spoke of the Jews' patriotism, their bond to the country.

The pessimistic turn of political thought, ill disposed to the Jews, was not echoed in Polish poetry. In only one instance, in the work of one poet, can we encounter a negative attitude toward Jews and echoes of the anti-Semitic journalism of the time. That poem is Zygmunt Krasiński's *Nieboska komedia* (The Undivine Comedy), but it is important to add that the Jews in this play were converts, Jews who had broken with their past and were seeking entry into the non-Jewish world. In his aversion to such Jews, Krasiński is not so much following in his father's footsteps as he is expressing the mood and prejudice then prevailing in France toward *homines novi* from the world of the Jews and in certain Polish circles toward the Frankists. Those he portrays are ex-Jews. In his time, religious Jews had not yet emerged onto the political stage. In this case, Krasiński the aristocrat was disturbed not only by *homines novi* of Jewish origin, but by *homines novi* of any sort.

Be that as it may, Krasiński's stance was an exception. In Polish poetry the Jews are viewed favorably, even by such poets as Kasprowicz, who in daily life showed them no goodwill.

Let us make another statement that is undoubtedly true: in Polish poetry, the few exceptions aside, the Jew is viewed as a part of the Polish landscape, both spiritual and physical. The poets see him as he participates in Polish life, separately from the Jewish milieu. What do we know about Jankiel outside the Polish-Lithuanian context of Soplicowo? Very little. In fact, only that he engaged in "Jewish" professions and was the assistant rabbi in the neighboring town. In *Pan Tadeusz*, Jankiel is seen exclusively in his Polish aspect (we might say, his Soplicowo aspect). Jankiel was a self-sacrificing and ardent Polish patriot. On behalf of "the patriots" he carried out secret political missions and was suspected by the Russians of being a spy. He was a mediator in the feuds between supporters of two families of noble stock in *Pan Tadeusz*, the Soplicas and the Horeszkos; both sides respected him and valued his opinion. He was Father Robak's trusted confidant. He performed certain cultural services: he was a source of news from the larger world, and it was thanks to him that songs from various areas of Poland reached Lithuania. In Jankiel, Mickiewicz has indisputably grasped a number of the basic objective functions that had fallen to Polish Jews. But Mickiewicz entirely omitted Jankiel's Jewish world, just as he omitted the world of the peasants. The author intended *Pan Tadeusz* to be a "gentry saga," as the subtitle has it, and so, by the nature of things, the nongentry world could be seen only from the vantage point of the gentry and as part of the gentry world of Soplicowo. In comparison with Jankiel, the peasant in *Pan Tadeusz* is much more a background figure.

That separation of the Jew from the Jewish milieu prevails in nearly all of Polish poetry. The Jew is seen and evaluated from the Polish point of view. The most important motif is that of his Polish patriotism, his ability to display the highest Polish virtues. If the motif of self-sacrificing patriotism is not dealt with directly, the Jews' contribution to Polishness is depicted. So it is in Syrokomla's poem about the book vendor or in Zofia Bohdanowicz's beautiful poem "Szałdy-Bałdyrowski" about an itinerant Jewish peddler, a humble and unpretentious link between the out-of-the-way Lithuanian countryside and the great world symbolized by the Puls Apparel Company of Warsaw. Here, too, the poet grasps very well one of the culture-creating functions of the Jew; but she too presents him entirely apart from the Jewish milieu.

Leaving aside poetry written during World War II or relating to it, earlier Polish poetry more than once lamented or described the sufferings of the Jews. In Wacław Szymanowski's poem "O Żydzie Boruchu" (The Jew Boruch), the Jew was always the victim no matter what he did, and the same was true of the peasant. Here the sufferings of the Jew are one fragment in the suffering of all the lower classes, who are victims of the license taken by the nobility. But here, too, the Jew is seen as a part of the overall Polish landscape and not in the context of his own sociocultural community.

The great Polish drama *Sędziowie* (The Judges) by Wyspiański introduces the Jewish world independently of the non-Jewish world. But the Jewishness in that play is rather incidental. Wyspiański's imagination had been roused by an actual event concerning a Jewish inn. However, the play is universal in its problems and more classical than specifically Jewish.

But there were attempts in Polish poetry to catch an intrinsically Jewish atmosphere, especially a mystical religious one, and they bore fruit in beautiful poems by Juliusz Wiktor Gomulicki, Jan Kasprowicz, and Jerzy Liebert. There the Jew was presented as a Jew, shown in the light of his own feelings, beliefs, and aspirations. Those were the exceptions, however, and there were relatively few such works in Polish poetry.

It is noteworthy that the Polish poetry of later times completely overlooked, as did Polish prose as well, the changes that were occurring in Jewish life. They simply went unnoticed. They were not even noticed by Polish poets of Jewish origin who, like Tuwim, Słonimski, Wittlin, and Hemar, used Jewish themes and motifs in their work. In the way they looked at Jews and Jewish affairs, those poets did not differ fundamentally from other Polish poets. No doubt personal factors were much alive in their poetry. There was a note of bitterness about the anti-Semitism that denied them the right to call themselves Polish poets. But their basic approach was in accord with the general model prevailing among Polish poets. In his depiction of a "usurer manqué" who was enraptured by the charms of Polish literature to the point of ceasing to lend money Słonimski does not depart from the basic direction taken by earlier poets. In "Polish Flowers" Tuwim includes some fragments of a Jewish milieu in his description of a summer resort outside Łódź. It is a rare attempt in Polish poetry to get inside the world of the Polish Jews. But for all its authenticity, Tuwim's description of that little world is another Soplicowo, a reflection of Poland among the assimilating Jewish middle class. We do not find a reflection of the trends and aspirations that had come to life in that period in Jewish society in Poland. Like other Poles—and he was a Pole and a great Polish poet—Tuwim knew very little about those things, was only slightly interested in them, and saw them as more comical than serious.

If Polish poets of Jewish origin suffered an inward tragedy because of the Polish-Jewish conflict, it was a consequence of the general atmosphere prevailing in Poland at that time. In poets of an earlier day—Antoni Lange, Franciszka Hanna Arnsztajnowa, and Jan Mieczysławski, for example—that conflict was either absent from or only weakly reflected in their work. Those poets were "accepted" by the Polish world and could find in it places for themselves. Such conflict would occur only later, when poets of Jewish origin were refused their place in Polish literature. That was the source of their bitterness, sarcasm, and even cynicism toward themselves, their own position, and the world around them. This created works both beautiful and painful, but it provided no vehicle for bringing the image of the Jew and his reality into literature. It allowed only for introducing certain aspects of the Jewish question in Poland, and even that only in relation to Jews who had ceased to be Jews.

We leave aside here those poets who, while writing in Polish, identified with Jewishness. Naturally, these writers were reaching out for a broad range of Jewish subjects, but they constituted a group apart, one little known in the larger Polish community.

V

It is not poetry but prose that is of fundamental significance in fixing the image of one community in the mind of another. The novel and the short story can always serve as splendid sources of sociological material. Their very form and subject matter create possibilities that infinitely exceed those of poetry. And thus the problem of the Jew's image in Polish prose fiction will be of particular interest to us.

And here we will make the same statement that we made when discussing poetry. The Jew appears frequently in Polish prose and for the most part is treated sympathetically.

Polish literature has a good many "Jewish" novels and stories based on Jewish subjects and describing Jewish life, or certain aspects and fragments of it. They originate with Niemcewicz's *Lejbe and Siora*, that sentimental correspondence between a pair of noble-minded lovers who strive for knowledge and virtue; and they culminate in Orzeszkowa's novels and stories, with *Meir Ezofowicz* chief among them. A whole series of Jewish novels were penned by minor writers, to name but Marian Gawalewicz, Artur Gruszecki, and that spinner of yarns Klemens Junosza. Of these novels by minor writers, Gawalewicz's *Mechesi* (The Converts) is of special documentary significance, and we shall deal with that work separately. The Jewish stories by Konopnicka, Szymanowski, and Swiętochowski, among others, achieved great popularity. Mendel Gdański nearly became a symbol.

Certain plays could also be included here, such as Gabriela Zapolska's *Małka Szwarcenkopf*, certainly not her best work but one of great sociological interest.

As background figures, Jews are common in Polish prose. They appear rather often in the works of the prolific Polish writer Józef Ignacy Kraszewski (1812–87) and the playwright Józef Korzeniowski (1797–1863). They play an important role in the positivist writer Bołeslaw Prus's work and appear in Żeromski's. Jews were not overlooked by Maria Dąbrowska (1889–1965) either, whose "Żydówka-bądźzdrówka" had a great influence on the fate of her novel's heroes.[1] Jews appear casually in works by Władysław Reymont (who received the Nobel Prize in 1924 for his novel *Chłopi* [The Peasants]) and Stanisław Przybyszewski. Henryk Sienkiewicz and Wacław Berent were probably the only eminent Polish writers who bypassed Jews in their work.

What is the image of the Jew in those Jewish novels, to what degree does it reflect reality? We can at once call the informational value of Niemcewicz's novel into question. That work, a beautiful demonstration of the author's elevated sentiments and convictions, was weak in reflecting Jewish reality in Poland. One might hear in it some echoes of the Haskalah movement that had begun to reach Polish Jews in that period. But there is not much evidence that Niemcewicz knew anything about that movement, or if he did, that he understood its significance. *Lejbe and Siora* is a belated product of the Enlightenment's rationalistic notion that all problems of social life can be solved through education. Niemcewicz also applied that notion to the Jews, concerning himself very little with the actuality of Jewish life. This is probably the reason that his heroes appear so wooden, schematic, and unconvincing.

It would be wrong for us, however, to disregard the significance of Niemcewicz's novel. It originated a type in Polish literature: the young Jew seeking education and dedicating his life to the cause of helping his fellow Jews become good citizens and thereby serve Poland as a whole. Meir Ezofowicz's predecessor was none other than Lejbe, and echoes of Niemcewicz's novel can be found even in Gawalewicz's *The Converts*. The noble-minded hero of that work, though living under completely different conditions, has in himself some traces of the tradition of Lejbe and Meir.

Eliza Orzeszkowa provided a much fuller image of Jewish life in her novels and stories. She was interested in Jewish life, though her field of experience was a limited one. On the one hand, it was confined to her observations of the local Lithuanian ghettos, and on the other hand, it came through her friendship with people of the Jewish Polonized elite like Leopold Meyet, the Nussbaums, the Lewenthals, the Eigers, and others. In her Jewish friends Orzeszkowa was able to see the promise made by Meir Ezofowicz fulfilled. Those were people who came from the Jewish world: their grandfathers, and even their fathers, had been religious Jews. Orzeszkowa's friends represented the highest cultural level; they were good Poles, and served the Polish cause self-sacrificingly. Orzeszkowa could be certain of their friendship, and she was wholehearted in her relationship with them.

The views of these people on the Jewish question in Poland did not depart from those of Orzeszkowa herself. They were not contemptuous of their forefathers' past; they found precious values in it. But at the same time, they rejected that past as something that had seen its day and was now an impediment to progress. They had left the caste and were no longer able to return to it. Having rejected the caste for themselves, they wished to help others who were in the process of leaving it.

Meir Ezofowicz cannot be considered an attempt at faithfully reflecting the reality of a small-town Lithuanian or Polish ghetto. It is questionable whether it was even Orzeszkowa's intention to write a "realistic" novel. The Ezofowiczes' family situation is itself exceptional. How many Jewish families in Poland had traditions like theirs? Historically speaking, the Karaite theme in the novel seems very unconvincing. Of Orzeszkowa's Jewish novels, *Eli Makower*, an inferior work, is more true to life than *Meir Ezofowicz*. Parenthetically we might add that the depiction of the Bohatyrowiczes, for example, is equally unrealistic.

There are, however, certain elements of realism even in *Meir Ezofowicz*. Orzeszkowa was able to capture the early struggle for the secularization of Jewish life in Poland. She was also able to grasp the meaning of the burgeoning aspirations of the younger generation. A great deal of what she wrote about the constant conflict between the *kahal* authorities and the rabbinate was right on the mark. In that respect she had given an image of Jewish life in Poland that was fuller and closer to reality than any in Polish literature.

That image became a model by which the Jews of Poland were perceived for many years. But even by Orzeszkowa's time fundamental departures from that image had begun to occur in the world of the Jews. Those changes were most pronounced in the large cities of the Congress Kingdom but were also observable in Lithuanian small-town ghettos. Even during Orzeszkowa's lifetime, at the end of the nineteenth and the beginning of the twentieth centuries, not much remained of the ghetto of Meir Ezofowicz. Those changes did not escape her attention. She was pained by the progress of Russification among the Lithuanian Jews, not realizing that, given the existing conditions, Russification was the only way to oppose the caste and to leave it. She took consolation in the progressing Polonization of the Jews in Poland proper, though she could not have foreseen that this Polonization was only a preliminary phase in the development of broader national emancipationist aspirations among Jews.

The number of novels and longer stories with Jewish themes increased toward the end of the nineteenth century. Of those authors only one, Klemens Junosza, attempted to render an image of the life of the Jewish masses in Poland. But Junosza's tales maintain the tone and nature of a nobleman's facetious yarn. He sees the comedy in Jews, and his portrayal of them adheres to the traditional patterns of the past. The Jews are "bloodsuckers," but at the same time they are vital to the landowning nobleman, who could not manage without them. Junosza's attitude toward Jews is neither friendly nor hostile; it is instead one of amusement. Junosza is struck by the Jew's comicality, a result of the disparity between the nobles' way of life and the Jews'.

Of much more importance than Junosza's yarns and Gruszecki's markedly anti-Semitic novels was Gawalewicz's lengthy novel *Mechesi* (The Converts). It attempts to portray the life of a certain Jewish milieu, that of the wealthy plutocracy who were abandoning the caste and striving to assimilate to the nobility and the aristocracy. Gawalewicz's novel—other novels with similar subject matter appeared in Poland around the turn of the twentieth century—reflects the change that was occurring in all Polish life and, in particular, in certain Jewish milieus.

Gawalewicz accurately captured the role of the Jews in the formation of the new urban plutocracy and well-to-do middle class in Poland. The action was, rightly, set in Warsaw, which was becoming the most important Polish center of industry, trade, and banking. Bound closely to Warsaw, he had the opportunity to observe the life of the Warsaw plutocracy directly, and he knew how to look. His novel is an invaluable document on the process of assimilation of the Jewish plutocracy at the end of the nineteenth century.

Gawalewicz did not fail to notice that the model that the wealthy Jewish middle class strove to adopt was that of the Polish aristocracy. And it was not the best elements of that model that were being adopted but the worst. Senseless luxury, living beyond one's means, snobbery, pretentiousness, arrogance—all that was zealously aped by the Jewish plutocracy. The ideal was to marry into an aristocratic or pseudoaristocratic family in straitened circumstances. The main plot of *The Converts* concerns such a marriage.

Gawalewicz's novel cannot be considered anti-Semitic. If the author is censuring the Jewish plutocracy, he is no less sharp in criticizing the Polish aristocracy or pseudoaristocracy. Moreover, it is in the Jewish milieu that he finds many types to praise, the hero, for example. The positive characters are precisely those who resist pressure from the world around them, seek their own way, and desire to create real values. There are some echoes of *Meir Ezofowicz* here but transposed to a completely different arena.

There can be no doubt that the novels of Orzeszkowa and Gawalewicz attempted to show the reader authentic fragments of Jewish life. They were, however, only fragments. In Orzeszkowa's work the fragments are stylized and adapted to that great writer's ideological premises. Gawalewicz's book presents a fragment that, properly speaking, is already outside the compass of Jewish actuality. The world he describes is not even Jewish in the religion it professes. That world's attitude toward Jewishness is expressed by its striving to cut itself off from Jewishness, to erase all traces of the past—if that were possible. This is a world of those who fled the caste, not of those who simply left it. Seen from that point of view, Gawalewicz's novel is a first-rate document, but it cannot serve as an illustration of Jewish life in Poland.

Like Polish poetry, the "Jewish" novel, both Orzeszkowa's and Gawalewicz's, looks at the Jews from the aspect of their participation in Polish life, and from a purely Polish point of view. No doubt in those novels the Jew is more than just a detail of the Polish landscape. But he is not seen as part of a vital community, one facing problems of its own and attempting to resolve them. The very existence of such problems found only the weakest reflection in Polish literature's Jewish novels. It is characteristic that even the factors of Jewish life that had profoundly universal aspects were reduced to the level of Polish patriotism or of a quite naive social utilitarianism. An example is the treatment of mixed marriage and its attendant conflicts in Gawalewicz's novel. Those were subjects with which the author was unable to cope. He could not transcend the provincialism of the Warsaw of his day.

VI

But Jews and Jewish motifs appeared in many Polish novels and stories whose themes and assumptions had nothing to do with Jews. This aspect of Polish literature, quantitatively the largest and qualitatively the most important, deserves close attention.

As we have indicated, Jewish figures appear frequently in Polish fiction. And that is understandable. In one way or another, Jews were a constant presence in various situations of Polish life, and naturally that presence could not be overlooked by the novel, the novella, or the short story.

The Jew could not be overlooked in a novel about landowners or, for that matter, in any novel connected to some extent with the world of the nobility. The same may be said of works that took peasant life as their subject matter. In both types of fiction, the Jew is depicted primarily as an innkeeper, a tavern keeper, a shopkeeper, an itinerant peddler or craftsman, and sometimes, as in Prus's *Placówka* (The Outpost), as an important merchant and even the squire's brother-in-law. Most frequently, however, the Jewish characters are reduced to their traditional functions in the countryside, as is true of *The Outpost*.

Here the Jew is portrayed in keeping with the traditional image of the Jew in the Polish village. Even as a background character, he plays an important role in the life of the manor house, the peasant hut, and even the presbytery. The inn is depicted quite rightly, as the center of important events in village life. Polish writers frequently portray the typical ambivalence felt toward Jews: the Jew is simultaneously held in contempt and considered someone whose opinion carries great weight. Polish prose writers frequently lay great stress on the positive aspects of the Jew's character. This applies to Prus and especially to Maria Dąbrowska, with her warmth in depicting a few Jewish figures from the village and from the town Kaliniec (Kalisz) in her novel *Noce i dnie* (Nights and Days). The negative aspects of the character of rural Jews are not concealed either. The innkeeper in *The Outpost* is not an attractive figure, but there are many other unattractive figures in Prus's novella.

It is not our task to discuss in detail all the instances in which Jews appear in Polish fiction dealing with village life. One clear generalization can be made, however: the Jew is always viewed from the Polish point of view—no matter whether the nobleman's or the peasant's—and is always a fragment of or a supplement to a picture of life in the Polish community. It can be said that, as a rule, he is an addition to the characters, issues, and situations described. He is a necessary addition, one that cannot be omitted, but one that is entirely subordinate to the Polish community. The life of a rural Jew within his own community is not portrayed. He is always viewed against the background of Polish life; we know nothing about his own affairs, expectations, aspirations.

To no less an extent, the same may be said of those works of Polish fiction that took their material from city life. In the novels and stories of the earlier period, the urban Jew is in fact the old village Jew transposed to the city and town. He performs similar economic functions, except that the dimension and scope of his activities are often considerably greater than those of the village Jew. Toward the end of the nineteenth century, the great Jewish banker appears on the scene, who, though breaking socially and culturally with the traditions of the village moneylender and innkeeper, is, economically, their continuation. Forms change, but the content remains comparable, though the scale of the activity undergoes a tremendous increase.

However, at the end of the nineteenth century, the Polish novel also begins to register a new type of Jew. Writers could not fail to notice that ever-larger numbers of Jews who had left the caste were now participating in the ranks of the Polish intelligentsia. And since the urban intelligentsia had increasingly begun to provide themes for literature, the Jewish intellectual had to assume a place of importance in the overall image of the Polish Jew.

Frequently such characters are physicians. So it is, for example, in Prus's *Lalka* (The Doll) and Żeromski's *Ludzie bezdomni* (The Homeless). But whereas for Żeromski that character is rather incidental, for Prus Dr. Szuman is a major figure in the novel. From the societal point of view, both doctors have much in common. Both have left the world of the Jews behind and are entering, or attempting to enter, a Polish milieu. Neither is having an easy time of it. They encounter problems and opposition, they drag their past along behind them, and they are constantly in the shadow of the caste. In Prus's novel this leads to a skeptical and rationalistic attitude on the part of the character, making him an eccentric, a recluse; in Żeromski it leads to cynicism. Żeromski's Jewish doctor is the counterpart of a doctor who has risen out of the lower classes. His fate and that of Judym reflect similar social conditioning. He seems to be like Żeromski's Judym but with the difference that he is divested of Judym's idealism; he is embittered and takes a cynical view of people and the world. Szuman has something of Judym's idealism, and something of the romanticism of Prus's Wokulski; yet in him they are imbued with bitterness, overrationalized, and tainted by an awareness of the dimensions of human madness.

A new type of Jewish character appears in Maria Dąbrowska's work—the student, the socialist, the political activist. Although such characters had already appeared in the works of some Polish writers, for example Zapolska's *Zaszumi las* (The Rustling Woods), they had been purely incidental characters, mere sketches. The figure in Dąbrowska is also incidental but it is full of expression. Moreover, this character does not come out of nowhere; he has his own social background and is seen not only from a Polish angle but also from within his own tragedy. Dąbrowska had met with prototypes of her hero in real life, and several were friends of hers. One senses this clearly in her novel.

Dąbrowska accomplished her artistic intentions within the limits she had set for herself. She brought Jews into her novel and gave them a certain social coloration, but her prime intention was not to write about Jews. The same, of course, can be said of Prus and Żeromski. When introducing Jews into their works, these authors portrayed them as the finished products of certain social and cultural processes, depicted them against a Polish background, and wanted them to be seen from the Polish perspective. There was in it a certain one-sidedness, for which the writers cannot be blamed. The one-sidedness was inevitable, given the very assumptions of the given works.

In all these works the Jew is part of the overall Polish landscape. Only rare attempts were made, by Dąbrowska and Prus, to portray him also from the point of view of the Jewish community—the old community if he had abandoned it, or the existing one if he still belonged to it. In *The Doll*, old Szlagbaum and Wokulski have an interesting conversation about Jewish pastimes and parlor games, whose intellectual character Wokulski finds striking. That small fragment of the novel is an attempt at showing the Jew from "within," but it is only a small fragment.

Judging by Polish fiction, one could determine beyond any question: that there were Jews in Poland, that they constituted a numerous community, that they performed certain economic functions that were sometimes harmful to society but were also sometimes helpful, that there were good people among them though there was no lack of bad ones, that there were many who deserved the greatest goodwill, that a considerable portion of them strove to identify with Poles, and that many were truly good Poles. But can Polish fiction aid us in obtaining a fuller image of Jewish society in Poland as it really existed, an image of its affairs and aspirations, and of the changes that were occurring in it? That is highly doubtful. In fact, Polish fiction spoke no more of Jewish society in

Poland than it did of any of the other national communities, representatives of which appear sporadically. Russians did appear in Polish fiction, but even in Żeromski they too were treated apart from their national milieu. The same may be said of Germans and Frenchmen, not to mention Ukrainians, Belorussians, or Lithuanians. They all appear as elements of the Polish landscape, they are seen in connection with Polish affairs and from a Polish point of view. While a reflection of the reality of Napoleon's France does somehow penetrate *War and Peace*, the same cannot be said of Żeromski's *Popioły* (Ashes).

The great emancipationist movements that had begun to emerge among Jews at the beginning of the twentieth century found no reflection in the Polish novel, not even indirectly. If anything was noted about them, it was given a false interpretation, one that was sometimes sheer fantasy. An example is Gruszecki's rather bad novel *Litwackie mrowie* (A Mob of Litwaks). There is no doubt that Polish writers knew very little about Jews as Jews and were not much interested in them. What interested them was the Jews in relation to Polish affairs and aspirations, Jews against the background of Polish life.

There was a serious nearsightedness here. In the end, even Jewish internal affairs could not be a matter of indifference to Poland. On the contrary, they had an influence on the whole course of Polish life. The same is true of the affairs and aspirations of the Ukrainians, Belorussians, and Lithuanians that also met with indifference and misunderstanding. In that respect, Polish literature only reflected the entire society's attitude toward the lives of those non-Polish national groups with whose fate the history of the Polish nation was bound up. Very little was known about those groups in Poland, and there was no desire to know more. And what was considered knowledge had little in common with the truth.

It must be said that Polish life found a relatively better reflection in Jewish fiction. We can take two Jewish novels, Joseph Opatoshu's *Yidn in di poylishe velder* (In the Polish Woods) and Sholem Asch's *Warsaw*, as examples. In these works there is much misunderstanding and mistaken interpretation of certain phenomena and processes of Polish life. As a whole, however, they contain incomparably more solid knowledge of Polish life and a greater understanding of it than can be found of Jewish life in Polish literature.

It is only very late, in the period between the two wars, that we find certain attempts to approach Jewish life in Poland. *Wiadomości Literackie* initiated a series of reports on Polish Jews, the most important of which were written by Wanda Melcer.

The exoticism of the subject was the decisive factor. A "dark continent" had been discovered in Poland, and Wanda Melcer's articles and others like them were a pendant to the literature of exotic travel, popular for centuries in all the countries of Western civilization. Now one could travel to a mysterious and exotic world without leaving the borders of Poland. Moreover, it was a world of people who were much talked about.

Undoubtedly, these articles, though by the nature of things written in haste and colored by journalistic interpretations, contained many accurate observations. Even so, they resembled descriptions of the colonial countries given by various European and American travelers. Those accounts dealt with the exotic, which appealed to the imagination of the author and the curiosity of the reader. But, most frequently, they overlooked the most important things (and still do today): the enormous social and cultural changes that had begun to occur in the colonial countries. Reading many of those accounts, some written relatively recently, one cannot understand the origin and power of that colossal revolution that has now embraced the "exotic" lands of Africa, Asia, and South America. The assumptions, the origins, the conditioning factors of that revolution went unnoticed, though they must have existed at the time. The writers' attention was focused exclusively on the exotic.

The same can be said of Polish journalism reporting on the dark continent of Jewishness. It overlooked the most important things, even though they were pronounced at the time and must have intruded themselves on the observer's attention at every step.

Thus we must be clear in saying that the image of the Jew as it emerged in Polish literature was markedly stereotyped, fragmentary, and inadequate. As a rule, that image was created apart from the entirety of the affairs, life, and aspirations of the Jewish community in Poland; Jewish life was treated as a fragment of purely Polish affairs and solely in relation to them.

There is, however, a striking disparity between literature and political journalism. That disparity, mild in some periods, was particularly striking after the beginning of the twentieth century. Political journalism became increasingly anti-Jewish in tone, culminating in a wave of prewar anti-Semitism. The hostility of journalism toward the Jews found a relatively faint reflection in literature. There was no anti-Semitism in Polish poetry, and in prose it appeared only in inferior writers like Gruszecki. In their journalism some writers succumbed to the anti-Semitic mood. This was true of Świętochowski at one time, and of Niemojewski and Nowaczyński as well. In the latter two this was more an extravagance of temperament. In the best Polish prose, the attitude toward Jews was not hostile, sometimes friendly, and in the case of both Orzeszkowa and Dąbrowska, very warm.

However, authentic Jewish life in Poland has found no reflection either in journalism or in literature. Until the end of their existence on Polish soil, the life of the Jews was a terra incognita. Objectively speaking, it could easily have been studied. In a few instances it was studied by men of science, mostly Jewish. On the whole, however, in Polish society the knowledge of the Jewish world was astonishingly minuscule, fragmentary, and, most frequently, distorted. That the knowledge of the world of the other non-Polish groups living within the Polish state was no better was small consolation indeed.

In the Service of Polish Culture

I

In his *Wspomnienia z Polesia, Wołynia i Litwy* (Memoirs of Polesie, Volhynia, and Lithuania), Józef Ignacy Kraszewski writes that, in the years of his youth, a landowner who was hiring a Jew as a tavern keeper would mention that, along with various other duties, the Jew was to inform him of any news of the world that he might hear. A variety of sources belonging to the world of the nobility and its mores confirms Kraszewski's statement. In the nobles' tradition the Jew was seen as particularly well informed, an unerring source of quickly spreading information. In Poland there was an expression the "Jewish mail." And as Sienkiewicz's Pan Zagłoba said, when a Jew sneezes by the Warta River, the *żydeks* in Lithuania answer "God bless you" a minute later. In *Pan Tadeusz* as well, Jankiel is an important source of information that, as he himself asserts, he receives from other *żydeks*.

The "knowing"—even more than that, the "all-knowing"—Jew became part of the image of the Polish Jew as a person (it also entered the image of the Jew in other countries as well), and remained a part of it almost to our day. The form and coloring of that "all-knowingness" underwent changes but the substance remained the same. It was generally accepted that Jews were always particularly well informed and received news from all over. In his story "Karabela z Meschedu" (The Scimitar from Mesched), Ksawery Pruszyński describes how his hero, a Jewish antiquary, keeps up relations with his fellow Jews throughout the world, receiving detailed information from them about antiquarian events. That was a specialized type of information, but the function was the same. That, too, was the traditional "Jewish mail."

Let us not overestimate the objective value of that Jewish mail. Its information was not as precise as that of the great information bureaus of today (and quite a few things could be said about the accuracy of the latter). But still, in the conditions of the time, it was information, and sometimes the only source of news about events occurring in the larger world.

We must take a basic fact into account: after the middle of the seventeenth century Polish society to an increasing degree became transformed into a number of local groups that were very isolated from each other. The nobleman was not inclined to travel distances. He was a homebody and proud of it. His interests were concentrated on his farm. Now and then, mainly as a young man, he would spend some time at the court of a magnate. Later on, his contacts with a somewhat larger world would be reduced to meetings of neighbors, regional councils, religious celebrations, and fairs. He seldom traveled farther than that. His reality was enclosed within the narrow confines of a small local area. The printed word seldom reached him; a prayer book, an almanac, and a dream book were sufficient. That situation underwent no great change even during the reign of King Stanisław. The nobles were, in the main, relatively mildly affected by the great changes. After Poland's loss of independence, the nobles became even more homebound. The former regional councils, a factor in creating somewhat broader contacts, ceased to exist. As late as Prus's *Kroniki* (Chronicles) one still encounters the type of provincial squire who ventures a journey to Warsaw and feels lost in the turmoil of the great capital (not so very great then).

The peasant's world was narrower still. It came down to his relations with family and neighbors and did not exceed the boundaries of his native village. It was only fairs and *odpusty* that increased his scope of contact somewhat beyond that of family and neighbors.[1] Considerably later, compulsory military service in the armies of the partitioning powers brought the young peasant to distant and unknown lands. Military service, and the mass emigrations somewhat later on, caused a breach in the Polish peasant's mentality.

A lack of mobility was characteristic of traditional Polish society, for both the lord and the peasant. Hence, it was isolated from the larger world and deprived of any information about it. In the peasant world, only itinerant beggars, going from one place of pilgrimage to another, offered an example of a certain mobility. They were a link with the outside world and a source of news. That, however, was specialized news, limited to matters of pilgrimage and religion, and rarely contained reports of greater latitude. Still, without those itinerant beggars, the Polish countryside would have been even more isolated than it was.

In general, the Jews were the most important physically mobile element in Poland. Obviously, one should not exaggerate this. A huge number of the Jews in Poland led the same sort of sedentary and nonmobile life as the bulk of Poles. But a relatively large number of Jews were mobile and had a strong connection with the rest of the Jewish masses. Moreover, their connection with non-Jewish society was also strong.

One who is engaged in trade has to be on the move, even if his business is a penny-ante one—or especially if it is. The itinerant Jewish peddler was a familiar figure in Poland almost until recent times. It is interesting that many Polish Jews who in the course of time emigrated to America attempted to work there, too, as itinerant peddlers. But in America they encountered strong competition from other immigrants from equally business-oriented communities, especially Italians and Greeks. In time that itinerant peddling grew into the great mail-order houses that were to play such an enormous role in the American distribution system. Jews from Poland had a certain part in that. In Poland itself, itinerant business, remaining on the level of primitive peddling, was an expressly Jewish domain, and non-Jews were but modestly represented in it.

Physical mobility allows one to come to know other people and their affairs, to establish contacts, and to obtain information. In trade, this is particularly important. A merchant who does not know the world, who does not acquire information about it, is doomed to failure. The very type of activity they pursued predestined the Jews to seek out and distribute information. It was not a matter of chance that over the course of time they came to play so big a role in two professions (and not only in Poland): that of the traveling commercial agent (traveling salesman), and that of the journalist. Both professions grew from the same soil: the need for physical mobility, and the need to acquire and distribute information. In the Anglo-Saxon countries, where business was considered an occupation worthy of the highest respect and was not relegated to a despised caste, the professions of traveling salesman and journalist have not become a domain of the Jews. That the Jews readily took to journalism in America is another matter. Two names, Pulitzer and Lippmann, attest to their contribution to the American press.

Alongside the itinerant Jewish peddler, the itinerant Jewish tradesman was also a common phenomenon in Poland. He too was an element of physical mobility and a source of information. He always had some news, he'd always heard something. And he was talkative. Silence didn't win customers.

In brief, the Jews in Poland became an instrument for spreading news and thereby were a positive factor in creating certain, albeit indirect, interpersonal contacts. In a world made up of isolated local societies, such a function performed by Jews was socially of particular importance.

It was primarily the nobleman who made use of the Jewish mail. From it he learned of political events, wars, happenings in Warsaw, economic developments. In a certain, though no doubt very incomplete, way this bound him with the rest of the country and reduced his isolation. This was a modest substitute for other contacts; but without it the consequences of the nobles' extreme attachment to home would have been even more grave.

The peasant village also made use of the Jewish mail. Echoes of the distant world, some information about events, some new experiences, reached the peasant by the way of the inn and through the itinerant peddler or tradesman. That was an important supplement to those contacts with the world that were brought by wandering beggars.

II

But the Jewish mail was only an adjunct to the basic function of the merchant or itinerant tradesman—the distribution of goods and economic services. Poland's distribution system was always in lamentable condition, a reflection of the country's economy. Even during the twenty years between the wars, it was still primitive. And even today it is a far cry from the models that are considered the norms in highly industrialized countries. Polish society's contempt for nonagricultural professions, the nobles' distaste for "weights and measures," had a serious influence on that state of affairs. Surowiecki was undoubtedly correct in maintaining that it was to the Jews that Poland owed the survival of what was left of trade and handicraft.

And the task of that scanty trade was to distribute economic goods and services, a task poorly done. The goods and services were not great in number, their selection was often absurd from a sensible economic point of view, and their distribution was very irregular. As a market, the peasant village was disproportionately smaller than the wealthy countryside of the landowners. Yet there was a peasant market. Even during the period of villein service, the peasants would buy something from itinerant peddlers, and they attended fairs readily and in large numbers.

Over the course of time the peasant's share as a buyer kept increasing, while the manor's share gradually decreased. Goods became more varied and were adapted to more diverse and refined needs on the part of consumers. In the second half of the nineteenth century, the Jewish peddler and itinerant merchant became channels through which machine-made products reached the countryside. In that way, the countryside came to know muslin produced in Lodz and even soap made by the Puls Company in Warsaw.

But every item of merchandise has two sides to it: it is both an economic good and also a value of certain social and cultural significance. A piece of muslin from Lodz bought by a village housewife introduced into her life new extraeconomic values that had wide-ranging impact. This is a question of both a new fashion coming to the village and a new need to adapt to the customs of the world beyond the village. The American experience shows clearly to what degree a mass distribution system for economic goods has influenced the fundamental social transformation of the entire nation, rooting its democratic attitudes even deeper.

Lovers of "folk ways" lamented that muslin was displacing the former peasant garb and held the "greedy" Jewish merchants responsible. Both the regrets and the accusations were ridiculous. Muslin was better adapted to the changes taking place in the village and, for its own part, helped facilitate those changes. Along with the muslin, the peasant was accepting, albeit timidly and slowly, a new way of life, one that broke with the past but was infinitely better suited to the new conditions. It is another matter that—as we shall have occasion to mention later—the Jews also had some influence on the development of Polish folk dress.

As it was throughout the world so it was in Poland: the merchant became an instrument of deep social and cultural change. Needless to say, in this he was not guided by idealistic considerations. The motive of his activity was profit. The accusation often leveled at Jewish merchants was that they were motivated by the prosaic considerations of profit. Such accusations were possible only in a country suffering from total atrophy of the economic sense. If the great founders of the American economy had not operated on the profit motive (and how they operated!), the United States would not be the country it is today, economically and socially. People, each of whom was motivated by the desire for profit, were at the same time the bearers of enormous social, economic, cultural, and political change whose consequences are to be seen at every step in America.

The Jewish merchant in Poland was not an idealist when performing his economic functions and did not think of himself as carrying out some mission. His desire was for profit. In the vast number of cases that was a paltry profit, just as Jewish trade was for the most part a paltry affair. Given Polish conditions, it could not have been otherwise. Nevertheless, Jewish trade was an agent of important and far-reaching changes.

This was not because specifically Jewish business was involved. It was because it was any business at all. In other countries, analogous functions were performed by non-Jews. In Poland only the Jews could perform them. And they performed them as well as they could, as well as conditions permitted. Sometimes they did a better, sometimes a worse job. They had to adapt to reality.

The Jews in Poland took over the distribution system, for that was what had been given to them. By engaging in that work, they fulfilled a great historical task. They were better prepared for it than others because other roads were closed to them, and they had to do what they could under the circumstances.

Did they contribute anything specific to Polish commerce, anything characteristic of themselves? Probably not a great deal. What was said about Jewish business in Poland is identical with what is said in Indonesia or Burma today about Chinese business. The sole difference is that the Chinese merchants are infinitely better organized than the Jews were, more acquisitive and monopolistic in intent. The Jewish merchant in Poland was no different from any other merchant who functioned under similar economic and cultural conditions.

There may, however, have been certain specific elements that Jews contributed to the Polish system of distribution and exchange. Jews had preserved certain traditional methods in the area of credit that they had brought with them from Western Europe. Jewish moneylenders were successful because they were more efficient than others (and Poland never lacked non-Jewish moneylenders) and because they were cheaper. Numerous historical sources support this point. In his extremely interesting *Pamiętniki* (Memoirs), Stanisław Stempowski quotes his father, who thought quite well of Jewish moneylenders. Stempowski's father "recalled warmly old Perla Makower . . . , who . . . would loan [Stempowski's father] a hundred roubles and more to pay for the harvest, charging him only 18 percent whereas the others took 48." The Polish banks that existed later on—the work of people like Kronenberg, Wawelberg, and Natanson—were an outstanding contribution to the modernization of Poland's credit system, especially in improving its efficiency.

One Jewish contribution to commerce in Poland deserves special attention. The book trade became a Jewish specialty, as it did in many other countries. The Jews were the people of the book. There was no period in history when the production of Jewish books—in Hebrew and later in Yiddish—ever came to a standstill. Venice and Amsterdam, Vienna and Prague, Lublin and Wilno, not to mention dozens of other cities, were great centers of Jewish publishing and printing activity. The selling of books naturally went hand in hand with all that. And not only Jewish books. The itinerant Jewish peddler in Poland always had some Polish books in his pack. Most often they were almanacs and dream books—this was what the market demanded. But in the course of time other books appeared as well. After all, Mickiewicz mentions the Jew who smuggled volumes of his works into Lithuania. Syrokomla, in his figure of the Wilno street bookseller, offers further evidence.

Great Polish booksellers of Jewish origin are a tradition that reaches from Glucksberg to Jacob Mortkowicz. Jacob Shatzky, a historian of Jewish Warsaw, wrote a beautiful essay on the Jewish booksellers in that city. The Polish book world is greatly indebted to them. No doubt, they were looking for profit, but there was more to it than that. If they had not sought profit, Polish book and publishing activity, small as it was, would have been even worse off.

And so, Jewish commerce, wittingly or not, fulfilled great historic tasks. To some extent, it reduced or overcame the isolation of local groups, created broader interpersonal contacts, and distributed certain values that were more than just material. By virtue of their economic functions, the Polish Jews played the role of connective tissue in the Polish organism. No one else was better suited for it. And in that sense, they performed an important task for Polish culture. As we have already indicated, because of their economic functions the Jews had an interest in a state government that was strong and efficient. To accuse them of anarchistic or antistate tendencies is absurd. There was a certain grain of truth in the accusation leveled at the Jews (e.g., by Adam Skierko, *Les Juifs et la question polonaise* [Paris, 1919]) that, in the time after the partitions, they gravitated toward the partitioning powers and were indifferent to Poland's national interests. But were the Jews, in this, any different from those large elements in Polish society that constantly preached the slogans of triloyalism? And for similar reasons. Why should the Jews be more Polish than the die-hard Lithuanian conservatives, for example? As a community that was economically active and that engaged in all aspects of exchange, the Jews always had an interest in a cohesive state organization and, within their means, tried to consolidate it. That the Jews produced many outstanding revolutionaries does not alter this thesis. They also produced many self-sacrificing fighters for Poland's independence.

III

Certain aspects of what we have just discussed in general terms are worth dwelling on further. Let us begin with the following question: Did Jews—merchants, peddlers, middlemen, small tradesmen—have any creative cultural influence on Polish folklore?

Given the current level of research little can be said with certainty. There are, however, indications that the Jews did play just such a creative cultural role.

Let us take an example. In the 1920s a new type of apron appeared in the Hucul villages lying within the Polish borders. It departed from the traditional design in that it had a weave of gold or silver thread. It was adopted very quickly, mostly for wear on festive occasions. The traditional garb of the Hucul woman underwent a change. Whether this was an improvement from the aesthetic point of view is doubtful, but the Hucul women liked the new aprons. In addition, they were cheap because they were produced in factories. Though they were based on the traditional design, they in fact departed greatly from it. The introduction and distribution of that new apron were the work of local Jewish merchants, who in this manner contributed to a new "fashion" in traditional Hucul dress.

Was that an isolated case? Most likely not. We know that folk dress is not static but undergoes numerous transformations and comes under the sway of "fashion." Such fashions are not at all of folk origin. On the contrary, their sources are outside the world of the folk. Łowicz peasant costume and the uniform of the papal Swiss Guard, mountaineer dress of the Tatry area and the uniforms of the Hungarian hussars are classic examples. Many others could be cited, at least in those cases where the genealogy of the innovation is known. It would have been an odd thing if a local tailor, who most often was Jewish, did not play some role in creating those fashions and in establishing those designs. And the local merchant, the supplier of various clothing accessories, must also have played some role in it. Painful as this might be for many "folklorists," there is every indication that the Jews had a considerable part in the development of folk dress in Poland.

But their influence was not limited to dress. We know that the Jews played a basic role in the wide acceptance and distribution of the paper cutouts from the town of Łowicz, and that in certain districts of Poland folk furniture owed quite a bit to Jewish carpenters. In a valuable work on Kraków's folk jewelry, Tadeusz Seweryn clearly determined the "Jewish" character of that branch of folk art. The principal makers of that sort of jewelry were mostly Kraków Jews who had descended from the old goldsmiths. Seweryn mentions by name a series of prominent Jewish manufacturers of folk jewelry in Kraków and writes of some with great appreciation. It would be futile to debate which were the "Jewish" and which the "Polish folk" elements in that jewelry. The original designs were most likely found somewhere far from Poland, but there is no question that the Jewish craftsman played a role in that branch of Polish folk art.

Did the Jews have any part in the development of Polish folk music, and, if so, what? It is an irrefutable fact that artists of Jewish origin constitute an important chapter in the history of Polish musical culture. The list of names is impressive. But what about folk music?

The historians of Polish music have very little to say on these matters. Only Sowiński provides a few indications. But there is no question that Jews were well represented among the musicians who played at the inns during parties or at celebrations or other fetes in the villages. Roving bands of Jewish musicians were a counterpart to the itinerant tradesman so characteristic of Polish Jews. Jan Piotr Norblin de la Gourdaine, the great illustrator of Polish late-eighteenth-century customs,[2] provides us with a splendid image of such a village band of Jewish musicians. They were a common phenomenon during his time, as well as during Chopin's. It was probably from musicians of that sort that Prince Karol Radziwiłł formed his famous Jewish orchestra, which he had dress in Turkish attire. Reiss states that this orchestra was peerless in its performances of polonaises and other Polish dances. Citing Maurycy Karasowski, Sowiński speaks of a Jew in Berdyczów who played an unknown and very interesting polonaise on his clarinet. He had supposedly learned it from his father, who had been a court musician in Prince Radziwiłł's orchestra.

But those are only indications. The part the Jews played in the prehistory of Polish music, in folk and court music, deserves serious study. Every argument suggests that they did play a part, and it is doubtful whether it could have been exclusively performing. Village bands played without sheet music. They would take a musical theme and develop it. Such improvisation allowed the musicians to impart something of themselves to the music.

We know of the influence non-Jewish melodies exerted on Jewish religious and secular songs, and even on melodies. Hasidism, in which song is of such great significance, made uses of various borrowings. And whether its songs, in turn, imparted something to others, would be worthwhile studying.

The excellent book written by Maria Piechotka and Kazimierz Piechotka on wooden synagogues demonstrates the harmony between the design in Polish synagogues and the designs prevailing in Polish wooden architecture in general. There is no doubt that Polish architecture had a direct influence on Jewish architecture. But was there no influence in the other direction as well? Cultural influence is never a one-way process. Usually such influence ensues from the adoption by both sides of a certain design which is then fixed by the craftsmen executing it wherever they happen to be working. Those craftsmen could include both Jew and non-Jew alike. It would be difficult to determine what of specifically Jewish character was contributed by the Jewish craftsmen, and the same would hold true for the Polish craftsmen's contribution of something specifically Polish. What mattered was that Jewish craftsmen participated in the process of creating culture and made some contribution of merit to it.

The thesis that the Jews played a part of no significance in shaping traditional Polish folk culture seems fundamentally false. Although we cannot at present establish the exact nature and extent of that contribution, we must accept that it did exist. Indeed, the Jews made an outstanding contribution to spreading many values through Poland, and not only purely material ones.

IV

Of course, cultural creativity within the Jewish community itself could be viewed as an element of general Polish national culture. That would, however, depend on first accepting a certain definition of national culture. In the United States native American folklore is understood to include Negro spirituals, Navajo rugs, products of cottage industry or legends of the Pennsylvania Dutch, the work songs of various groups speaking foreign languages, and whatever else those groups created in their own languages on American soil. The foreign-language press; literature in foreign languages; the religious beliefs of all denominations; and works of art, decoration, and music are all components of American culture, with no regard paid to language, origin, race, or local features. It is of no significance that certain groups, primarily blacks, still maintain caste traits. A very broad concept of nation and a very broad concept of national culture are accepted.

That was the inevitable consequence of this vast country's entire history, of the role of various ethnic and religious groups from the world over in building the United States. That was also the consequence of the ideology that was accepted as the moral foundation for the new nation. It held that the mission of American democracy was to create a common home for a variety of people united by common ideals expressed in the Declaration of Independence and the Bill of Rights.

Similar concepts also arose in other large societies that were carrying out the idea of commonwealth in political terms, like the English and the French. Modern India is attempting to build its civilization in the same spirit.

In Poland it was the age of the Jagiellons that favored the development of that type of philosophy. *Natione Polonus* but *gente Ruthenus* contained the seed of a new concept of national culture. That concept was not fated to develop further. It was replaced by one that narrowed the ideas of nation and national culture to the limits of one ethnically, even religiously uniform community. This led to extremist mystical nationalism, to the idea of a "national" state, which had such fundamental influence on Poland in the period between the wars.

Given that narrow concept, the culture specific to the Jewish community found itself outside the acknowledged orbit of Polish national culture. It was an alien culture of which nothing was known, and no knowledge was desired. That culture was held in universal contempt. It was held in contempt also by those Jews who had left the caste and were attempting to identify completely with the Polish national cultural community. Yiddish was still spoken of contemptuously as a jargon. Without the slightest embarrassment, the English acknowledge that their language was originally a jargon and still preserves certain traits of a jargon. But that language produced one of the world's most splendid literatures and is itself an excellent instrument for human communication. In reality, a great number of languages were jargons in their initial phases of development. What else was the *lingua romana* from the point of view of Latin?

The entire corpus of religious and philosophical work done in Hebrew by the Jews was also outside that sphere of Polish culture. Only certain individuals, like Ksawery Korczak-Branicki, were aware of its significance. But his interest was viewed as the whim of a great lord who was a bit mad, a bit eccentric. Few people apart from the Jews were aware of the existence of great rabbinical centers in Poland. What those centers produced was relegated with contempt to the Talmud and Talmudism. It is only now, as a result of research in which the part played by Poles is minimal, that we are beginning to understand that those centers of Polish Talmudism not only engaged in nonsensical hairsplitting but also dealt with interesting philosophical ideas; and that those ideas did not arise in complete isolation from Polish life and culture.

But we can only mention all this in passing. Let us hope that the history and development of the spiritual culture of the Polish Jews will someday meet with serious treatment by Polish scholars.

V

If, given the current state of research, one may speak of the Jews' contribution to the development of Polish folk culture only in general terms, and if this is an area replete with hypothetical assumptions and open questions, the same cannot be said of the Jews' contribution to the culture of Poland's "higher" classes, the culture considered representative of the Polish national community, its "official" culture. Here the part played by people of Jewish origin is beyond dispute.

Julian Tuwim remains a star of the first magnitude in Polish literature. And that literature would be poorer without Bolesław Leśmian, Słonimski, Józef Wittlin, Adam Ważyk, and Mieczysław Jastrun, not to mention a long list of other less famous names. Julian Klaczko, Wilhelm Feldman, Ostap Ortwin, and Juliusz Kleiner are names that will long remain in Polish literary criticism. Polish historiography was enriched by Askenazy, Marceli Handelsman, and Józef Feldman. In Polish music, Jews were among the greatest performers. The list of outstanding Jewish names in Polish art ranges from Maurycy Gottlieb to Henryk Kuna, Eugeniusz Zak, Mela Mutermilch, and Roman Kramsztyk. Jews were well represented among Poland's eminent lawyers. Polish medicine, science, and technology owe a great deal to people who had left the Jewish caste. Not all those scientists were able to find an area for their activity in Poland. Many, to name but the famous mathematician Leon Lichtenstein or Kazimierz Fajans, found it abroad. But despite the difficulties, they felt a bond with Poland and its culture and must be counted as part of that culture.

Were there any fields in Poland in which people of Jewish origin did not leave their mark? Julian Klaczko's influence on Polish conservative thought was probably no less than that of Feliks Perl on Polish socialist thought, and possibly even greater. Klaczko's biographer and admirer was none other than Count Stanisław Tarnowski. Polish middle-class liberalism, weak as it was, was greatly in the debt of people like Stanisław Kempner.

People of Jewish origin contributed to the development of the Polish theater, to mention but Arnold Szyfman. In the world of actors, Stanisław Stanisławski was considered brilliant at portraying archtypal Polish roles and his Polish was thought unsurpassed. And Polish journalism? A strong list could be compiled of Polish journalists who had left the caste, and with a number of eminent names among them.

Thus, the statement that Polish culture was being "Jewified" was entirely correct. The contribution by people of Jewish origin to "official" Polish culture was beyond any doubt considerable. And in that sense Polish culture had been Jewified. The value placed on that Jewification and the conclusions then drawn were another matter.

None of the people whom we have just mentioned were actually Jews. They were of Jewish origin and constituted the contribution Polish Jewry made to Polish culture, but they neither considered themselves Jews nor could they be so considered. In his youth Julian Klaczko wrote poetry in Hebrew. Wilhelm Feldman learned to speak Polish relatively late in life and had his "accent" to the end, which even the satirist Tadeusz Boy Żeleński poked fun at (in England no one ridiculed Conrad's accent and many people even found it "charming"). But both Klaczko and Feldman had broken entirely with Jewishness and had fully identified with things Polish. They viewed the Jewish masses as material from which future Poles could be made. Other figures had come from circles in which the connection with Jews, even that of religion, had been lost, in some cases for several generations. If those circles maintained certain remnants of the traditional Jewish ethos, that usually came down to a high respect for intellectual values, a cult of the book. None of those people knew the Talmud, and most frequently their fathers had not known it either. They all lived in the world of Polish values and attempted to represent those values in their creations.

If some of these people dealt with Jewish subjects, they viewed them from a Polish point of view, at best infusing them with greater warmth. Maurycy Gottlieb's paintings are full of Jewish subjects, but their treatment owes infinitely more to Jan Matejko (Gottlieb was his favorite pupil) than to traditional Jewish art. Of contemporary writers, Adolf Rudnicki writes within the sphere of Jewish subject matter, a result of the shock he suffered from what he experienced during the war and from the annihilation of the Polish Jews. His being of Jewish origin no doubt makes for special emotional power in his work. But what he writes about and how he writes could also have been the work of an author with a different origin. Rudnicki's thought, technique, and literary vision are all dominated by Polish traditions, and it would be difficult to discover anything specifically Jewish about them.

In prewar Poland considerable ink was expended to prove that Tuwim was a Jewish poet who wrote (and wrote badly!) in Polish. Many Herostratian efforts were made to remove from Polish culture a large number of eminent figures who had helped create it. There were attempts to purge the culture of "alien" and "harmful" influences, that is, to impoverish and cripple it. A "pure" national culture, free of "alien" influences, is a dead culture. All the great cultures are always to some degree syncretic and owe their development to influences from every side. Nazi German literature purged of non-Aryan influences and contemporary Soviet literature purged of bourgeois influences are vivid examples of the consequences of such purification.

All attempts to prove that the contribution to Polish culture made by people of Jewish origin were "Jewish" and "alien" to Polishness were obvious absurdities. The traits ascribed to the work of Tuwim, Leśmian, Wittlin, or Słonimski grew out of the entire history of Polish poetry, had their counterparts in other Polish poets (starting with Jan Kochanowski [1530–84]), and had very little in common with the traditions of Jewish culture.

A contribution made by "aliens" is to be found in every great national culture, and to an enormous extent, those cultures owe their greatness to those contributions. From every side flow streams that strengthen and shape the great river of a national culture. The most valuable streams are those that bring in their own specific elements and thus become agents of innovation, enriching the main current. Only on a limited scale was this the case with Jewish literature in Poland. When flowing into the great river, that stream had already been shaped by the river's current and become similar to it. All the same, it enlarged that river and enriched it. One may think that Polish culture would have been more fortunate had its contributors of Jewish origin brought more of specifically Jewish values with them, had they truly been "Jewifying" it.

We can see examples of this in American culture, where the Jewish contribution is more original, more strongly bound to Jewish traditions, and thereby more enriching of American national culture as a whole. But in America the Jews did not form a caste and were accepted as an integral part of the entire national society.

That was not the case in Poland or indeed in many other European countries. In order to make any sort of contribution, the Jew had to escape the caste, to cease to be a Jew. And when, in the modern period, the caste system began to break down from within, new problems, connected with the atmosphere of the period, came into being. The Jew could either serve Jewish culture exclusively or seek a way into the other culture on condition that he leave Jewry behind. In Poland some people attempted to participate in both cultures, Jakub Apenszlak, for example. In conditions of intensive cultural development, for an individual to participate in more than one culture is possible and highly gratifying. It enriches his personality and well serves each of the cultures in which he participates. But in times of great turmoil, widespread panic, and a breakdown in traditional value systems, such efforts are doomed to failure. In Poland, the people who sought places for themselves in both cultures became comic figures. In reality, they were profoundly tragic.

VI

But was there really nothing "Jewish" in what people of Jewish origin contributed to Polish culture? Fortunately, there were certain traits that, though not necessarily Jewish, were nevertheless the product of the specific experiences of Polish Jews.

We have spoken of one of those traits at various points in this book—the tradition of the written or printed word, the tradition of the book. Wisdom and knowledge were primary values in the Jewish ethos. This had a great influence on the process of assimilation in certain Jewish milieus and to a tremendous degree explained why Jews entering the intelligentsia were so numerous. That tradition was the source of the Jews' fondness for thought and reasoning as such—for pure speculation in all fields—and of the intellectuality characteristic of many Jews. Pragmatism was not a specifically Jewish trait, since it was an Anglo-Saxon one.

There is no question that, throughout their history, the Jews displayed great physical and social mobility. They were an active element both in the economy and in the domain of thought. That, however, was primarily a consequence of their specific social position and resulted more from necessity than from an ideological program. In order to achieve anything in life, the Jew had to change places. The very professions Jews usually practiced imposed this necessity on them. They had to take risks and seek out new ways. In their boldest endeavors, they had to attempt to change their entire social condition. Personal advancement did not come easily to a Jew, yet he sought it more frequently and with greater boldness than did, for instance, the peasant, who found no smaller obstacles on his path to social advancement. The motive force of the Jews was a sense of their charisma, of their intellectual superiority issuing from their pursuit of wisdom. It was not important whether any intellectual superiority really existed. What was important was that the Jews possessed a sense of their own mission and of their own intellectual worth.

But we should not exaggerate when speaking of Jewish mobility. Mobility was displayed by only a part, and by no means the largest part, of the Jewish community. The masses lived a passive life in their local ghettos for centuries on end. They did not seek change and did not desire it. The aspiration for change came to them late, when general emancipationist currents began to arise. A great number of Polish Jews never stuck their nose outside their native ghetto. But even among those masses certain intellectual traditions, the cult of the book and of wisdom, were preserved. Often these traditions assumed degenerate form and were reduced to a cult of those who interpreted the books and the wisdom, the scholarly rabbis or tsadeks. Still, possibilities remained that were foreign to other elements of Polish society.

In that society, intellectual traditions, the traditions of books and thought, were very weak. The traditional Polish cultural model, especially that of the nobility, gave pride of place to entirely different values: valor, honor, agriculture, hospitality, and so on. Until the end of the eighteenth century, the circle of educated people enamored of books and knowledge was very narrow in Polish society. It expanded somewhat in later times but was always marginal. This situation persisted even when respect for skills taught in schools had risen considerably and when the intelligentsia and semi-intelligentsia began to play an ever-increasing role in Polish life.

Beyond any doubt, assimilating Polish Jews adopted the ethos and values of their new milieu. It was not rational considerations (in Poland many called it "self-interest") that impelled young Jews to join the ranks of the insurgents in the Uprising of 1863 and the Legions in 1914. Their guiding motives were no different from those of others who took part in those struggles. Still, while taking on the cultural model and ethos of Polish society, assimilating Jews did preserve some of the intellectual traditions of their former milieu.

In many instances this led to a conflict between the new model and the old: both internal conflicts within the individuals themselves, and broader, interpersonal conflicts, born of the clash of different social values.

An internal conflict between the rational and the "romantic" approach to life was common among intellectuals of Jewish origin. That sort of conflict is not, in general, rare among intellectuals of any sort. However, among Polish-Jewish intellectuals it had a particular coloration as the expression of a basic disparity between the traditional deep-rooted attitude and the model one sought to adopt. Signs of such conflict can be found in the work of many writers of Jewish origin, as well as in the life histories of many scholars and public figures. In some cases, the conflict expressed itself in a violent rejection of intellectual values and rational methods in the way one acted, in the striving to yield to emotions. At times this was accompanied by an ironic attitude of one's own sensibility that was emphasized with exaggeration and affectation.

More serious and socially more far-reaching were the external conflicts. Jewish "overbraininess," Jewish "hairsplitting," "Talmudism," criticism, and the bent for analysis did not agree with the nobles' attitude. Those sorts of accusations were repeated often. How many malicious remarks of that kind were made of Słonimski! There were objective grounds for such accusations, since reflectiveness, intellectuality, criticism, and a bent for rational analysis were what the Jews contributed to Polish culture. Obviously, not all Jews, and not only Jews. There was no shortage of "romanticism" among Polish-Jewish intellectuals, and no shortage of rationalist criticism among non-Jewish intellectuals. If, however, a relatively large portion of the intellectuality of Polish life was the contribution of Jews, that stands to their obvious merit. It was, after all, an element no culture can do without, and Polish culture had no surfeit of it.

It was surely no accident either that Jews had a considerable hand in various broad educational ventures in Poland. There were a striking number of Jewish names among popularizers of knowledge. Stanisław Michalski (who in time became one of the most fanatic anti-Semites) was greatly indebted to people of Jewish origin for their financial and editorial aid in creating his first-rate *Poradnik dla samouków* (Guide for the Self-Taught). The excellent periodical *Wiedza i życie* (Knowledge and Life) was under constant criticism for being "Jewified." Roman Kramsztyk, Hilary Nussbaum, Ludwik Wertenstein, Rudniański, Bardach, to mention but a few, hold places of honor in the history of the popularization of scientific thought in Poland. Bruno Winawer did the same but in a different way.

Once again, it would be absurd to say that it was only Jews who were active in this field and that the chief merit should be ascribed to them alone. But their contribution was considerable and at times pioneering. And all the data indicate that this was closely connected to the intellectual traditions that had been alive for centuries in the world of the Jews.

VII

There is one more element that must be included in this examination of the Jewish contribution to Polish culture. I refer to a quality that was not so much the issue of age-old Jewish traditions as it was the result of the Jews' existing within the confines of a caste organization and of individuals' attempting to leave those confines. This requires somewhat broader treatment.

In every caste system the lower caste occupies a marginal position vis-à-vis the upper caste. The Jews were a marginal element to the Polish nobility. The margin was not isolated, for the Jews could have access to various areas in the nobility's life, just as they did to various areas in peasant life. But as a whole, as a caste the Jews were at the margin of what determined the essence of the noble Poland's history.

That marginality did not disappear in the case of Jews assimilated to Polish culture; to a certain extent, it even increased. But certain essential changes occurred in it.

Every individual who leaves a group with its world of values and attempts to enter another group with its world of values finds himself in a marginal situation. That individual is already outside the former group but has not yet been accepted by the new one. Judym had ceased to be a worker. He was treated as alien by his immediate family, as someone who, if not entirely outside the sphere of their affairs, was at least marginal to them. But Judym was treated with mistrust by his new environment as well. Here he was still an intruder. He was on the margin of that environment's life, affairs, and values.

These are common phenomena in all ages and all civilizations. Immigrants to America sense the marginality of their situation in their new homeland for a long time, often until the end of their lives. This is felt particularly by intellectuals who have played an outstanding role and held central positions in their former country. And even though American society is extraordinarily inclusive, the newcomer is here for a long time, often for the rest of his days, outside the mainstream of life: he feels rejected; he lives on the margin. For many this is an especially painful experience, that of being déclassé, tossed overboard.

Marginality can occur in the most varied situations and can be conditioned by various social situations. It is to be observed in "border" areas where various systems of cultural values clash with each other. It can be the result of social or economic decline. Not infrequently it occurs with older people who retire after a very active life. And at times people may even voluntarily impose it on themselves. That is the case with all "internal emigrations," caused by the individual's nonconformity with the prevailing rules. For example, the so-called beatniks were a marginal element in America. In Russia, there are a number of nonconformist writers who were on the margin, to name but Boris Pasternak and Anna Akhmatova. There is no doubt that, in the Poland of today, certain intellectual elements choosing "internal emigration" are shifted to the margin of life. Various groups of bohemians in literature, art, and politics are another example of marginality. In brief, there is no all-inclusive formula: "marginality" applies to a variety of situations and social conditions. What is common to all of them is that individuals or entire groups are left on the margin, beyond full and unconditional participation in the life of the dominant social group.

Marginality creates in its participants certain moral stances and a certain attitude toward life. This is particularly striking in milieus with a high intellectual level, in urban milieus, and in instances of nonconformism, whether assumed voluntarily or imposed from without. Marginal people, not being actively engaged in the life of the larger community and by maintaining a certain distance from it, are usually more objective observers of that community's affairs and perceive in it things that elude the notice of its active participants. In people of high intellectual attainment, this marginality often gives rise to criticism of the larger community, to irony and skepticism. At times that leads to revolutionary activity, while at others it is reduced to sarcasm, humor, or *Galgenhumor.*

The role of marginal people in the great social and cultural processes of the present time is tremendous. And not only of the present time. Great movements in thought and art, social revolutions, and changes in accepted value systems all usually had some connection with the actions of marginal people. Those people are a fermenting agent, the "yeast" without which culture would not be able to develop and the world would seem dead. What was said in Poland about the Jews—"difficult with them, boring without them"—can be applied to marginal people in general.

In Poland those who left the Jewish caste found themselves at the margin of Polish national society. If it were possible to conceive of the entire Polish margin in numerical terms—which is clearly unfeasible—the share of people of Jewish origin in it would, no doubt, be huge.

That was an element that had not chosen marginality of their free will. In Poland, Jewish marginality was the inevitable consequence of the entire caste system. Anyone who left the caste system could not avoid landing on the margin. In the overwhelming majority of cases, those who left the Jewish caste experienced their marginality as difficult, painful, even tragic. They did not want to be on the margin and sought ways out of it. But it was rare that they succeeded. In some cases they even behaved as if they were not marginal. This was the same thing we referred to when speaking of those who acted as if they had never had a caste background. That was make-believe life, an attempt to play a role that was not acknowledged by others.

In practice, the consequences were obvious: among Jews, and particularly among the Polish-Jewish intelligentsia, this inevitably led to the formation of attitudes that are characteristic of all marginal people—keen perception of others and their affairs, criticism, skepticism, irony, and sarcasm. Difficult with them, boring without them. Willy-nilly they became an agent of ferment and unrest. And in that lay their great cultural role, the source of their contribution to Polish culture. Without the part played by marginal people, no matter what their origin, any national culture is in danger of ossifying and lapsing into boredom. Contemporary Russian literature, from which all marginal individuals are being systematically removed, is terribly boring. It is the literature of conformism triumphant, of banal platitudes. The fact that Pasternak was marginal—fortunately for the future of Russian literature—makes *Doctor Zhivago* an intense experience for the reader.

Conformists are not overly friendly toward people on the margin. Sometimes, though, this is masked by tolerance, especially when the marginal man is not treated very seriously or when the conformists do not feel too sure of themselves. In the eyes of conformists, the margin may even look amusing. The Parisian bourgeoisie considered Montmartre a part of the Parisian landscape, a place for amusement, not to be taken too seriously. The average New Yorker once had a similar attitude toward Greenwich Village. But conformists are always suspicious of "bohemians" or of other representations of marginality. They know that they are challenged from that quarter; they know it is the source of sarcasm, mockery, and sharp criticism.

And that was why it was difficult but not boring with the Jews in Poland. The difficulty was greatest for the most extreme conformists. And from that side came the severest accusations about the Jews' destructive qualities and their natural subversiveness. At bottom among many of those "subversives" there was a longing for conformity and a dream of togetherness with their opponents. Wherever Jews cease to be marginal as Jews—in Israel, in the United States—they accept the conformism of the larger community. They cease to be difficult and begin to be boring. Of course, there too they provide recruits for local margins, but as individuals, not by compulsion, and within the framework of the general construction of marginal milieus. No one in America has taken an interest in delving into this question, but I do not have the impression that Jews were represented in especially large numbers among the beatniks.

In Poland those who left the Jewish caste were compelled to the margin as a result of the distrust and opposition they encountered on the part of the larger community. The latter attempted to maintain some distance between themselves and the Jewish *homines novi*. This had far-reaching consequences, and—as so often happens in history—ones different from those that were intended. The margin produced its own attitudes and tendencies, which exerted a profound influence on the attitudes and tendencies of the larger environment. And that influence was creative. What is more, it outlived the existence of the Polish Jews and the Polish-Jewish margin.

The sarcasm, irony, and skepticism that characterize the intelligentsia's mentality in Poland today are, in the form they take and in their essential expression, a living reminder of what before the war was considered typically Jewish. Current Polish political humor, scathing and sometimes cynical, is a clear continuation of the old *shmontses*. It must be acknowledged, however, that conditions in Poland today also provide fertile ground for such humor: a considerable portion of Polish intelligentsia have now become a marginal element vis-à-vis the conformism of the ruling group. The irony those elements of the Polish intelligentsia direct against themselves is socially conditioned in a way similar to that which influenced the nature and form of the old Jewish humor.

It is my impression that the influence of the old margin is not limited to this alone but also embraces considerably broader areas. It would be extremely interesting to examine from this angle the characteristics of contemporary Polish literature and art, as well as that dimension of political journalism and sociology that eludes the clichés of obligatory party doctrine.

Once again let us stress what we have already indicated: in all the stages of our civilization's development, the culture-creating role played by marginal elements has been prominent and fertile. They were the yeast without which new values could not rise. Among the great creators of Euramerican culture the number of marginal people was enormous. Those were people rejected in one way or another by society, or people who themselves rejected society. Most often, theirs was a personally tragic fate. They had no "success in life." It is not even known where some of them are buried. That was the terrible price they had to pay for what they gave to humanity by grace of their genius.

Needless to say, not every creative person has to share that fate. Julian Tuwim, the Polish Jews' greatest contribution to Polish literature, died a famous and successful man. But how highly influenced by his marginality was all of Tuwim's creation! And when viewing the Polish-Jewish intelligentsia, we must acknowledge that their marginality contributed a great deal to Polish culture. This was one of those paradoxes with which human history abounds.

Afterword

This book is neither an obituary for Polish Jewry nor an attempt at an exhaustive study of its role in Polish culture. Although there are no longer Jews in Poland, the achievements of the Polish Jews and their contributions to Polish culture remain. Thus, there is no place for an obituary. And it is still too early to write an exhaustive study. That cannot be done by one man, especially one who for years has been far from Poland.

This book's task is to open the discussion, pose the problems, and discuss the methods that can be used in their solution. Further work should be taken up by others.

It would be a grievous thing were those others not to appear. Undoubtedly, the old prejudices of the past still dogging the heels of the present will be the obstacle here.

This book was written by one who has always considered himself a marginal man. And perhaps even more so now. When youth has passed, everyone is, by the nature of things, thrust to the margin. Especially when one is an émigré. For I have not ceased to be one even though the country in which I settled received me with such friendliness and though I am connected to it by such strong and cordial ties. I hope that my marginality has been reflected in this book and that, while maintaining its objectivity, the book also contains some ferment that will compel its readers toward thought and debate. If that be so, then I bless my marginality.

The principal motive of this book is to portray the Polish Jews as a social caste. In my judgment, it is this fact that gives rise to the other, fundamental elements of what in Poland was called the "Jewish question." To the best of my knowledge, no attention has been paid thus far to the caste nature of the Jewish community in Poland (and in other countries as well). I have been aided in this perception by coming to know the real life of my second homeland, the United States. Excellent research done here in the field of intergroup relations—between races, ethnic groups, classes, and so on—and the enormous literature that arose in that context have allowed me to view the Jewish question in

Poland from yet another angle. This book is primarily the fruit of my American experience. America, the splendid work of American scholars, and the work of European scholars who, like Gunnar Myrdal, were provided with ideal conditions for unrestrained research, played an outstanding role in the creation of this book. And for this I offer my humble thanks to my second homeland.

Notes

The Sabbath Candles Have Gone Out

1. Joseph Opatoshu (1887–1954) was an American Yiddish writer, born in Mława, a Polish town.
2. Maria Czapska (1894–1981) was a historian of literature, author, and translator.
3. The author refers here to Ibrahim ibn Yaqub, a Jewish merchant, traveler, and writer from Spain of the tenth century, and Jewish coiners who minted money with Hebrew inscriptions for Polish kings of the First Royal Dynasty in the eleventh and twelfth centuries.
4. Antoni Słonimski (1893–1985) was a Polish poet, writer, and human rights activist of Jewish descent. His grandfather, Chaim Zelik Słonimski, was the founder of *Hatzefira*, a Hebrew-language newspaper.
5. The Polish (*Bóżnice drewniane*) and the English editions were published in Warsaw in 1957 and 1959, respectively.
6. To date the multivolume *Historia Polski* (History of Poland) prepared by the Institute of History of the Polish Academy of Sciences consists of four volumes, published between 1957 and 1972.
7. *Dyplomatariusz dotyczacy Żydów w dawnej Polsce* (Documents Relating to Jews in Poland), Warsaw, 1910.
8. The above-mentioned works by the well-known Polish-Jewish historians Majer Bałaban, Jakub Szacki, Yitskhok Schipper, Rafael Mahler, Emanuel Ringelblum, and Philip Friedman are noted in two recently published bibliographies: Gershon David Hundert and Gershon C. Bacon, *The Jews in Poland and Russia: Bibliographical Essays* (Bloomington: Indiana University Press, 1984); and George J. Lerski and Halina T. Lerski, *Jewish-Polish Coexistence, 1772–1939: A Topical Bibliography* (New York: Greenwood Press, 1986).
9. Stanisław Vincenz (1888–1971), Polish writer and folklorist, is best known for his great work *Na wysokiej połoninie: Obrazy, dumy i gawędy z wierchowiny huculskiej* (In the Upper Highlands), Warsaw, 1936.
10. Tadeusz Czacki (1765–1813) was a Polish historian and statesman. His *Rozprawa o Żydach i Karaitach*, published in Vilna in 1807, was the first comprehensive historical survey of Polish Jews.
11. Eliza Orzeszkowa (1842–1910) was one of Poland's great novelists. Among her many novels on Jewish themes are *Eli Makower* and *Meir Ezofowicz*, published in 1875 and 1878, respectively.
12. The questionnaire appeared in *Kultura* in the issues of September 1956 and January–February 1957.
13. An allusion to the outcry by the extreme nationalistic and clerical elements in Poland after the assassination of Gabriel Narutowicz, the first elected president of the Polish Second Republic. It was the Polish nationalists, associated primarily with the parties

of the Christian Democrats and National Democrats, who were against Narutowicz, whom they accused of being too liberal and pro-Jewish. During the presidential election campaign in the winter of 1922 those parties were the organizers of a vicious fight against Narutowicz. Five days after he was sworn in as president, Narutowicz was assassinated by a nationalistic extremist. In order to evade responsibility for creating this kind of political climate before and after the election, Stanisław Stroński, one of the leaders of the National Democrats, published in his party paper an appeal: *Ciszej nad tą trumną* ("Keep silent beside this coffin").

14. Stanisław Szczepanowski (1846–1921) was a Polish economist, businessman, and political activist.
15. Andrzej Niemojewski (1846–1921) was the author of *Dusza żydowska w zwierciadle talmudu* (The Jewish Soul as Mirrored in the Talmud), Warsaw, 1920.
16. Joachim Lelewel (1786–1861), a historian and professor at Wilno and Warsaw universities, was the first to introduce modern methods into Polish historiography. He was one of the leaders of the Polish National Uprising of 1831; after its suppression by the Russian troops, he went to France and Belgium, where he became the leader of Polish democratic emigrant societies.
17. Mateusz Butrymowicz (1745–1814), political activist of the Reform Camp during the Four-Year Sejm (Diet) of 1788–92, was the author of a bill concerning Polish Jews.
18. Julian Ursyn Niemcewicz (1757–1841), prolific historical novelist and essayist, was the leader of the Reform Camp and aide-de-camp to Tadeusz Kościuszko at the time of the uprising of 1794.
19. Positivism was both a literary and an intellectual and sociopolitical movement among the Polish intelligentsia and liberal bourgeoisie that developed in Poland at the end of the nineteenth century; it was based on the philosophy of Comte as well as Poland's geopolitical situation as a country occupied by three foreign powers. The positivist creed was to develop Poland—its economy and culture—without any political collaboration with the occupiers.
20. Jan Czyński (1801–67), publicist and political writer, was a participant in the uprising of 1831. After its suppression, he settled in Paris, where he became one of the leaders of Polish émigré political organizations. While in Paris, he was a constant contributor to the Jewish periodical *Archives Israëlites*.
21. Esterka was the legendary Jewish mistress of the Polish king Kazimierz the Great, who reigned in the years 1333–70. Szmul Zbytkower (173?–1801) was a banker, merchant, and army purveyor. Berek Joselewicz (177?–1809) was a Polish soldier and patriot who was appointed colonel of his Jewish Legion by Kościuszko during the Polish uprising of 1794. He later took part in Napoleon's war against Russia as an officer in the Polish Legion.
22. After the final partition of Poland by her three neighbors (Russia, Prussia, and Austria) in 1795, some semi-independent or quasi-autonomous Polish governments came into being. The first was the Great Duchy of Warsaw (1807–12), established and under the protection of Napoleon. Then, at the time of the Congress of Vienna, after Napoleon's defeat, three entities were created: Congress Poland, or the Polish Kingdom (1815–1915), under Czarist Russia; the Great Duchy of Poznań (1815–1918/9), part of Prussia; and the Republic or Free City of Kraków. The latter was abolished and added to Galicia, the southern part of Poland which was taken by Austria at the time of the first partition in 1772.
23. A pogrom in fact took place in Warsaw December 25–27, 1881.
24. Baron Maurice Hirsch (1831–96), German financier and philanthropist, founded the Jewish Colonization Association (ICA).
25. Jakub (Izaak) Cylkow (1841–1908), Conservative rabbi and preacher, was the first Jew to translate the Bible into Polish.
26. Ludwik Gumplowicz (1838–1909), Polish sociologist, lawyer, and historian of Jewish descent, was the author of *Prawodawstwo polskie względem Żydów* (Polish Legislation Concerning the Jews), Kraków, 1867.
27. The National Democrats (the League was its forerunner) was the commonly known name for an entire political movement and party founded at the end of the nineteenth century. With time and under the leadership of Roman Dmowski and Zygmunt Balicki,

the ND and its splinter groups became the most anti-Semitic forces on the Polish political scene.

28. General Jan Henryk Dąbrowski (1755–1818) was the founder of the Polish Legion in Italy, which fought alongside Napoleon's army in the hope that it would free Poland from the Russian, Prussian, and Austrian occupying forces. The mazurka was a song dedicated to General Dąbrowski that later became the national anthem of Poland.
29. Józef Piłsudski (1867–1935), politician and soldier, was the founder and commander of the Polish Legion in World War I. He was Marshall of Poland and Head of State of the Second Polish Republic.
30. Wilhelm Feldman (1868–1919) was a Polish literary critic of Jewish descent. Under his editorship *Krytyka* became the main magazine of the Młoda Polska (Young Poland) movement.

The Kindred and the Alien

1. Mikhail Nikiforovich Katkov (1818–87), who was the editor of *Moskovskiia Viedomosti*, was considered one of Russia's most reactionary and nationalistic journalists of his time.

Caste

1. In prepartition Poland, the governing board of the Kehillah was, most often, represented by the learned (or traditionally educated) and wealthy people.
2. Frankism was a sect founded in southeast Poland by Jacob Frank (1726–61), a messianic pretender. After he and his followers were excluded from the Jewish community, the Frankists embraced the Islamic and then the Christian faith, although some of the sect's rituals and practices were upheld.
3. *Meches* is a pejorative word for a Jew who had converted to Christianity. It came to the Polish language from the Hebrew and literally means a fee, dues, or charge.
4. Kazimierz Wyka (1910–) was a historian and literary critic and essayist. The essay mentioned here was later republished in *Życie na niby* (Abnormal Lives in German-occupied Poland), Warsaw, 1959.
5. One of the most difficult problems in the work on this translation was how to translate *cham, tyk,* and *parch*. Finding exact equivalents in English proved simply impossible. Of course, their meaning can be described, but their exclusively Polish aura cannot be conveyed. In addition, all three words must be short, only one syllable to be barked out in anger. *Parch* literally means "scab." Thus the popular Polish (and Russian) appellation *parszywy Żyd* (scabby Jew) is the counterpart of the English "dirty Jew" and the French *sale juif*.
6. The Cossack uprising against the Polish gentry and Jews under Bohdan Chmielnicki occurred in 1648.

Those Who Leave the Caste

1. After the creation of the Commonwealth of Poland and Lithuania in 1569, the united country consisted of two somewhat autonomous parts: *Korona* or the Crown (Poland) and *Litwa* (Lithuania), or *Pogoń* (Chevy), the emblem of the old Principality of Lithuania.
2. Count Fryderyk Skarbek (1792–1866), economist and historian, writer and journalist, was professor of political economics at Warsaw University and author of books on a variety of topics.
3. Count Stanisław Tarnowski (1837–1917), literary critic and historian, was professor and Rector of the Jagiellonian University.
4. The Order of the Golden Fleece was one of the oldest decorations in Europe and, in Austria and Austria-Hungary from 1713 to 1918, the highest decoration.
5. The Natansons were a leading banking house in Warsaw established by Zelik Natanson in 1866.
6. *Biali* (The White) was a political camp or party of liberal landowners and the upper

middle class and the intelligentsia, founded before the Polish National Uprising of January 1863. On the other side of the political spectrum were the so-called *Czerwoni* (The Reds), who advocated a more radical and revolutionary course against the Russian occupiers.

7. Julian Klaczko (1825–1906) was a Polish poet and writer, publicist, and historian. In 1842, after the death of his father, an Orthodox Jew, he converted to Catholicism.

Within the Caste or Outside It?

1. Jakub Apenszlak (1894–1950) was editor of *Nasz Przegląd* (Our Review), a Zionist-oriented Polish-language newspaper (1923–39).
2. Hipolit Gliwic (1878–1943), a former chargé d'affaires of the Polish Embassy in Washington, was Minister of Industry and Commerce (1926–28) and Vice-speaker of the Polish Senate.
3. Ksawery Branicki (1814–79), a descendent of the family of a Polish magnate whose coat of arms was Korczak, was a financier, politician, and publicist.
4. The reference is to two characters in the fiction of Stefan Żeromski.
5. Jakub Epstein was the progenitor of the Epstein banking family.

Against the Caste

1. Litwaks were Jews from the Pale of Jewish settlements in Russia, especially from the Wilno and Minsk gubernias, who settled in Congress Poland at the end of the nineteenth century. Many of them were under the influence of Russian culture and language.
2. Jędrzej Cierniak (1886–1942) was an educator and author. Both Bujak and Cierniak came from peasant families.
3. Młoda Polska (Young Poland) was a modernistic trend in Polish literature and the arts at the turn of the nineteenth century (1900–1918).
4. As part of the Mickiewicz Polish Legion in the Italian-Austrian military campaign of 1848–49.

The Crisis

1. This is a reference to the imprisonment of leaders of the parliament opposition to the government at the Brześć Fortress in the autumn of 1930.
2. The sixteenth-century religious movement, the Reformation, attracted in Poland only some small segments of the nobility and the urban population. The highest point of the Polish Reformation, especially the formation of Calvinist and Lutheran churches, was during the reign of King Sigmund August (1548–72).

The Image of the Jew

1. *Żydówka-bądźzdrówka* cannot be translated. Literally, *Żydówka* means "Jewess," and *bądź zdrowa* is a greeting: "be in good health" or "keep well." *Żydówka* is a diminutive of "Jewess" and a rhyme of *bądźzdrówka*.

In the Service of Jewish Culture

1. *Odpust* means a church fete when absolution of sins takes place. It is always connected with a fair, crowds arriving from various neighborhoods, and so on.
2. Jan Piotr Norblin de la Gourdaine (1745–1830) was a French painter who for many years lived in Poland as a guest of Count Adam Czartoryski.

Index